Cash Flow Analysis
and Forecasting

Cash Flow Analysis
and Forecasting

*The Definitive Guide to Understanding
and Using Published Cash Flow Data*

Timothy D.H. Jury

A John Wiley & Sons, Ltd., Publication

Library of Congress Cataloging-in-Publication Data:

ISBN 978-1-119-96265-6

Set in 10/12pt Times by Aptara Inc., New Delhi, India
Printed in Great Britain by TJ International Ltd, Padstow, Cornwall, UK

To my mother and father,
brother and sisters for always being there

Contents

Introduction

This book is the definitive guide to cash flow analysis. It is designed to be the definitive first reference on all aspects of historic cash flow analysis. It also provides an incisive overview of the risks to be managed in preparing cash flow forecasts.

It has been written from a cash flow-centric point of view. Other financial and analytical information is introduced whenever relevant to support the process of cash flow analysis.

This book is designed for people trying to understand and analyse cash flows, probably in a professional context. Whilst it contains some theoretical content, the primary objective is to offer a practical handbook of cash flow analysis.

Ideally, it should first be read like a novel and then dipped into chapter-by-chapter as required; a detailed guide to the contents of each chapter follows this introduction. Much of the information in the book has been laid out to facilitate direct reference from the index; also allowing it to be used as a pure reference text.

Considerable effort has been expended to make the book as user friendly as possible. It has been designed to be relevant and useful both to persons who are coming to cash flows for the first time, and to those who are more experienced in the perils of financial statement analysis! I have paid particular attention to the needs of those who are not native English speakers. I have tried to keep the use of English as clear and concise as possible whilst avoiding the use of unnecessary complexity.

Whilst the book is written primarily for those employed as financial analysts, I have identified four other major user groups whose needs are specifically dealt with in different sections of the book. They are:

- Novices in financial analysis and other persons new to, or relatively unfamiliar with, cash flows in general and their analysis in particular, in all fields of endeavour, who wish to improve their understanding of cash flow.

- Bankers, credit analysts and others involved in business lending and the management of credit exposures and credit risk.
- Investors, fund managers and credit analysts involved in taking investment decisions.
- Entrepreneurs, managers and business people involved in controlling business entities.

The guide to the book, which follows this introduction, provides an indication of the content of each chapter and its relevance to different users. For example, persons who have no desire to actually perform the analysis of the cash flows of a business themselves, but who still wish to understand cash flow, will initially gain little from Chapters 4 and 5 as they are written for persons who are seeking to practically apply the technique for the restatement of published cash flows.

THE LOGIC OF THE BOOK DESIGN

Years of experience as a financial trainer have taught me that people acquire technical knowledge in a very random way from a variety of sources as they come across information relevant to their needs. This sometimes results in a partial, incomplete and often inaccurate understanding of the particular subject in issue. As a trainer and author my objective is to organise the information relevant to a subject or task in a logical and structured way to facilitate and ease the assimilation process. The metaphor I like to use is that of a jigsaw. My audiences will typically have many of the pieces of the jigsaw already in their possession; however, until I facilitate the process of assimilation they have not previously assembled the pieces into a complete picture. When working as a trainer not only do I assist in completing the jigsaw, I also provide the missing pieces, which are different for each participant!

For this reason the book has been organised into specific blocks of knowledge. It can be read sequentially. It can also be used as a reference to provide answers to specific queries and problems by dipping into the relevant part of the book.

COMPLEXITY

The word complex is regularly misused to mean difficult, or beyond the users present comprehension. When things labelled complex are analysed it often becomes clear that what is actually meant is there is a lot of information to assimilate before comprehension of the whole can be gained. The information itself is not particularly demanding to comprehend; there is, however, a lot of it! Writing computer software or learning a musical instrument or foreign language are typical examples.

My strategy for this type of assimilation problem is to chop the information up into lots of little bits that are sufficiently elemental that they can be adequately digested by the person seeking to assimilate the whole area of knowledge and then build the knowledge in a pyramid form by adding blocks and layers in an ordered way. This is the approach I have taken in writing this book.

THE USE OF CASE STUDIES IN THE BOOK

Once the initial chapters have introduced the concepts upon which the analysis of cash flows rely, the book includes a number of case studies that illustrate the use of the technique for cash flow analysis offered. Most of these cases are based on financial information taken from the accounting statements of real business entities. I prefer to do this because there is then no challenge as to the reality of business behaviour. If I create fictional cases for the book there is a risk users will question my conclusions about them and cash flow analysis in general on the basis that the examples are fictionalised and therefore do not represent a reasonable representation of business reality.

However, this inevitably results in problems with dates! The question of how to deal with dates in the book is one that has vexed me significantly. The problem for the publisher and I is that the book will soon appear dated if we show the years from which the case studies were taken in the original. Users may wrongly assume the message and content of the book is somehow less relevant because the material used to illustrate the logic of the technique offered is ageing.

The logic of the cash flow analysis technique offered in the book is essentially timeless, it should work virtually anywhere and anytime financial information is available to perform the analysis. For this reason I have partially disguised the original dates of the material used to illustrate the cases. The timeline of most of the case studies offered is incidental; the examples are there to illustrate the use and benefits of the cash flow analysis technique that is the basis of this book.

Experienced analysts will know that in performing any business analysis the economic context in which the company operates is sometimes highly relevant. Matters such as inflation, interest rates and the state of the economy may affect the conclusions drawn about the relative performance of a business. For this reason, in a small number of cases and where the context of the example warrants it, I have left the dates as they were originally. This allows the reader to put the case into the context of the economic conditions prevailing at the time.

Considerable effort has been expended to keep the various examples, tables and other information both numerically and factually correct, however, it is inevitable in a work of this length that, despite our best efforts, errors may still creep into print. Please do not hesitate to bring these to my attention, to further improve the book as it develops.

I hope this book changes your life. For those whose job is to analyse cash flows for a living it may actually do so!

Capitalisation

Throughout the book, where you see CAPITALISED WORDS, these refer directly to key words in tables and figures that are being discussed and explained in the text.

GUIDE TO THE BOOK

The book is organised into two sections, the first dealing with the analysis of historic cash flow data, the second dealing with the forecasting of cash flow information.

Section One – Historic Cash Flow Analysis

Chapter 1 – Understanding How Cash Flows in a Business

Level basic – the chapter is designed as a layperson's introduction to the whole subject of cash flow in business. In addition to introducing the cash flow patterns seen in business, it outlines a number of other fundamental issues and risks that managers must overcome in order to trade successfully. No prior knowledge of cash flow is assumed. The material is presented from the ground up through the use of straightforward examples.

Despite being offered as a basic introduction everyone seeking to utilise the cash flow analysis technique presented in the book should read this chapter as it introduces and defines part of the terminology used throughout the book.

Chapter 2 – Understanding Cash Flows Properly

Level intermediate – this chapter explains the knowledge and the steps required to analyse cash flows properly. It then commences the process by explaining all the terminology used in a simple cash flow example and introduces the analysis technique for the first time.

Chapter 3 – Start-up, Growth, Mature, Decline

Level intermediate – this chapter introduces the non-financial information needed to get the most out of the cash flow analysis technique offered in the book. Everything offered in this chapter is covered in more detail in Chapters 6 to 10.

Chapter 4 – Restating the Cash Flows of a Real Business

Level advanced – readers without some prior knowledge of financial statement analysis and accounting will find this chapter demanding. Considerable effort has gone into explaining the accounting and analytical knowledge required to properly utilise the cash flow analysis technique offered. The example chosen to illustrate the process being taken from a business preparing its accounts using International Financial Reporting Standards.

Chapter 5 – Restating US GAAP Cash Flows

Level advanced – this follows on from the previous chapter by taking an example of the technique based on a business following US financial accounting rules in the preparation of its financial statements. It is necessary to be familiar with the content of the previous chapter in order to get most benefit from this one.

Chapter 6 – Analysing the Cash Flows of Mature Businesses

Level advanced – this chapter defines the term 'mature' and presents the information required to comprehensively analyse the cash flows of a mature business.

Chapter 7 – Analysing the Cash Flows of Growth Businesses

Level advanced – this chapter defines the term 'growth' and presents the information required to comprehensively analyse the cash flows of a growth business.

Chapter 8 – Growth and Mature – Further Analysis Issues

Level advanced – this chapter presents two important further issues relevant to the analysis of both growth and mature businesses.

Chapter 9 – Analysing the Cash Flows of Start-up Businesses

Level advanced – this chapter defines the term 'start-up' and presents the information required to comprehensively analyse the cash flows of a start-up business.

Chapter 10 – Analysing the Cash Flows of Decline Businesses

Level advanced – this chapter defines the term 'decline' and presents the information required to comprehensively analyse the cash flows of a decline business.

Chapter 11 – What to do about Bad Cash Flows

Level advanced – this chapter offers a variety of strategies to make decisions about cash flows that are bad. It suggests a number of questions that the analyst should seek to answer, before coming to conclusions about bad cash flows.

Chapter 12 – Cash Versus Profit as a Measure of Performance

Level advanced – this chapter explains in detail the differences between profit and cash generation as a measure of performance. It points out the pitfalls of using profit alone as a performance indicator.

Chapter 13 – Cash Flow Analysis and Credit Risk

Level advanced – this chapter explains how to tailor the cash flow analysis technique offered specifically to the needs of bankers and others who are exposed to credit risk.

Chapter 14 – Cash Flow Analysis and Performance Measurement

Level advanced – this chapter looks at ways the cash flow analysis technique offered in the book can be used for business performance measurement.

Chapter 15 – Analysing Direct Cash Flow Statements

Level advanced – this chapter deals with the differences between direct and indirect cash flow statements and how to deal with them in applying the cash flow analysis technique. It is necessary to be familiar with the earlier content of the book in order to get the most out of this chapter.

Chapter 16 – Generating a Cash Flow Summary from Profit and Loss Account and Balance Sheet Data

Level advanced – this chapter illustrates how to arrive at a summary of the cash flows of a business entity that does not produce a cash flow statement as part of their financial information. It is essential to be familiar with all the earlier content of the book in order to get the most out of this chapter.

Chapter 17 – Summarising Historic Free Cash Flow

Level advanced – this chapter illustrates how to identify the historic free cash flow of a business entity from the cash flow information derived by using the cash flow analysis technique presented earlier in the book. It is necessary to be familiar with the earlier content of the book in order to get the most out of this chapter.

Section Two – Forecasting Cash Flows

Chapter 18 – Introduction

Level advanced – this chapter discusses the risks and benefits of forecasting when compared to the analysis of historic information.

Chapter 19 – Spreadsheet Risk

Level advanced – this chapter introduces spreadsheet risk and offers strategies to minimise the problem.

Chapter 20 – Good Practice Spreadsheet Development

Level advanced – this chapter introduces a number of techniques to reduce spreadsheet risk through good modelling practice. It illustrates four examples of common cash flow forecasting models.

Chapter 21 – The Use of Assumptions in Spreadsheet Models

Level advanced – this chapter offers guidance on dealing with assumptions in spreadsheet forecasting models. It then discusses the use of scenarios for risk analysis using spreadsheet forecasts.

Section One
Historic Cash Flow Analysis

1
Understanding How Cash Flows in a Business

INTRODUCTION

This chapter is designed to enable those with less direct experience of the operation of businesses to grasp the fundamental financial and economic logic that governs how successful businesses operate. It represents the starting point for our journey through the landscape of cash flow analysis. In order to gain benefit from this chapter no prior knowledge of either cash flow or business is required.

We start our journey by developing a model of how the cash flows in a simple business work. We then develop our knowledge of cash flows by incrementally adding complexity to this model.

Whilst developing this model based on the cash flows of a business we also introduce some fundamental logic about what different types of business must do in order to be successful.

THERE IS NOTHING NEW ABOUT BUSINESS

Humans have been engaging in trade for thousands of years, initially through some sort of barter process. Archaeologists have discovered ancient manufactured goods such as pottery and metal objects that have travelled vast distances from their point of manufacture. There are numerous examples of early Greek and Roman shipwrecks being discovered in many different parts of the Mediterranean dating back 2000 years or more. In the 1960s evidence was finally discovered that proved that the Vikings were the first Europeans to discover America some 500 years before Columbus. The remains of a Norse settlement at L'Anse aux Meadows on the northern tip of Newfoundland have been authenticated and dated to around 1000AD. During the excavation of the site over 100 objects of European manufacture were unearthed.

A more recent development in human history was the introduction of money in the form of coinage and, later, notes. Whilst there is much debate about what should be recognised as the first coin, a good candidate would be a small lump of electrum (a natural alloy of gold and silver) stamped with a design and minted around 600BC in Lydia, Asia Minor (now known as Turkey). Paper money seems to have emerged in China at about the same time.

This innovation, together with many others such as agriculture, settlements, the wheel and writing led to the modern, technologically based world economy we have today. Trade or business, in one form or another, has probably been part of the human condition from our earliest origins.

UNDERSTANDING MONEY IN BUSINESS

We are going to start with two simple examples of business activity. The first one represents one of the simplest forms of business. (More complex business examples follow over the next few pages.)

The Simplest Form of Business

Newspaper vending, by which I mean the activity of selling newspapers to passers-by on a street corner, is a good example of a really simple business. The vendor, or businessman, buys the newspapers from the publisher or a wholesaler and then retails them to passers-by for a price that gives him a margin over the cost of purchasing the newspapers.

A second example of a really simple business is an antique dealer, someone who buys and sells old objects. We will work with this example from now on.

The Debate About the Purpose and Objectives of a Business

The varying cultures around the world place different emphasis on how the benefits generated by a successful business should be shared amongst its stakeholders. I do not propose to examine the merits or otherwise of these views. There is considerable literature on what measures should be used to assess success or failure in business. Both growth and profit increase look like good candidates but fail as measures of success if the improvement in growth or profits is achieved by investing disproportionate amounts of cash. I do not propose to go much further with this debate other than to say that increasing the value of a business over time is now considered the most appropriate measure of success. This is achieved by continually improving the present and future cash flows of a business on an ongoing basis.

So, at this point in my explanation, I am assuming that the business I am describing is being run with the objective of wealth maximisation for the owners. For the purposes of this book I define that as maximising the future cash flows of the business.

The Objective of Being in Business is to Generate *More Cash*

It is important to introduce the purpose of a business here because specifying the objective of the business defines the task of the business person, entrepreneur, manager or other business controller (which is to get *more cash*). In both the business examples introduced so far we have a trader or dealer who buys and sells, typically without changing or modifying the items traded in any way. This is the simplest form of business.

The trader's objective is to generate more cash than they started with. (Note that I have not used the terms *profit* or *gain* as we are developing a model containing only items that represent the cash flows in a business. What we mean by profit is actually quite an abstract concept. This is dealt with in more detail in Chapter 12.)

How Does a Trading Business Add Value?

An initial observation might be that these businesses make money by buying things for less than they can sell them. While this is an accurate observation of what a successful trading business does, this fails to explain why or how the business is able to achieve this beneficial outcome.

What is the key skill for an antique dealer? Is it knowledge of the antiques traded in? Whilst this may help, much of this information is available from books. Is it renovation skills? Again this may or may not add value to the items being renovated depending on consumer taste at the time. The key skill is probably, knowing where to buy cheaply and where to sell expensively. Here is an example of what I mean.

For many years the typical vehicle of choice for a British antique dealer has been the Volvo estate, which is used to travel to distant parts of Scotland and Wales so that the dealer can purchase furniture and other antiques from remote house sales and auctions where they are often sold cheaply. The goods purchased are then transported to London where they can be auctioned through the major auction houses or retailed to wealthy collectors at collectors' fairs or from retail premises.

What this antique dealer is doing is relocating the goods traded from a place where they can be bought cheaply to a place where they can be sold more expensively. It's all about the relocation of the goods. Why is this so important?

Consider what happens when you get up in the morning. Do you travel to Java for your coffee beans, Florida for your orange juice, Jamaica for your sugar, and to your local farm for your milk?

This is unlikely. What most of us do is go to the nearest convenience store, which may be just down the street and buy what we wish to consume for our breakfast. So, what then is the owner of the convenience store doing to add value? What he does is relocate a range of goods he knows we are likely to consume for breakfast to a place convenient for us to make our purchases as consumers. The convenience of the location is the most important thing, the goods offered are in a sense irrelevant, they are whatever we want to consume.

So, the key to most trading, retail and wholesale businesses is location. What these businesses do is relocate goods from their places of production or, if second-hand, their present location, to a location convenient for the target consumer to consume them. It follows that there is little point in locating a business in a remote part of the world as there are few consumers there! The ideal location for newspaper vending is directly outside a major railway station in central London or any other major city in the world, this is where you will have thousands of potential consumers passing by every hour of the working day. In other words, you will sell more newspapers. The location is the essence of the business's ability to generate cash.

So, the cash flows of our simplest business look like the model shown in Fig. 1.1. Overheads is the term commonly used in business to refer to all the costs of trading other than inventory costs.

Using CASH the trader makes purchases of goods, which he holds as INVENTORY. Some time later he resells the goods acquired for more than he paid for them, receiving cash in exchange for the items. He will typically incur some OVERHEADS in the process, in our example of the antique dealer these will be transport, location and communication costs.

This is effectively all a trading, retail or distribution business does, repeating the journey round the circle many times. Now let us look at a more complex business, one where work is performed on the purchased inputs of the business.

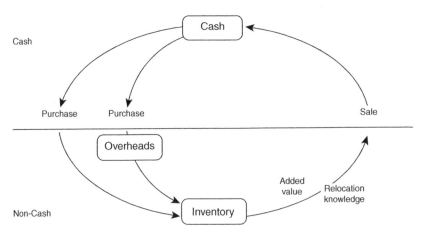

Figure 1.1 Diagram of the cash flows of a simple trading business

THE SIMPLE MANUFACTURING BUSINESS

In my other life as a financial trainer I have travelled all over the world offering training seminars on financial analysis and related subjects. One of the places I have visited on my travels is Nairobi in Kenya. When travelling from Nairobi airport to the training location I noticed business people selling beds and other simple items of furniture outside their workshops by the side of the road. This then is the next example we will examine; a simple manufacturing business.

How Does a Simple Manufacturing Business Add Value?

What do manufacturers do to create wealth for themselves? They take raw materials and change them into something more useful; economists talk about adding utility. For example, I could sleep on a log. However, this would not be particularly comfortable, the bark would make my back itch and I might roll off! If the log is cut up into timber and then turned into a bed frame I am likely to be willing to pay more for it in this form. Now, I could of course do this myself with the aid of a saw and a few basic woodworking tools, so why do I not normally bother? There are three reasons: time, quality and cost. I could make the bed, but it would take me three days whilst the manufacturer does it in half an hour. Secondly, the result I achieve might not have the quality of the professionally manufactured alternative and, finally, it would almost certainly be more expensive when the opportunity cost of my time as well as the cost of the raw materials is taken into account.

So, manufacturers do not just convert things (raw materials) into more useful things (finished goods), they are experts at the process of doing so. Successful manufacturers do it very quickly and efficiently to a very high standard. The key word here is *expert*. If you are analysing the performance of a manufacturing business and find that it receives many customer complaints and returned goods due to manufacturing defects, or is experiencing significant difficulties actually producing goods, this suggests they are not experts. To use a metaphor: it implies they are amateurs rather than professionals. Any business being operated in a non-professional way is at a higher risk of poor financial performance and eventual failure than its more professional and competent competitors. The extreme levels of professionalism required just to be competitive in most manufacturing activities is simply a consequence of competition over long periods of time.

So the cash flows of our simple manufacturing business look like the model shown in Fig. 1.2.

Using CASH the manufacturer makes a purchase of RAW MATERIALS and does work on them, so converting them to WORK IN PROGRESS and eventually FINISHED GOODS. These items being akin to INVENTORY in our previous model. Some time later he resells the finished goods for more than the cash costs of producing them, receiving cash in exchange for the items. He will typically

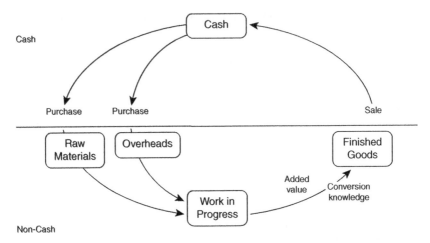

Figure 1.2   Diagram one of the cash flows of a manufacturing business

incur some OVERHEADS in the process of conversion, these being purchasing, manufacturing, premises, and selling costs in our example.

This is what the cash flows of a new small manufacturing business look like. Cash is generated by repeating the journey round the circle many times. Now let us see how this develops as the business evolves over time.

Developing Our Model – the Next Step

Continuing with our example of an African entrepreneur who has recently established himself as a manufacturer of furniture, let us assume his new business is successful. Our entrepreneur is working many hours a day and all the product he produces sells well. What is likely to be his first major issue in developing his business?

Given his location his next move is most likely to be adding labour to the business to increase output and hence cash flow. This is because there is much labour available and, given the emerging market location of the business, this labour is available relatively cheaply (Fig. 1.3).

LABOUR now joins overheads as an item purchased and consumed by the business to add value to raw materials.

If our entrepreneur furniture designer was in Munich in Germany the decision might be quite different. In this location the economic environment is different to that in Nairobi in Kenya. In Germany labour costs are significantly higher per hour and employees are protected in many ways by a mass of social legislation

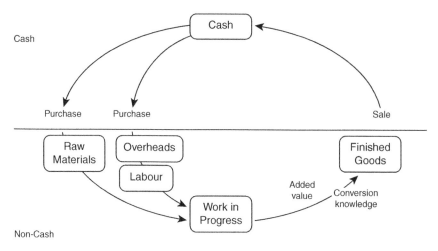

Figure 1.3   Diagram two of the cash flows of a manufacturing business

giving them extensive rights and obliging employers to compensate employees in the event of job losses. From an economic point of view the cost of labour is higher and the cost itself is less variable. In Germany the first major initiative to build our business is more likely to be the purchase of machinery (i.e. fixed assets) to increase output and hence cash flow, rather than the addition of more labour (Fig. 1.4).

Why is the decision different depending on the location of the business? This is because the economic environment is different. Factors that affect the decision of whether to employ labour or purchase fixed assets would be things like, the law and regulations affecting the cost and flexibility of labour, the local environment governing labour and investment in fixed assets, and the availability and quality of labour.

There are other issues that might inform or determine the decision. Machines have certain characteristics that could arguably make them superior to labour in many situations. They do not go on strike; they can, assuming they are properly maintained, produce a succession of perfect and identical output 24 hours a day without requiring sleep or food. But, there are also some key negative characteristics of machines. They usually require infrastructure such as electricity, gas, compressed air and water constantly available without interruption. They are very good at doing the same thing again and again; they are not so good when the required output keeps changing. Any change to the product manufactured may necessitate hours of re-engineering and re-programming of the machine before productive output recommences.

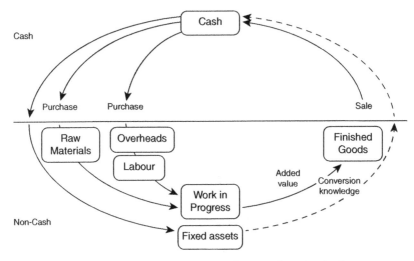

Figure 1.4   Diagram three of the cash flows of a manufacturing business

Labour, despite its imperfections, is very flexible. It can make the tea, collect the raw materials, deliver finished product and paint the wall, in addition to being available to produce product as required. It copes well with a succession of variable tasks. The negatives are that it can go on strike, it requires a safe and healthy working environment and protection from the risk of injury or death (known collectively as health and safety). It also needs constant breaks for food and rest, and it can produce substandard and defective work if not properly trained and supervised.

So, labour is flexible but inconsistent, machinery is inflexible but consistent. As our example business grows, whether situated in Kenya or Germany, labour and fixed assets will be added as required according to their relative utility to cost in the local environment.

You may have noticed the use of a dotted line to denote the sale of fixed assets. This is because when we acquire fixed assets we intend to keep them to assist us in the process of producing or trading our goods and services. We do not intend to sell them or trade them during their useful lives. Only when they are no longer of operational use to us do we sell them if we can. The cash flow we get when we sell them is usually small relative to the cash flow spent on new assets.

The Consequences of Growth and Success

As the business develops it becomes more complex, typically because growth means an increase in everything. The numbers of labour, machines, products, customers and suppliers can all increase. With this complexity comes new risks. When a business is small it can be controlled by one person. As it grows this becomes more and more difficult because too many things that require control are happening simultaneously. Delegation of authority to others is required, which implies the creation of a management structure.

Similarly the cash flows involved in the business all get larger. Turnover, costs, investment, debtors and creditors all increase. At this point it is sensible to consider limiting the risk of the owner. How can this be achieved?

The owner can sell the business to a limited company owned by him or herself. Until this point our example business has been trading as a sole trader. In English law there are three different ways a person can trade, as a sole trader, as a partner in a partnership and through the use of some sort of company owned by the person.

As a sole trader or partner an individual's risk is unlimited. Should there be any negative event that results in significant liabilities for the business in which they are involved, the sole trader and any partner are personally liable for the full amount. Should a business operating as a limited company suffer an event that leads to huge liabilities the company itself is the party responsible for the liabilities, not the owners. The owners are only liable to the extent they have subscribed for shares, (in other words they may lose the equity they own in the company). As long as the directors have acted lawfully they cannot be made personally liable for the liabilities of the company. This means if the company collapses into bankruptcy the director owner can keep his house, pension fund and other personal assets that are separate from the limited company in which the business resides.

So, from a risk management viewpoint, are companies a good idea or a bad idea? For society as a whole they appear to be a good idea, partly because they facilitate the pooling of investment for new projects. A developed nation has extensive infrastructure in the form of roads, railways, airports, pipelines, communications, electricity and oil and gas infrastructure which requires the capital of hundreds of thousands of individuals to create. By issuing shares to millions of people, each of which is a part owner of the business, these beneficial assets for society can be created and maintained. They also encourage risk-taking in the form of new business creation because entrepreneurs can protect their personal assets by using a limited company as the vehicle for their new ventures.

The negative aspects of companies arise if you are a creditor of a company. Banks, suppliers and employees lose money when companies fall into bankruptcy. In extreme situations a limited company can be used deliberately to acquire the cash flow of a business, which is then stolen by the owners. This is of course criminal and fraudulent. This is why it is essential that stakeholders who are creditors monitor the creditworthiness (or credit risk) of any company they are involved with as a creditor.

Figure 1.5 introduces equity (and debt) to the model.

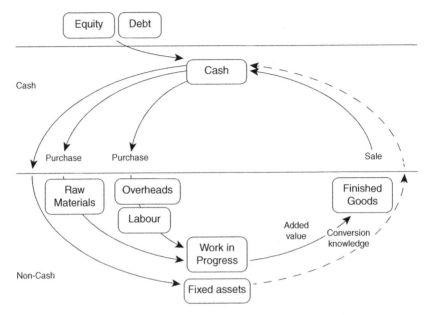

Figure 1.5   Diagram four of the cash flows of a manufacturing business

The business is now owned by an independent legal entity (a company) that is separate from the person or persons who formerly owned it. Their interest is represented by their shareholding in the EQUITY of the company. The company may also have raised cash to invest in the company by borrowing, perhaps from a bank, which is recognised in Fig. 1.5 as DEBT.

Debt, in the form of loans or leases may be used by the company to acquire fixed assets such as factory premises and machines. Debt may also be used to provide working capital in the form of an overdraft facility or via the use of factoring or invoice discounting.

Having introduced these new sources of capital we need to add further items to the model to keep it consistent with reality. Cash borrowed from banks is not lent for nothing. Banks charge INTEREST (essentially a rent) for the period that the money is advanced to the borrower. Similarly, if the company is successful it may pay DIVIDENDS to its shareholders. Finally, most governments demand that the company pay TAXATION on any taxable profits from trading or other investment income generated by the company.

These potential cash outflows do not represent operating costs because they arise for reasons that differ from the other cash outflows required to operate the

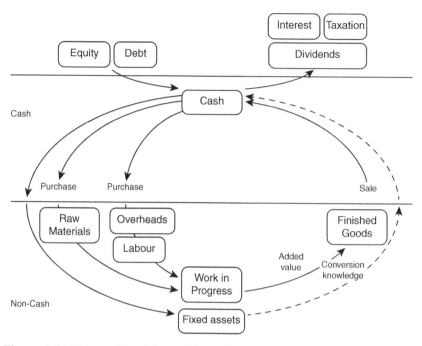

Figure 1.6   Diagram five of the cash flows of a manufacturing business

business. DIVIDENDS and INTEREST represent rewards paid to financiers as a consequence of their investment. TAXATION is a government levy on surpluses generated by the company. All the other operating costs of the business should be incurred because they are necessary in order to generate the operating cash flow of the business. When we add these items our model of the cash flows of the business looks like Fig. 1.6.

The Implications of Supplier and Customer Credit

So far we have assumed that all transactions in the business take place in cash. In the real world this is not so. There is often a difference between the time we take physical delivery of something we have purchased and when we pay for it. Conversely, it is common to sell something to a customer allowing them a period of time to pay, the cash due on the sale of the product being received some time later.

Let us consider the example of our business of our African entrepreneur some years on. He is no longer manufacturing furniture outside his home; he now has a substantial factory full of machinery and labour, owned by a limited company controlled by him.

When he buys timber he does not collect it on foot with a handcart any more. He telephones his timber merchant and asks him to deliver three truckloads of timber. When the timber arrives he does not pay for it, he signs a delivery note. A CREDITOR (or PAYABLE) is created at this point (being the money due to the supplier in payment for the goods) which may be settled (paid) one to three months later.

Similarly when the business sells a bed it is no longer sold for cash on the side of the road. Instead the beds are now manufactured in the form of flat packs, stuffed in a container and sent to IKEA, a major global discount furniture retailer. When IKEA receive the beds they do not pay cash, they sign a delivery note for the goods and create a DEBTOR (or RECEIVABLE), (being the money due from the customer for the goods sold to them) which may be settled one to three months later.

So, CREDITORS effectively grant the business a short-term interest-free loan whilst the liability to them remains unpaid. Conversely, our furniture business essentially lends its DEBTORS short-term, interest-free funds for the duration of the period whilst the debt owed to the furniture business remains unpaid.

These time delays have a substantial and important effect on the cash flows of a business and must therefore be incorporated in our model. Our model now evolves further (Fig. 1.7).

The model is now essentially complete; it contains all the cash flows relating to a single business entity. We can see clearly how the cash flows round a business. Having constructed this model, we can now work with it to develop our understanding of cash flow and business practice. What else is important to our understanding of cash flow?

The Working Capital Cycle

We can now see that cash flows round the business as follows:

1. The business orders goods and services (these being either RAW MATERIALS, LABOUR or OVERHEADS).
2. The goods and services are delivered, creating a CREDITOR. They enter production or are consumed in the production process.
3. The RAW MATERIALS are converted into WORK IN PROGRESS and finally FINISHED GOODS.
4. The FINISHED GOODS are then sold, creating a DEBTOR.
5. The DEBTOR pays the invoice some time later providing CASH to the business.
6. The CASH is used to pay CREDITORS as they fall due.

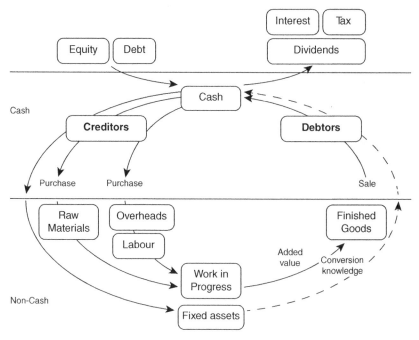

Figure 1.7 Diagram six of the cash flows of a manufacturing business

This movement of cash and resources around the business is known as the WORKING CAPITAL CYCLE. It represents the most active and volatile set of cash flows through most businesses. It is the most demanding area of cash management to control. Experienced managers know that managing the working cash flows is a demanding exercise. Most of the daily tasks of management arise from problems achieving the timely supply of goods and services at the right level of quality to the business, and the problems of manufacturing the product right first time without quality defects. Both tasks have to be satisfactorily completed before delivery and invoicing can take place in turn resulting in cash flow from customers to the business.

The investment requirements of a business and the amount of business risk inherent in a particular business are both affected by the nature and behaviour of the working capital cycle. Understanding the working capital cycle is therefore very important. The main problem is recognising the risk implications – of the impact of time – on the business.

You may be wondering what time has to do with all this. *Timing is the essence of working capital management* which, in turn, is the key component of cash flow management. Let us take two examples:

On day one Tesco plc (a leading UK supermarket group) orders a truckload of beans from Heinz plc (a major global food manufacturer). The beans arrive at Tesco's distribution depot on day three and arrive in the store on day four. By the end of day five all the beans are sold to customers for cash or credit card payment with Tesco in possession of cleared funds by day seven. Tesco then holds the cash for 53 days before paying Heinz for the beans. Contrast this with Airbus Industrie (a major civil aircraft manufacturer) who are constructing an Airbus A380 for a major airline.

Following years of negotiation Airbus receives an order for a number of aircraft, this in turn initiates the thousands of orders necessary to obtain the various components and sub-assemblies required from their respective suppliers. Over a period of many months raw materials are received and the aircraft is assembled (being work in progress at this point, which takes about 12 months), then completed and tested (becoming finished goods at this point). Finally, after further performance tests by Airbus and the purchasing airline the aircraft is accepted into service and paid for. The journey round the working capital cycle takes between one and two years.

What conclusions can we draw from these two deliberately extreme examples? If Tesco has agreed 60 day settlement terms with Heinz they will be able to sell the beans and hold the resultant cash for 53 days before settling their liability to Heinz. In other words Tesco plc *generates cash from the working asset cycle as a consequence of trading. No external finance is required to trade. All the cash required comes from credit provided by suppliers.* The operating creditors of Tesco exceed the inventory and there are no debtors. Where the operating creditors of a business exceed the amounts invested in the inventory and operating debtors of a business we say the business has *negative* net working asset investment. In this situation the more turnover *increases* the more *cash is generated* from working assets. Another way of illustrating the benefits of this is that Tesco would have the benefit of this cash for 53 days and be able to earn interest on it even if Tesco *sold the goods acquired with trade credit at the same price they were purchased from the supplier.*

Airbus Industrie enjoys much less favourable working asset behaviour. They have to invest many millions of euros in the working capital cycle to manufacture each Airbus A380. The funding of the working capital requirement for each major contract is a major undertaking. Each aircraft sells for approximately $US320 million. The more successful Airbus is at selling the Airbus A380 aircraft the more cash has to be found to invest in working capital. *Airbus has to invest vast sums into the working asset cycle in order to trade. Increased trading requires more cash to be invested in the working capital cycle. Airbus has positive working asset investment. No cash is generated from working assets; as the business grows cash is typically absorbed by working asset investment.*

Investing in Fixed Assets

Cash is also required to invest in FIXED ASSETS as required. The need for investment is determined largely by the nature of competition in the markets in which the business operates. In a competitive market, changes in consumer expectations and technology will constantly drive suppliers to design better and cheaper products to satisfy consumer needs, the fixed asset investment needed to do this must then be committed before production can take place. Depending on the nature of the fixed assets acquired, it may be possible to borrow much of the funds required to finance acquisition or construction.

Timing is also important when investing in fixed assets. Invest too early and you may not achieve sufficient utilisation to recover your investment, invest too late and your competitors may have already captured markets and reduced operating costs ahead of you.

HOW DOES ANY BUSINESS GENERATE CASH?

In order to generate cash the business must go round the WORKING ASSET CYCLE at least once. Every time the business completes a circuit more cash is generated. It follows from this that it makes sense to get very good at going round the working asset cycle very quickly as this will generate more and more surplus cash! This is what good businesses seek to optimise. Delays in completing a circuit can wipe out the extra cash simply due to the cost of financing the working asset investment. If you can regularly make a circuit round the WORKING ASSET CYCLE faster than your competitors you have a competitive advantage.

What Causes Businesses to Fail?

There is only one answer to this question. *It is because they have run out of cash.*

In a crisis all the boxes in the model become temporary or short term sources of cash, fixed assets can be sold, inventory reduced, creditors increased, overheads reduced, and so on. However, there is a natural limit to this process, there comes a point where the assets left in the business and overheads remaining are those without which it cannot continue to trade. As the business is distressed equity providers and lenders are no longer interested in supporting the business. At this point the business has run out of sources of cash.

More specifically, businesses fail because two adverse events take place simultaneously. A creditor demands payment in respect of a liability and the business does not have the cash available to pay as is demanded. As a result the creditor successfully forces the business into bankruptcy.

The rules regarding the actions to take when a business becomes insolvent vary depending on the location of the business. In countries with Roman law legal

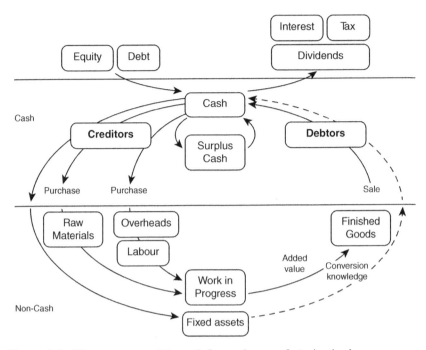

Figure 1.8   Diagram seven of the cash flows of a manufacturing business

systems the directors may be obliged to apply for court supervision and direction when the business becomes insolvent.

In Anglo-Saxon law countries it is usually an offence to trade whilst knowingly insolvent. However, exactly what constitutes this condition is not tightly specified. So, if there is no creditor who has any interest in forcing the business into bankruptcy it is unlikely to happen, irrespective of the state of the balance sheet or the availability of liquidity.

Remember the only sustainable (and most important) source of cash generation is the cash generated from operating the business (for which I use the term the OPERATING CASH MARGIN), which is the extra cash generated each time the business goes round the inner circle in the model (which I have labelled the WORKING CAPITAL CYCLE). This is shown in Fig. 1.8.

THE COMPLETE REAL BUSINESS MODEL

Our model is now almost complete. We see the WORKING CAPITAL CYCLE, we see cash spent on FIXED ASSETS and we see the sources of the cash invested in the business, these being labelled EQUITY and DEBT in the model.

For the purposes of this model and any further discussion in this book, DEBT represents all forms of borrowing, such as loans, mortgages, commercial paper, bonds, lease finance, hire purchase, factoring, invoice discounting and any other form of external debt financing. Basically, if the company pays interest in some form or other in exchange for the loan of the cash, the liability that results is a debt liability.

Any cash surpluses generated that are not paid out are retained in the business as SURPLUS CASH. When this is added to the model the model is complete. This represents an accurate and comprehensive representation of all the significant cash flows of a single business entity. The descriptions on the left-hand side of the diagram refer to the nature of the items shown in the model. Debtors, creditors and cash are items generally denominated as cash values. The non-cash items, inventory, overheads, labour and fixed assets all represent real as opposed to monetary items.

SUMMARY OF THE CHAPTER

Running a business is all about cash. More specifically it is about generating as much cash as possible from going round the working capital cycle again and again. The primary objective is to receive more cash when we sell goods or services than we paid out in fixed asset investment, overheads, labour and raw materials to make or create them.

Businesses *receive cash* from the following sources:

- From successful trading (this being the OPERATING CASH MARGIN)
- From owners in the form of EQUITY
- From lenders and other cash providers in the form of DEBT
- In certain businesses (such a supermarkets) from the WORKING CAPITAL CYCLE itself

Businesses *spend cash* in the following ways.

Within the trading cycle of the business to pay for:

- RAW MATERIALS, LABOUR and OVERHEADS
- Investing in the WORKING ASSET CYCLE
- Investing in FIXED ASSETS

They also make payments to external finance providers and the government in the form of:

- INTEREST
- DIVIDENDS
- TAXATION

- Debt repayment
- Equity buy backs and redemptions

Any cash held but not invested in the operations of the business is defined as SURPLUS CASH. This cash may be the accumulation of historic surpluses or be debt and equity not yet invested in the business itself. It may be retained in order to display that the business has adequate liquidity to operate in the future and to reinforce its credibility as a reliable counter-party.

CONCLUSION

Irrespective of the level of your prior knowledge you should now have an under-standing of the way a business operates from a cash flow centric point of view. You should also now appreciate some of the fundamental logic that underpins business operation. The purpose of this chapter is to provide an adequate grasp of the fundamentals of business, and more specifically cash flow, to assist in the assimilation of the more advanced material that follows.

2

Understanding Cash Flows Properly

INTRODUCTION

It is human nature to seek short cuts when engaged in any repetitive process. The main purpose of these shortcuts being to save time and expense.

In my other life as a trainer I have observed experienced financial analysts adopt a number of strategies to try to reduce the amount of time they spend evaluating financial statements in order to come up with the required output. Many use pre-prepared spreadsheet models and groups of ratios with which they are familiar.

Less experienced analysts generally seek to oversimplify the task, ignoring important information they do not yet understand and placing too much emphasis on what they believe are the most important numbers. The tendency is to overemphasise and over-analyse what they know about and to underemphasise the source information that is beyond their current level of comprehension.

However, there comes a point where omitting to gain a proper understanding of the task and then failing to complete the analysis fully leads to the wrong conclusions.

I have added the word 'properly' to this chapter heading in order to emphasise that it is necessary to acquire a solid understanding of cash flow analysis, accounting theory, business strategy and financial control issues, before drawing conclusions about a business entities cash flows. Those seeking immediate short cuts are going to be disappointed! Although I would always encourage users of this book to read as widely as possible around the subject, this book contains all the knowledge required in order to complete this task.

There are three discrete steps involved in the process of analysing the reported cash flows of a business. These are as follows:

1. We need to be able to understand a published cash flow statement.
2. We need to know how restate it into a more user-friendly format.
3. Finally, we need to understand what the restated values and totals signify.

This chapter deals with these tasks.

THE NATURE OF THE BEAST

We will start by familiarising ourselves with the basic anatomy of a cash flow statement. Table 2.1 is a fairly simple cash flow statement. This is in the format of a typical cash flow statement prepared in accordance with International Accounting Standard 7 – Cash Flow Statements (IAS 7).

Table 2.1   A typical cash flow statement

Simple Limited Cash Flow Statement For the year ended 31st December 20XX	Euros '000	Euros '000
Cash flows from operating activities		
Profit before taxation	5600	
Adjustments for:		
Depreciation	550	
Increase in operating provision	30	
Investment income	−500	
Interest expense	350	
	6030	
Increase in trade and other receivables	−600	
Decrease in inventories	1100	
Decrease in trade payables	−1690	
Cash generated from operations	4840	
Interest paid	−310	
Income taxes paid	−1800	
Net cash from operating activities		*2730*
Cash flows from investing activities		
Acquisition of subsidiary X net of cash acquired	−650	
Purchase of property plant and equipment	−460	
Proceeds from sale of equipment	30	
Interest received	350	
Dividends received	320	
Net cash used in investing activities		*−410*
Cash flow from financing activities		
Proceeds from issue of share capital	400	
Proceeds from long term borrowings	360	
Payment of finance lease liabilities	−110	
Dividends paid	−1450	
Net cash used in financing activities		*−800*
Net increase in cash and cash equivalents		1520

Looking at the statement in its entirety the first thing that is evident is the cash flow is split into three main sections. These have the following headings:

• Cash flows from operating activities,
• Cash flows from investing activities, and
• Cash flows from financing activities.

These primary headings have been used since the first standards on cash flows were introduced in 1987. It appears the choice of these headings was quite arbitrary, the objective being to make the cash flow statement more logical for the user.

Remember that the cash flow statement is still a relatively new invention when compared to the balance sheet and profit and loss account. They have been around for hundreds of years.

Let us see what each section contains.

CASH FLOWS FROM OPERATING ACTIVITIES

This section of a cash flow statement discloses two things:

1. The cash generated by the business, which is derived from generating more cash from selling goods or services than the cash costs of production.
2. The amount invested or generated from the net working assets of the business.

In this example both these values sub-total to an item headed 'Cash generated from operations'. This section also contains the cash interest paid and the cash taxes paid.

What is the Cash Generated from Operations?

In Chapter 1 *Understanding How Cash Flows in a Business* I introduced a cash flow model, which I call the complete real business model. I offered the observation that modern financial theory implies that the purpose of running a business is to generate cash flow by selling goods and/or services for more cash than it costs to produce them. Typically this is achieved in a manufacturing business by purchasing raw materials and other inputs such as labour and overheads, which are combined into finished products and then sold.

Notice I am talking solely in terms of cash, not profit. Profit and cash flow are not the same thing. Over the past few decades the issue of what is profit has become very complex. This will be discussed in more detail later in the book.

For a single product the cycle begins when we purchase the raw materials and ends when the debt relating to the sale of the finished goods to the customer is paid. In an established business it is usual to enjoy a period of credit from suppliers when purchasing raw materials and other overheads. To summarise, in order to generate a cash flow from producing products we typically do the following:

1. Purchase inputs, typically RAW MATERIALS, LABOUR and OVERHEADS, being granted credit by suppliers (and so creating a CREDITOR) in the process.
2. Process these inputs through WORK IN PROGRESS into FINISHED GOODS.
3. Sell the FINISHED GOODS to a customer, typically granting them a credit period as well (so creating a DEBTOR).
4. Collect the cash due from the customer at the appropriate time.

Intuitively it appears obvious that the cash generated from operations is likely to be the value of the cash value received from customers when they have purchased finished goods minus the cash costs of purchasing the inputs required to produce them, such as raw materials, labour and overheads. There is, however, something else we have to do in order to get this cash flow from customers.

We need to recognise that we have to invest cash in raw materials, work in progress and finished goods. We also have to invest cash in lending money to our customers until they pay us. Offsetting this is the fact that we get an interest free loan from our suppliers for the period that they grant us credit when we purchase goods from them. The amount invested in the inventory and debtors minus the amount invested in operating creditors is known as the amount invested in net working assets.

At the beginning of the reporting period we already have cash invested in these items. As we proceed through the year it may be necessary to adjust the values invested making them higher or lower depending on the flow of work through our business and changes in the price and credit period granted in respect of inputs to our business and the effects of changing our prices and the credit we give to customers.

So, the effects of these changes to net working assets are also recognised in the cash flow statement. They are to be found in the cash flow from operating activities section of the cash flow statement together with the cash generated from operations value.

To summarise, the business generates cash by going round the circle (Fig. 2.1) at least once (and ideally many times) in a given period.

The business also needs to have cash invested in DEBTORS and INVENTORY, less any contribution from CREDITORS, in order to trade. These three values may also increase or decrease in any given reporting period.

Let us now go through this section in detail to understand its contents more thoroughly.

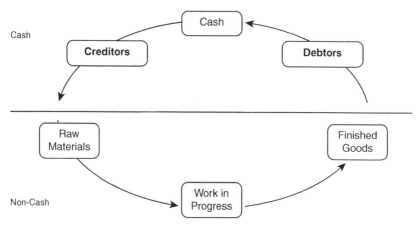

Figure 2.1 Diagram of the working asset cycle

CASH FLOWS FROM OPERATING ACTIVITIES – DETAILED REVIEW

Profit Before Taxation

The first item shown is the profit before taxation. You may be wondering what a profit number is doing in the cash flow. Most published cash flows are prepared using the *indirect* method. This means the reported cash flows are identified by deriving them from data contained in the profit and loss account of the business for the period and by identifying changes between the values disclosed in the opening and closing balance sheets for the same period.

> There is a second method of preparing a cash flow statement in published accounts known as the *direct* method. This method is explained in more detail in chapter 15 – Analysing direct cash flow statements.

When preparing an indirect cash flow statement the process commences by taking one of the profit values disclosed in the profit and loss account. This is then converted into the value of the operating cash flow by adjusting the profit value for non-cash items that have already been added or deducted. Non-cash expenses are added back and non-cash income items are removed. In this particular example the cash flow statement begins with the profit before taxation value from the profit and loss account of Simple Limited.

Indirect cash flow statements can start from other profit values in the profit and loss account. This depends on local GAAP variations and local custom in preparing cash flow statements. Usually the starting value is either the profit before interest and tax (also known as earnings before interest and tax 'EBIT', or operating profit) or the profit after tax (also known as net income). These variations are explained in more detail later in the book

GAAP stands for Generally Accepted Accounting Principles. This acronym being used to encompass the laws, regulations, standards and customs used in a particular jurisdiction to arrive at a set of published accounts.

A non-cash item is an income or expense item that appears in the profit and loss account for which there is no corresponding cash flow. Typically, the most substantial of these is the amount charged in the period for depreciation (also known in some regions as amortisation). Depreciation is a non-cash item. You do not write a cheque to anyone for depreciation!

Depreciation

Depreciation is an accounting adjustment. Its purpose is to charge the original cost of purchasing an asset to the profit and loss account in a series of instalments over its estimated useful life. Depreciation was invented by accountants a long time ago to make the profit and loss account more meaningful as a document seeking to communicate the annual performance of a business to its owners. If we did not have depreciation in accounts and capital expenditure was simply a cost, the business would show losses every time a substantial number of new fixed assets were acquired and much higher profits in periods when no fixed asset expenditure took place.

The effect of depreciation is to spread the cost effect of acquiring capital assets over their estimated useful life. This is a reasonable way of dealing with fixed assets because we continue to have the use of the fixed assets to assist us in producing goods for the duration of their useful life. Another way of considering the nature of depreciation is to think of it as a notional rent for the use of the fixed assets from the balance sheet to the profit and loss account, which is charged each year of the life of an asset to the profit and loss account.

The cash flow statement deals solely with cash flows. Depreciation is not a cash flow. We must therefore adjust for the value of depreciation charged to profits in identifying the cash flow generated from operations because it is a non-cash item.

When depreciation is deducted in the profit and loss account it is a cost or expense item. Thus, when we adjust for it in the cash flow statement we are adding it back to the disclosed profit before taxation value from the profit and loss account in the process of arriving at the operating cash margin. This is why depreciation appears as a positive value when disclosed in the cash flow statement.

Increase in Operating Provision

In a typical indirect cash flow statement there may be a number of further items listed representing other non-cash items of income or expenditure in the profit and loss account. In this particular example, in order to arrive at the correct value for the cash generated from operations we are also adjusting the profit before taxation value for an increase in operating provision. This label is a little vague. It does not tell us exactly what operating provision is involved. For example, it might be a provision relating to warranty claims on the years production, or further costs to be incurred in respect of a recent product recall.

Vague labels of this type crop up again and again in published cash flow statements. The fact that the label is vague is merely irritating, it will not affect our ability to analyse the cash flow statement as long as we know what to do with the item. As this item appears within the section of the cash flow statement labelled 'adjustments' we know it represents another add back to the profit before taxation value required in order to arrive at the cash generated from operations value. It is listed as an adjustment because movements in provisions do not represent cash flows. They represent the recognition in this period's accounts of the value of a future expected cost related to activities within the current accounting period, (an example of this might be the future warranty costs arising on this year's production).

The recognition of an expected future cost in the current periods profit and loss account is not a cash flow. The fundamental accounting concept known as the *prudence concept* requires that we recognise this future expected cost as soon as we are aware of it. However, we do not expend any cash flow in respect of this item until customers actually claim from the business in respect of warranties. The cash costs involved therefore arise in future accounting periods and are shown as such in the cash flow statement at that time.

The value of an increase in operating provision is shown as a positive number in the cash flow statement. This is because, once again, we are reversing an item that originally represented an increase in a future expected cost when charged to the profit and loss account.

Conversely, the value of a decrease in operating provision is shown as a negative number in the cash flow statement, this is because we are reversing an item that originally represented a reduction in a future expected cost in the profit and loss account.

Investment Income

This value represents the amount of investment income recognised in the profit and loss account in the current period. Once again we are showing it here in the cash flow statement as a reversing item because we need to remove it in order to arrive at the correct value for the cash generated from operations.

As we have mentioned before this cash flow statement commences with the value profit before taxation. The investment income of the business has already been recognised in the profit and loss account before arriving at this value. In order to arrive at the correct value for the cash generated from operations we need to remove this value. This doesn't mean that the investment income is left out of the cash flow statement. It is included in the cash flow statement elsewhere. We find it in the investing activities section where it appears as dividends received.

You may recognise that the value shown in the cash flows from investing activities as dividends received of 320 from the example cash flow statement of Simple Limited (Table 2.1) does not match the value of investment income adjusted for in the cash flow from operating activities section of minus 500. Again, differences of this type crop up regularly in cash flow statements; the rules for recognising income and expense in the profit and loss account are different from the recognition of the underlying cash flow itself.

The fundamental accounting concept known as the *'accruals concept'* requires us to match revenues and costs consistently as time passes. It may be possible then that the business has accrued investment income in the profit and loss account (perhaps because a dividend has been declared and approved for payment in a company in which the business has an investment). However, at the period end, the relevant dividend has not yet been paid and therefore is not recognised in the cash flow statement even though it is recognised in the profit and loss account. This is because the cash flow statement only deals with cash flows.

Interest Expense

This value represents the amount of interest expense recognised in the profit and loss account in the current period. Once again we are showing it here in the cash flow statement as an add back item because we need to adjust for it in order to arrive at the correct value for the cash generated from operations.

As we have mentioned before this cash flow statement commences with the value profit before taxation. The interest expense of the business has already been recognised in the profit and loss account before arriving at this value. In order to arrive at the correct value for the cash generated from operations we need to remove this value. This does not mean that the interest expense is left out of the cash flow statement. It is included in the cash flows from operating activities section further down where it appears as interest paid.

You will note that the value shown in the cash flows from operating activities as interest expense of 350 from the example cash flow statement of Simple Limited does not match the value of interest paid further down the same section of minus 310. Again, differences of this type crop up regularly in cash flow statements; this is due to the different rules for recognising income and expense in the profit and loss account. The fundamental accounting concept known as the accruals concept requires us to match revenues and costs consistently as time passes. It may be possible then that the business has accrued interest expense in the profit and loss account (because interest is accrued but is not yet due for payment). Only interest actually paid in the period should be recognised in the cash flow statement because the cash flow statement only deals with cash flows.

The First Total of 6030

This represents the cash generated from selling goods or services less the cash costs of production. It is an important measure of performance and a key component of the cash generated from operations. The term OPERATING CASH MARGIN is used in this book to describe this item.

Increase in Trade and Other Receivables

This represents the difference in value between the trade and other receivables (i.e. DEBTORS) at the beginning and end of the accounting period to which the cash flow statement relates. When the value in the cash flow is negative it represents an increase in the value invested in providing credit to the business's customers. In order to lend our customers more cash we have to invest more cash in trade and other receivables.

Decrease in Inventories

This item is equal to the change in the value of the inventories in the business between the beginning and end of the accounting period. In this example the inventory value has decreased, so resulting in a cash inflow to the business. This means less cash is invested in inventory at the end of the period than at the beginning. We have recovered some of the cash invested.

Decrease in Trade Payables

This item represents the change in the value of the trade payables (i.e. CREDI-TORS) between the beginning and end of the accounting period. In this case the amount owed to trade creditors has reduced. Cash has been expended to achieve this. To reduce the amount invested in the creditors of a business it is necessary to pay out cash to repay some of the trade credit granted by the supplier.

Cash Generated from Operations

This is the first major summary total appearing in this example. The cash generated from operations is 4840. This represents the difference between the cash cost of inputs to the manufacturing process and the cash received in respect of outputs, as well as the changes in the amount invested in the net working assets of the business.

The contents of this section of the cash flow so far are summarised in Table 2.2.

Table 2.2   Analysis of the cash generated from operations total

	€'000
Cash generated by the business from the cash margin on its products	6030
Cash invested or generated from the net working assets of the business	(1190)
Cash generated from operations	**4840**

These are the two key totals normally to be found in this section. When we come to introducing the recommended method used to analyse cash flows, the reasons why this split is extremely important will be made clear. For the moment let us say that the split is important because different causative factors affect each value:

- The cash generated by the business from the cash margin on its products is affected amongst other things by macro economic conditions, sector fundamentals, input cost issues, customer demand, manufacturing efficiency, and competitive pressure on output pricing.
- The cash invested or generated from the net working assets of the business is affected by the style of production (lean, just in time, etc.), the need to carry inventory to satisfy consumer needs and the typical sector structure of working assets. (For example, retailers generally sell for cash and therefore do not need to invest in providing credit to their customers.)

As a consequence each key total communicates different information to the analyst about the state of the business when analysing the cash flows of the business.

There are two remaining values left in the cash flows from operating activities section. They are the interest paid and the income taxes paid. IAS 7 makes it clear that both interest and dividends can appear in any of the three main sections, as there is no consensus on the classification of these cash flows for entities other than financial institutions. Taxes are generally shown in this section unless the cash tax paid relates to an investing or financing activity in which case the relevant amount of tax may be allocated to those sections as appropriate. What do these values represent?

Interest Paid

This is the amount of cash interest paid in the accounting period. This number may not match the profit and loss account charge for interest paid because there are different rules for the recognition of interest in the profit and loss account. The major difference is that it is normal to accrue for interest due but not paid in the profit and loss account. It is also normal in the profit and loss account to accrue the notional interest on other forms of debt with non-typical features such as deep discount bonds where no interest is paid during the life of the instrument.

Income Taxes Paid

This is the value of the cash taxes paid during the financial period. This number is normally different to the value shown in the profit and loss account because taxes are usually paid in arrears. In small- and medium-sized businesses the cash taxes paid in the current period often relate to the trading of the previous period. For large businesses the law often requires quarterly payment of Corporation Tax during the period to which it relates with one final balancing payment in respect of the accounting period after the period end. This means there is unlikely to be any significant relationship between the current period's cash generated from operations and the taxes shown in the same cash flow statement.

Cash Flows From Operating Activities – Summary

The first section of most published cash flow statements deals with the cash flows from operating activities. Whilst there may be a bewildering array of adjusting items, the bulk of the content can be summarised by two key totals: the cash generated by the business from the cash margin on its products (known as the operating cash margin); and the cash invested or generated from the net working assets of the business (known as the movement or change in the Net Working Assets). In Table 2.1 the cash interest paid and the cash taxes paid are also disclosed in this section. The sum of all these cash flows is labelled the net cash from operating activities. We may also refer to these as the cash flows relating to TRADING.

CASH FLOWS FROM INVESTING ACTIVITIES

This section of a cash flow statement also discloses two things:

1. The cash spent on purchasing or creating tangible and intangible fixed assets, and the cash received on disposing of obsolete or unwanted tangible or intangible fixed assets.

2. The cash spent on purchasing other businesses or investing in other businesses as associates or joint ventures or buying shares in other businesses as investments or to gain influence or to speculate and the cash received on disposing of businesses or shares in associates or interests in joint ventures or investments.

These represent the main elements of the investing activities section. In this particular business example we also find the cash interest received and the cash dividends received.

The headings in this section are reasonably self-explanatory. Typically we find two types of investment transaction in this section. The first relates to the purchase, creation or disposal of tangible and intangible fixed assets. By tangible fixed assets we mean items such as property or land and buildings, plant and machinery, fixtures and fittings, computer hardware and software, vehicles, ships and aircraft. Typically these represent the pool of tangible fixed assets used by the business to generate operating cash flow.

More rarely we may also encounter the purchase, creation or disposal of certain intangible fixed assets such as patents and know how and overheads relating to the creation of capital assets which have been capitalised as permitted by IAS 38. We may also refer to both of these as ASSET level cash flows.

The second type of investment transaction is where a business purchases or disposes of an interest in another business. This may range from, buying one share in (or lending one euro/dollar/yen/pound sterling to) the business, up to purchasing the whole of the business outright. Similarly it also encompasses disposing of the same. The interest may be an investment, recognised as an associate or joint venture, or giving control to the acquirer in which case the business acquired will be consolidated after acquisition as a subsidiary. We may also refer to all of these as BUSINESS level cash flows.

CASH FLOWS FROM INVESTING ACTIVITIES – DETAILED REVIEW

Acquisition of Subsidiary, X Limited, Net of Cash Acquired

This represents cash expended on the acquisition of a new business, X Limited. This will represent the purchase of a majority of, or all of, the share capital of X Limited. Goodwill will have been created if Simple Limited has paid more than the net asset value (less cash) of the balance sheet of X Limited. The goodwill will subsequently appear in the consolidated balance sheet of Simple Limited.

You may be wondering why this is shown net of cash acquired. To put this simply there is no point in acquiring cash when buying a business. The reason for this is you would be exchanging cash for cash if you bought cash, which is pointless. If, for some reason, cash is acquired in the balance sheet purchased it simply becomes part of the new groups cash pool. This is why it is normal to see the words 'net of cash acquired'.

> The value of €10 today is €10. How much would you give me for €10? Answer €10!

As a consequence of this, it is normal practice for the vendor to strip any surplus cash out of a business to be disposed of prior to the sale, usually by paying a dividend.

Purchase of Property Plant and Equipment

This represents the cash expended in the accounting period on the purchase of new property, plant and equipment. Analysts and others commonly refer to this value as capital expenditure. It is often abbreviated to the term Capex.

Proceeds from Sale of Equipment

This represents the cash received when we have disposed of equipment that is no longer required. Typically this is because it is obsolete or worn out.

> Do not confuse the proceeds from sale of equipment with the profit on sale of equipment, even though the two terms sound very similar. The profit on sale of fixed assets is an adjustment value to the cash generated from operations and is explained in more detail later in the book.

The proceeds of sale value is often insignificant in the context of the other cash flows. When summarising cash flows for analysis it is common to offset it with the period Capex to arrive at the value known as net Capex. Net Capex is the capital expenditure on new fixed assets minus the proceeds of sale of old fixed assets.

Interest Received

This value represents the cash interest received on cash surpluses held in the business during the accounting period. These surpluses may be recognised in the notes to the cash flow and accounts as cash and cash equivalents. The definition of cash equivalents varies across different GAAPs.

IAS 7 defines cash equivalents as short-term, highly liquid investments that are readily convertible to known amounts of cash and which are subject to an insignificant risk of changes in value.

This definition is designed to distinguish between investments that are very near to cash in nature and investments that may suffer from material price (or value) changes in the period over which they are held, even if this is relatively short term.

Dividends Received

This value represents dividends received from all interests in other business held by Simple Limited other than interests in subsidiaries. When a subsidiary pays a dividend to its parent company the transaction cancels out on consolidation. This means it will not appear in the consolidated statement of cash flows.

This amount will typically be reported in the profit and loss account as investment income.

Cash Flows from Investing Activities – Summary

This second section of most published cash flows deals with the cash flows relating to investment activities. Once again the section can usually be summarised by two key totals: the cash flows relating to ASSET level transactions; and the cash flows relating to BUSINESS level transactions.

In this example the cash interest received and the cash dividends received were also disclosed in this section. The sum of all these cash flows is labelled the net cash used in investing activities.

CASH FLOWS FROM FINANCING ACTIVITIES

The final section of the cash flow statement discloses two things:

1. The cash flows relating to changes in the business's equity capital.
2. The cash flows relating to changes in the business's debt position.

These are the main elements of the section. In this particular example we also find the cash dividends paid.

This section of the cash flows deals with the funding and liquidity of the business. If the business is using cash it reveals to us how this has been financed. If the business is generating cash it reveals what the cash surplus has been used for (reducing debt for example). Generally it is useful to summarise this information into two main values: the change in equity and the change in debt.

CASH FLOWS FROM FINANCING ACTIVITIES – DETAILED REVIEW

Proceeds from Issue of Share Capital

This represents the cash received from the sale of new shares to investors; it may be shown net of issue expenses, although these are usually disclosed if they are material.

This value shown in the cash flow statement may not agree with the change in share capital in the balance sheet as the shares may have been issued at a premium or discount to their par value. Any premium over par value is usually shown in the balance sheet equity as share premium or its local equivalent.

Proceeds from Long Term Borrowings

This value represents the cash received from banks or investors in respect of an increase in long-term borrowings. In other words this represents a debt increase.

Payments of Finance Lease Liabilities

This value represents the reduction in the liability outstanding in respect of finance leases entered into by Simple Limited. As a finance lease represents an interest bearing liability this item is part of the changes to debt in the accounting period. In other words this represents debt repayment.

Dividends Paid

This value represents the cash dividends paid out to investors in Simple Limited during the financial period. This value may not agree to the amount of dividends shown in the profit and loss account due to timing differences between the dividend being proposed, approved and paid. For example the final dividend for period one is usually paid in period two.

Cash Flows from Financing Activities – Summary

The final section of most published cash flows deals with the cash flows relating to financing activities. The section can usefully be summarised down to a change in EQUITY and a change in DEBT. In our example in Table 2.1, the cash dividends paid are also disclosed in this section. The total of all these cash flows is labelled the net cash used in financing activities.

Cash and Cash Equivalents

The final value in the cash flow statement is the net increase in cash and cash equivalents. This represents the increase or decrease in cash and cash equivalents held by the business in the period. In this example it is an increase of 1520.

THE NATURE OF THE BEAST – CONCLUSION

We have now examined, in some detail, the basic anatomy of a cash flow. We have learned that all the values disclosed represent pure cash flows, and that many of them do not agree to their corresponding values in the profit and loss account and balance sheet for technical reasons.

However, it is not enough to know what each value means. This is simply a starting point. We need to know what to do with each of these values in order to learn something useful about the business. The sort of questions we seek to answer are as follows:

- Is the business performing satisfactorily?
- Can we lend more money to this business?
- Can this business pay me if I supply it?
- Should I invest in this business?
- Is this business good or bad?

Unfortunately, the published cash flow does not answer these questions by providing convenient, user-friendly disclosure in an appropriate format. We have to work for our supper! In the next section we look at ways to overcome this problem.

SUMMARISING AND RESTATING CASH FLOWS FOR ANALYSIS – INTRODUCTION

Now that we understand what the contents of a simple cash flow statement represents we can now start to consider how best to summarise and restate these cash flows in order to best understand what is going on in the business.

Before we start to get radical, let us consider what we can glean directly from the information offered. For convenience the cash flow statement of Simple Limited is repeated (Table 2.3).

Table 2.3 A typical cash flow statement

Simple Limited Cash flow statement For the year ended 31st December 20XX	Euros '000	Euros '000
Cash flows from operating activities		
Profit before taxation	5600	
Adjustments for:		
Depreciation	550	
Increase in operating provision	30	
Investment income	−500	
Interest expense	350	
	6030	
Increase in trade and other receivables	−600	
Decrease in inventories	1100	
Decrease in trade payables	−1690	
Cash generated from operations	4840	
Interest paid	−310	
Income taxes paid	−1800	
Net cash from operating activities		*2730*
Cash flows from investing activities		
Acquisition of subsidiary X net of cash acquired	−650	
Purchase of property plant and equipment	−460	
Proceeds from sale of equipment	30	
Interest received	350	
Dividends received	320	
Net cash used in investing activities		*−410*
Cash flow from financing activities		
Proceeds from issue of share capital	400	
Proceeds from long term borrowings	360	
Payment of finance lease liabilities	−110	
Dividends paid	−1450	
Net cash used in financing activities		*−800*
Net increase in cash and cash equivalents		1520

The initial and most obvious way of summarising the cash flows disclosed is to examine what the totals of each section communicate as in (Table 2.4).

Table 2.4 Unadjusted cash flow section totals

Simple Limited – Summary cash flow: Year ended 31st Dec 20XX	€'000	% of operating cash item
Net cash from operating activities	2730	100%
Net cash used in investing activities	(410)	15%
Net cash used in financing activities	(800)	29%
Net increase in cash and cash equivalents	**1520**	**56%**

On the face of it these values look healthy. Simple Limited appears to be generating a healthy surplus from operations after dealing with the cost of working asset investment, interest paid and taxes. Investment and financing needs appear modest with the resulting increase in cash and cash representing over 50% of the net cash from operating activities. However, by summarising to this level we are losing a lot of potentially valuable information.

In investing activities the Capex and business level investment has been offset by substantial amounts of interest and dividends received, which implies this business has a substantial non-operating surplus of cash, cash equivalents and investments in its balance sheet.

In financing activities we have in fact increased the amount of cash invested in the business. This has been offset by the substantial dividend paid by the business.

IAS 7 allows those who prepare financial statements to show dividends paid as either a financing cash flow or an operating cash flow. Let us see what happens to the summary cash flow if we make this one adjustment (Table 2.5).

Table 2.5   Adjusted cash flow section totals

Simple Limited – Summary cash flow. Dividends paid shown as part of cash flow from operating activities rather than financing activities: Year ended 31st Dec 20XX	€'000	% of operating cash item
Net cash from operating activities	1280	100%
Net cash used in investing activities	(410)	32%
Net cash used in financing activities	650	51%
Net increase in cash and cash equivalents	**1520**	**119%**

The cash flows in the summary have changed dramatically. More importantly, the apparent relationship between the values is now different. Whilst Simple Limited still appears healthy, the amount of net cash from operating activities expended in investing activities now appears to have doubled relative to the first example. The net cash used in financing activities has become net cash generated from financing activities. The increase in cash and cash equivalents now appears to be derived partly from operations and partly from new finance.

CONCLUSION

In Table 2.5 we have only made one simple adjustment, a variation that is allowed by IAS GAAP. The result is to change completely the apparent relationships between the numbers. Remember that it is also acceptable to show interest paid and interest and dividends received in any of the three sections and corporate taxes can appear in sections other than operating if they relate to an investing or financing activity.

These permitted variations make a mockery of attempting to analyse cash flow performance directly from a published cash flow statement. This also means there is no direct comparability between cash flow statements, as their layout can vary markedly without contravening IAS GAAP.

So, how do we get around this problem? The answer is to use a standard layout.

What characteristics should this layout have? We need something that is sufficiently simple to allow us to assimilate quickly and effectively what the cash flows represent in terms of performance. However, we also require sufficient detail to enable us to avoid the distortions that would arise if we net off too much information as we did in the earlier example.

It is imperative to use a standard layout in order to gain comparability and eliminate the layout distortions arising from IAS GAAP alternatives. What is this layout?

The recommended template is shown in Table 2.6.

Table 2.6 Jury's master cash flow template

Simple Limited Summary group cash flow statement Year ended 31st December 20XX	Euros '000
OPERATING CASH MARGIN	6030
(INVESTED)/GENERATED FROM NET WORKING ASSETS	−1190
NET CAPITAL EXPENDITURE	−430
TAXATION	−1800
CASH AVAILABLE TO SATISFY FINANCE PROVIDERS	**2610**
NET INTEREST	40
NET DIVIDENDS	−1130
OTHER NON-OPERATING INCOME/(EXPENDITURE)	−650
NET CASH GENERATED/(ABSORBED) BEFORE FINANCING	**870**
Financed by:	
INCREASE/(DECREASE) IN EQUITY	400
INCREASE/(DECREASE) IN DEBT	250
(INCREASE)/DECREASE IN CASH	−1520
TOTAL CHANGE IN FINANCING	**−870**

What follows is an introduction to the template. After we have reviewed this we will revisit our analysis of the cash flows of Simple Limited to see if this layout is any more helpful in assisting us in understanding the business.

Later in the book we will develop our understanding of the power of this approach and develop our knowledge of the meaning of each line item as we examine a number of examples of the use of my template. This chapter merely serves as an initial introduction to my template.

Operating Cash Margin

This represents the cash generated from selling goods or services less the cash costs of production. It is derived from values disclosed in the cash flow from the operating activities section of a published cash flow statement. You will notice that the value is the same as that shown by the first total in the Simple Limited cash flow statement. In the Simple Limited example it is the value of the profit before taxation together with the sum of the four adjustments below it.

This value can essentially be considered as the cash flow equivalent of profit. It measures the success with which a business generates a cash flow surplus from doing things! Businesses with negative operating cash margin are receiving less cash for the goods and services they sell than the cash costs of materials and cash overheads suffered in producing them.

This value is the equivalent to the cash generated from going round the circle in the complete real business model.

(Invested)/Generated from Net Working Assets

This represents the net change in the amount invested in the net working assets of the business. The amount invested in the net working assets is the amount invested in inventories and the trade and other debtors, less the amount of interest free credit received from suppliers and other creditors because the business is trading.

Inventories represent the amount invested in raw materials, work in progress and finished goods less provisions for slow moving, damaged and obsolete items.

Seeing this value as a distinct total, independent of the cash generated from operations total, is important because the amount invested or generated from net working assets can be volatile and is affected by different drivers of change to the operating cash margin. Movements in this value convey a lot of useful information to the cash flow analyst about management quality, sectoral investment needs and relative efficiency.

Net Capital Expenditure

Represents the amount invested in new fixed assets in the period less the proceeds of selling old fixed assets. This is where we show the cash flows relating to ASSET level transactions.

The level of capital expenditure in a business is influenced by a number of factors, such as the market and business growth rate, technological change, changes in consumer demand and the need to invest to maintain competitiveness.

Taxation

This represents the taxes actually paid in the period.

Cash Available to Satisfy Finance Providers

This total represents the cash available after the business has satisfied its fixed and working asset investment needs and paid its taxes. In the long run a business needs to generate sufficient cash in order to satisfy finance providers, to service its interest burden, repay debt due in the period and provide the expected dividend to shareholders.

This value represents a key total for the cash flow analyst. Intriguingly, it doesn't appear at all in a published cash flow statement!

Net Interest

This is the value of the cash interest paid, less the value of any cash interest received. Essentially this communicates to the analyst the cost to the businesses of its net debt financing position. Net debt is the amount of interest bearing liabilities less the value of cash and cash equivalents.

Net Dividends

This is the value of the cash dividends paid, less the value of the cash dividends received.

Netting off dividends in this way simplifies the cash flow summary without losing much information. There are arguments that the net dividend cost is a more useful value to examine (the shareholders indirectly own the dividends receivable anyway!)

If more detail is required it is available from the source cash flow statement used to make the template. The template can of course be expanded should this be needed. It is up to the user how best to summarise the raw data for analysis.

Other Non-Operating Income/(Expenditure)

This is where we capture the BUSINESS level cash flows, such as the cash spent on purchasing other businesses or investing in other businesses as associates or joint ventures or buying shares in other businesses as investments and the cash received on disposing of businesses or shares in associates or interests in joint ventures or investments. We would also introduce here any grants, subsidies or other government assistance received in respect of business acquisition or development. Again, the title is meant to be largely self-explanatory. If it is not an operating cash flow item or an item related to the purchase or disposal of fixed assets it probably goes here!

Net Cash Generated/(Absorbed) Before Financing

This is the second key total. This total represents the cash surplus or deficit for the period after all cash costs incurred in the period have been satisfied. The remainder of the template deals with the impact of changes in the financing of the business. Again, it is unusual for this value to be stated implicitly in a published cash flow statement.

Increase/(Decrease) in Equity

This represents the net cash change in equity during the period. Businesses raise new equity by issuing shares and, in most countries, larger businesses are able to buy back or cancel some of their equity should they wish to do so.

Increase/(Decrease) in Debt

This represents the net cash change in the total debt of the business in the period. By netting in this way we eliminate the effects of re-financing (this being replacing old debt with new debt) leaving us with a view of the actual debt change in the period.

(Increase)/Decrease in Cash

This represents the change in the value of cash and cash equivalents during the period. Notice that in my template the signage of this value is reversed compared to the value disclosed in a typical published cash flow statement. An increase in cash and cash equivalents is shown as a negative number, a decrease in cash and cash equivalents is shown as a positive number.

It is necessary to reverse the sign of the last number to take advantage of a property of the cash flow statement that is not obvious from the published version and is particularly valuable to the analyst. *A cash flow statement balances just like a balance sheet.* As is clear from the master template the net cash generated/(absorbed) before financing is always equal in value to the financing cash flows themselves (after adjusting the signage of the cash and cash equivalents). This balancing property enables us to confirm that we have not made any arithmetic errors or omitted any of the values from the original cash flow statement, so improving accuracy. Bear in mind that having balanced the cash flow template it is still possible to make errors of allocation by entering a source value into the wrong heading.

Why is the signage of the last cash and cash equivalents number in a typical cash flow statement different to the signage used in the template?

Cash Change Signage – Algebraic Explanation

It has to do with the way a published cash flow statement is laid out. As you can see from Simple Limited the published cash flow statement is not laid out as a balancing statement. The cash flows are summarised and then added up to arrive at a final total or difference. The effect of this layout is to make the signage of the last number only in the cash flow incorrect should we wish to make a layout with the balancing feature. This is a problem with virtually all published cash flows irrespective of their national origin.

We can show this algebraically. A typical published cash flow is laid out like this:

$$O \pm I \pm F = C$$

where

O = The cash flows from operating activities
I = The cash flows from investing activities
F = The cash flows from financing activities
C = The change in cash and cash equivalents

In the template, in order to have two balancing totals which cancel each other out to zero we bring the cash value to the left side of the formula so it looks like this:

$$O \pm I \pm F - C = 0$$

So, in order to make the layout in my template mathematically consistent it is necessary to change the sign of the final cash value shown in the published cash flow.

Cash Change Signage – Double Entry Explanation

A second explanation relies on the process of double entry accounting to illuminate what is actually going on. If you have any familiarity with book keeping you will know that every transaction in a set of double entry accounts has two entries. These two entries for each transaction are known as a debit entry and a credit entry. At the end of a period all the entries are added up, if no arithmetic errors have been made all the debits and all the credits will total to the same value. In other words they will be in balance.

Balance Sheet

Debit side	Credit side
ASSETS	LIABILITIES

When I designed the template I had a choice as to how I dealt with the signage of the equity, debt and cash numbers. I chose to represent an increase in equity as positive, because for most people this is the intuitive signage to use for an increase, as debt is also on the same side of the balance sheet (a liability item) an increase in debt must also be positive, which again is largely intuitive for most people.

Cash, however, is not a liability. It is an asset item, this means an increase in cash must have the opposite signage to the equivalent equity and debt value for the three numbers to set off correctly in arriving at the balancing total. This inevitably means that showing the cash increase as negative is not particularly intuitive for most people, however, I believe it is preferable to reversing the signage of the other two items – equity and debt – because it leaves us with only one value whose sign is counter-intuitive rather than two.

Balance Sheet

Debit side	Credit side
ASSETS	LIABILITIES
Cash	Debt and Equity

If you mentally take the values shown above for the equity, debt and cash of Simple Limited and insert them in the above diagram it should become clear why it is necessary to change the sign associated with cash.

I have provided two explanations as to why it is necessary to change the last number only of a published cash flow in order to balance the master template. Increased familiarity by the user with the restatement of published cash flows will inevitably reinforce this point until it is no longer an issue in the mind of the user.

To summarise, unless the published cash flow statement is laid out as a balancing statement (something I have observed on a few rare occasions) it will always be necessary to reverse the sign of the last cash number in the cash flow statement only in order to get the master template values to balance correctly.

ANALYSING THE CASH FLOWS IN THE MASTER TEMPLATE

So, we have successfully summarised the published cash flows into the template. What does it tell us?

By having a standardised layout we have eliminated the distortions that might arise due to positional differences in the disclosure of interest, dividend and taxation values. We have also laid out the values in such a way that two key totals not shown in the original published cash flow statement are exposed for analysis and assessment (Table 2.7).

Table 2.7   The completed Jury's master cash flow template for Simple Limited

Simple Limited Summary group cash flow statement Year ended 31st December 20XX	Euros '000
OPERATING CASH MARGIN	6030
(INVESTED)/GENERATED FROM NET WORKING ASSETS	−1190
NET CAPITAL EXPENDITURE	−430
TAXATION	−1800
CASH AVAILABLE TO SATISFY FINANCE PROVIDERS	**2610**
NET INTEREST	40
NET DIVIDENDS	−1130
OTHER NON-OPERATING INCOME/(EXPENDITURE)	−650
NET CASH GENERATED/(ABSORBED) BEFORE FINANCING	**870**
Financed by:	
INCREASE/(DECREASE) IN EQUITY	400
INCREASE/(DECREASE) IN DEBT	250
(INCREASE)/DECREASE IN CASH	−1520
TOTAL CHANGE IN FINANCING	**−870**

Here is an explanation of what the cash flows of Simple Limited might reveal to an analyst experienced in the application of the analysis techniques explained in more detail as we proceed to the more advanced parts of the book.

Simple Limited appears to enjoy a healthy operating cash margin with approximately 20% of it being absorbed in working capital changes. Net capital expenditure appears low (we know this because we can compare it with the depreciation value in the adjustments part of the cash flows from operating activities), net capital expenditure is 78% of the period depreciation charge. IAS depreciation is based on writing off assets over their estimated useful life and therefore provides a crude estimate of the amount required each year to replace fixed assets. Thus it appears the business is investing less in fixed assets than it needs to compensate for the wearing out of the existing assets each year.

Taxes appear consistent with a business with no net debt. The taxation value is 28% of the operating cash margin, which may not signify anything if the taxation paid this year relates to cash generated in the previous year. If taxes are in arrears the tax paid implies the business's last accounting period enjoyed a similar operating cash margin value assuming no net leverage. The cash available to satisfy finance providers is a surplus of €2610.

The net interest value is positive, implying no net debt on average over the year, the net dividend is a substantial outflow even after offsetting dividends received. Simple Limited has made a small acquisition during the year. The remaining surplus of €870, together with the net increase in equity and debt has resulted in an increase in cash retained in the business of €1520.

These cash flows are typical of an established and successful mature business. Notice that everything mentioned above has been derived solely from the cash flow statement, no reference is made anywhere to any other value available in the full set of accounts.

THE STATE OF PLAY

So far we have started to address the nature of a cash flow statement and what this tells us about the cash flows of a business. Secondly we have introduced Jury's Cash Flow Template and restated the cash flows of Simple Limited into the template.

Finally, we have scratched the surface of what we can glean from the restated cash flows. It is now time to develop a deeper and more thorough understanding of this process. In the next chapter we introduce a further element of the knowledge set required to fully grasp cash flow analysis.

3
Start-up, Growth, Mature, Decline

INTRODUCTION

In order to gain further benefit and insight from the results of our cash flow restatement we need to understand what a typical set of 'good' cash flows should look like.

The typical 'good' pattern of cash flows varies dramatically between different businesses. The most important reason for this variety is to do with where the business is in its life cycle.

In this section we look at the typical cash flows of a business at start-up, in the growth phase, the mature phase, and finally the decline phase. To make this section as useful as possible to the analyst I have included a short discussion of exactly what we mean by the terms start-up, growth, maturity and decline when applied to business analysis.

Later in the book there are separate chapters on each of the four phases. They go into more detail about various aspects of analysis relevant to that particular phase. All cash flow values quoted in the text from the examples represent thousands.

THE START-UP PHASE

When does business commence?

As any entrepreneur knows, there are a number of steps that precede the commencement of trade.

Most entrepreneurs start with an idea for a new product or service. They then research the viability of the idea, the initiatives required, assess the feasibility of operations, the business risks involved and develop a business plan. This part of the process can take years. Assuming the viability of the project looks good, the entrepreneur at some point raises capital and invests in the necessary initiatives to develop the product or service.

At some point, once operations are established on a commercial scale, sales commence to customers of the business. This is when the first cash inflows from operations arrive. Prior to this point we do not have a true business. You could say we have a charity! Some person or persons (the project sponsors) are giving money to other persons to do things for them.

Why is this issue of what constitutes a true business so significant?

In the past I have observed numerous situations where entrepreneurs and businessman have claimed to be running a business, but in fact there is no true business there. There may be products, factories, employees, sales literature and administration. What missing is sales and hence cash flow from customers! In other words demand for the product or service provided has not yet been proven to exist.

I recollect visiting a start-up business that had developed a new form of solar heating device, I was shown a completed version of the product, met employees and was shown a factory containing various machinery purchased to manufacture the product. However, at this point, there was no sales activity at all! The business closed having run out of cash before any material level of sales had been achieved.

So, for the purposes of analysing cash flows, my definition of 'a start-up business' is the achievement of regular operating cash flow from customers. The business may not be proven to be viable in the long run at this point; however, some important milestones will have been passed.

1. The product or service is being delivered successfully.
2. Someone, somewhere (a customer) is willing to pay for it.
3. Customers are continuing to consume the product or service after their first purchase (there are repeat purchases).

The business will almost certainly still be cash negative and loss making at this point. The long journey to success is not yet complete. However, the basic credibility of the business model has been demonstrated. In the later chapter on the start-up phase we will discuss in more detail what happens in the period before this point.

So, in this initial example, my start-up business has already designed the first product or service to be sold and invested sufficiently to deliver this. Customers are starting to buy the product.

The cash flows of a start-up business could look like the example in Table 3.1.

Let us assume that an entrepreneur has recently started a new business. The business is manufacturing some sort of consumer product that requires an investment in machinery.

The restated cash flow summary reports the cash flows over the first year of operation. Let us review what the template tells us about the business.

The operating cash margin is negative as the business is still producing goods for more cash cost than they receive in sales income. This is because the volume through the plant is still too low to capture the necessary economies of scale to be profitable. The workforce is still learning to manufacture the product to the required levels of quality in an efficient manner. Production is not yet particularly efficient.

The business is investing in the net working assets it requires. The business has to invest in inventory; it must have sufficient raw materials, work in progress and

Table 3.1   The cash flows of a start-up business

Start-up example Restated cash flows Year 1	Dollars '000
OPERATING CASH MARGIN	−10
(INVESTED)/GENERATED FROM NET WORKING ASSETS	−200
NET CAPITAL EXPENDITURE	−500
TAXATION	0
CASH AVAILABLE TO SATISFY FINANCE PROVIDERS	**−710**
NET INTEREST	30
NET DIVIDENDS	0
OTHER NON-OPERATING INCOME/(EXPENDITURE)	300
NET CASH GENERATED/(ABSORBED) BEFORE FINANCING	**−380**
Financed by:	
INCREASE/(DECREASE) IN EQUITY	500
INCREASE/(DECREASE) IN DEBT	0
(INCREASE)/DECREASE IN CASH	−120
TOTAL CHANGE IN FINANCING	**380**

finished goods to be able to satisfy customer needs as required. In addition it will be obliged to provide trade credit to its customers (invest in debtors) as it acquires them if this is normal practice in the market in which the business operates. It will enjoy little if any trade credit from its suppliers, however, due to the newness of the business and lack of track record on which the suppliers could base a credit assessment. Most raw material purchases will be in cash.

The business is investing in fixed assets. In this year the entrepreneur has purchased the first machine required to commence production as well as other fixed assets needed to package and distribute the product.

The business pays no taxes at this point, as it has never made a profit, indeed there is likely to be a tax loss carried forward at the end of the year.

The cash available to satisfy finance providers is a substantial negative. This is typically what we expect to see at this point in the start-up businesses development.

The business has a small amount of interest received due to the having a net cash position in its balance sheet. There is no interest payable as the business has no debt at this point in its development.

The business does not pay a dividend at this point because any cash available at this point is used for investment and because it's probably illegal! In many countries dividends can only be paid out of positive revenue reserves. At this point the revenue reserves of the business are negative in the balance sheet.

The business receives a substantial grant from the government because it is creating employment in its location. The entrepreneur has employed five persons on start-up.

The net cash absorbed before financing at the end of the first year's trading is $380. This is financed by the introduction of $500 in equity from the entrepreneur, her family and other investors. At the end of the period $120 of this new equity remains in the business cash account unspent.

This is a typical set of start-up cash flows. Generally the business is cash negative, the shortfall being financed by investors.

THE GROWTH PHASE

The next three most important objectives are to achieve a positive cash flow position, to break even and to make this sustainable into the future. Ideally these objectives are achieved in the first two to three years of the life of the business. The business then enters the growth phase.

What exactly do we mean by a growth business? We mean a business whose VOLUME of output (or if it is a service business, its scale of operations) is growing. Inevitably this requires investment in both working assets and fixed assets (Table 3.2).

Table 3.2   The cash flows of a growth business

Growth example Restated cash flows Year 4	Dollars '000
OPERATING CASH MARGIN	1000
(INVESTED)/GENERATED FROM NET WORKING ASSETS	−400
NET CAPITAL EXPENDITURE	−900
TAXATION	−300
CASH AVAILABLE TO SATISFY FINANCE PROVIDERS	**−600**
NET INTEREST	−100
NET DIVIDENDS	0
OTHER NON-OPERATING INCOME/(EXPENDITURE)	100
NET CASH GENERATED/(ABSORBED) BEFORE FINANCING	**−600**
Financed by:	
INCREASE/(DECREASE) IN EQUITY	300
INCREASE/(DECREASE) IN DEBT	210
(INCREASE)/DECREASE IN CASH	90
TOTAL CHANGE IN FINANCING	**600**

Let us assume our example manufacturing business has successfully negotiated the start-up phase, the business is now growing strongly. How does this change what we see?

The operating cash margin is now positive and the business is generating a healthy cash surplus against its cash costs every time it sells its product to customers.

The business is still investing in net working assets because it is growing its unit output strongly. It therefore requires investment in increasing its inventory and its debtors. The business is now able to obtain some trade credit from its major suppliers as it is trading profitably and has a three-year track record available for analysis. This offsets some of the investment required in inventory and debtors.

The business is still investing in fixed assets because it is still growing; further machinery is purchased as required to increase output as the business expands. Periodically the factory itself may require expansion.

The business is now paying some taxes; however, the liability is not large. As a consequence of the capital investment there is substantial tax depreciation available to reduce the tax liability.

The cash available to satisfy finance providers is still negative. Again, this is typically what we expect in a growth business. The reason it is negative is that the business is making the fixed and working asset investment required to keep pace with growth in demand for its products faster than it is generating cash from the operating cash margin. The presumption when the investment is made is that the investment in fixed and working assets in the current period will yield more operating cash margin from the resulting increases in the volume of output in future years as the business continues to grow. Investors are prepared to finance this if they believe the future increase in operating cash flow as a result of the investment will be sufficient to recover or exceed the cash they invest in the new fixed and working assets.

The business is now paying interest. In our example, finance leases have been used to acquire some of the machinery and represent part of the capital expenditure. The young business in the growth phase is still too risky for most commercial banks to consider lending medium-term finance. However, leasing companies are less concerned about the business risk issues as they have the security of the machinery (against which they have lent) to rely on should the business cease to make the monthly payments required for any reason.

No dividends are being paid at this time, as the business is still cash negative. All surplus resources are focused on continuing the rapid growth of the business.

The business continues to receive grants from the government in respect of employment creation as it continues to take on more new employees for the first time.

The net cash absorbed before financing at the end of the fourth year's trading is $600. This is financed by the introduction of $300 in equity from growth stage investors and the introduction of $210 of debt being the principal outstanding in respect of the finance leases on new fixed assets. The remaining $90 required has come from cash and cash equivalents already in the business as the beginning of year four.

This is a typical set of growth cash flows. The business is still cash negative in this stage, because it is investing more in fixed and working assets in a given period than it is generating in operating cash margin. The shortfall is financed by growth investors, lenders with an appetite for lending to such businesses and the cash, which was retained in the business from previous periods.

THE MATURE PHASE

In a business analysis context the term 'mature' is somewhat ambiguous. All businesses want to grow if they can, including businesses considered by investors and analysts to be mature. They continue to invest significant amounts of management time and effort in seeking ways to increase turnover, profits and cash flows.

So, what exactly do I mean by a business that is mature? I will start by defining a business that is mature as one that is no longer growing the VOLUME of its output. This means that the new investment in fixed and working assets to grow the output of the business is no longer required. In a successful mature business the overall cash flows are positive (Table 3.3).

Table 3.3   The cash flows of a mature business

Mature example Restated cash flows Year 9	Dollars '000
OPERATING CASH MARGIN	3500
(INVESTED)/GENERATED FROM NET WORKING ASSETS	−600
NET CAPITAL EXPENDITURE	−1000
TAXATION	−1000
CASH AVAILABLE TO SATISFY FINANCE PROVIDERS	**900**
NET INTEREST	−400
NET DIVIDENDS	−400
OTHER NON-OPERATING INCOME/(EXPENDITURE)	0
NET CASH GENERATED/(ABSORBED) BEFORE FINANCING	**100**
Financed by:	
INCREASE/(DECREASE) IN EQUITY	0
INCREASE/(DECREASE) IN DEBT	−100
(INCREASE)/DECREASE IN CASH	0
TOTAL CHANGE IN FINANCING	**−100**

Let us assume our example business is now mature. The business has reached a position in the geographic markets in which it chooses to compete where it controls a significant market share and enjoys adequate competitive advantages to sustain its position. At this point it has no immediate plans for further new investment or growth in the planned volume of its output.

The operating cash margin is now substantial, the business is generating a healthy cash surplus against its cash costs each time it sells its products to customers. It has thousands of customers spread over a wide geographic area. It has learned how to manufacture its product in a highly efficient way and has used capital expenditure over many years to lower costs and improve quality. It is selling its product in millions of units a year. The volume of output is not growing or is growing very slowly.

The business is still investing in net working assets. Why is this?

The business does not require further investment in net working assets in respect of volume growth because there is none! However, there is one other external variable affecting the business that may still trigger a need for further investment each year. This is the effect of inflation on the business. If the economy in which the business operates suffers inflation at say 2% a year this means that it will cost 2% more at the end of the year to replace the same physical inventory that was present at the beginning of the year. The same logic applies to debtors. Conversely the interest-free loan that represents supplier credit will increase 2% a year in respect of the same physical purchasing. So, even in a mature business, it may be necessary to invest in net working assets each period to offset inflation effects.

The business is still investing in fixed assets. Again, it may not immediately be obvious why. The business is no longer growing so it does not require fixed asset investment to provide increased output capacity. As with the net working assets there is a second driver of investment at work. Machines wear out, vehicles and computers need replacing regularly. We have a name for this type of capital expenditure (this term often being abbreviated to Capex). This is known as maintenance or replacement Capex. This distinguishes it clearly from growth Capex, which is new capital expenditure made with the intention of increasing output or operations.

So, when a business stops growing its output Capex doesn't drop to zero. It drops to a lower number representing the maintenance or replacement Capex. For a business to maintain its productive capacity it needs to keep its fixed assets in appropriate productive condition. Competitive and technological changes may also stimulate fixed asset replacement even in conditions of no growth of output. So our mature business will still have net capital expenditure, this being devoted mainly to maintenance or replacement Capex.

The business is now paying a substantial amount in cash taxes, as there is less capital expenditure to reduce the tax bill through accelerated tax depreciation.

Remember that the amount shown in respect of taxes in this year's cash flow statement may in some countries relate to the previous year's profits and this means the value may have no direct relationship with this year's operating cash margin.

The cash available to satisfy finance providers is now positive. This is what we expect to see in a successful mature business. All mature businesses should be producing a positive cash flow available to satisfy finance providers. If the cash flow is negative at this point it means the business is not generating sufficient operating cash flow to cover investment needs and taxes, *a situation that is not sustainable*. The business is probably distressed and without significant change may collapse at some point in the future. If a business cannot meet its maintenance investment needs and pay its taxes from the operating cash margin it is in serious trouble. Remember that this measure of performance is before we consider the additional cash outflows relating to the servicing of debt and providing dividends to investors. Neglecting either of these will also result in problems in the future.

The business is now paying interest. It is now nine years old and has built up a substantial balance sheet full of assets. It should be an attractive lending opportunity for most lenders and the business should have little trouble in raising any kind of debt as it requires it. Our example business now has bank debt in its balance sheet as well as finance leases.

The business now pays a dividend. Whist the decision to pay a dividend is largely a matter of tax efficiency in a private company it would be essential in a mature public company if the business were to sustain a reasonable share price. Corporate finance theory suggests mature businesses should be distributing cash back to investors because they no longer require their cash surpluses for investment in the business.

Other non-operating income/(expenditure) is zero as the business is not engaged in the acquisition or disposal of other businesses or investments and is no longer receiving any grants.

There is a small cash surplus before financing at the end of the ninth year's trading of $100. There is no longer any need to introduce further new equity to the business. If the business required investment for any reason it would normally borrow to fund it. In this example the $100 has been used to reduce the debt outstanding. Other than that required for day to day liquidity there is no cash in the business as it now has a net debt position. This is why there is no movement in the cash change value.

This is a typical set of mature cash flows. The business is generating cash at both the cash available to satisfy finance providers total and the net cash generated/(absorbed) total. It now has net debt and pays dividends. Other than maintaining its fixed and working assets its investment needs are minimal.

THE DECLINE PHASE

The word 'decline' is used by analysts for a variety of purposes. A business that is suffering poor performance may be referred to as being 'in decline'. In this sense a business can be in decline in any of the four phases. The whole issue of bad performance in each of the four phases is dealt with the later in Chapters 6–11, which go into more depth about what constitutes 'good' and 'bad' cash flows.

What we are going to examine here is the effect on the cash flows of being a successful business whose product or service markets are in decline. That is to say they are reducing in size year on year. This implies that the volume of output produced by the business is falling year on year. What will the cash flow look like now?

This is not a poorly managed business or failing business. What is illustrated in Table 3.4 is a successful business in a declining market. The best example available at the moment is probably a cigarette manufacturing company. In Europe cigarette consumption is declining at about 3% a year. The cash flow decline example is included at this point to illustrate to the reader what should be happening to the behaviour of the cash flows in such a situation in a successful business.

Table 3.4   The cash flows of a decline business

Decline example Restated cash flows Year 20	Dollars '000
OPERATING CASH MARGIN	7000
(INVESTED)/GENERATED FROM NET WORKING ASSETS	1000
NET CAPITAL EXPENDITURE	1500
TAXATION	−3200
CASH AVAILABLE TO SATISFY FINANCE PROVIDERS	**6300**
NET INTEREST	−1000
NET DIVIDENDS	−3000
OTHER NON-OPERATING INCOME/(EXPENDITURE)	0
NET CASH GENERATED/(ABSORBED) BEFORE FINANCING	**2300**
Financed by:	
INCREASE/(DECREASE) IN EQUITY	−1000
INCREASE/(DECREASE) IN DEBT	−1300
(INCREASE)/DECREASE IN CASH	0
TOTAL CHANGE IN FINANCING	**−2300**

We expect to see something along the following lines: The operating cash margin is substantial. The business is generating a healthy cash surplus against its cash costs each time it sells its product to customers. It has learned how to manufacture its product in a highly efficient way and has been exploiting a significant position in its market for decades. It is selling its product in millions of units a year. Turnover is declining at a few percent a year. The operating cash margin is still substantial but is falling slowly year on year.

The business is now recovering its investment in working assets. As the business turnover declines the need to invest in inventory and debtors – less the interest-free loan from suppliers – disappears and, as the amount invested in working assets declines, the cash invested in working assets in the growth phase of the business returns to the business as a cash inflow.

The business is now recovering its investment in fixed assets. As volume output reduces manufacturing capacity is rationalised. Factories that are not required are closed and where possible the plant and machinery is sold to others or relocated. As the factory was built decades ago in or near centres of population the land on which it sits may be very valuable for redevelopment. Production is concentrated in the lowest cost and most modern facilities, further increasing margins. Maintenance Capex may still be required. However, this is minimal due to the availability of surplus assets elsewhere to substitute for it. The proceeds of sale of fixed assets exceeds the replacement Capex, so resulting in a cash inflow from net capital expenditure.

The business pays a very substantial amount in cash taxes, as there is minimal capital expenditure to reduce the tax bill through accelerated tax depreciation.

The cash available to satisfy finance providers is now massively positive. This is what should be happening in a successful decline business. Not only are we receiving the operating cash margin, we are recovering the investment in net working assets and fixed assets.

In our example the business now carries a significant amount of debt and now pays a lot of interest. If the business is large the management may be increasing the debt in the business periodically and using the cash inflow to buy back equity, so supporting the share price. The massive operating cash flow is used to service interest and repay debt. Every few years the process of adding more debt to buy back equity may be repeated.

In our example the business also pays a massive dividend. If the business is listed this is the only reason to invest in the business as there is no longer any expected future volume growth. Investors assess a share in such a company on the basis of its dividend yield relative to debt yields.

Other non-operating income/(expenditure) is zero as the business is not engaged in the acquisition or disposal of other businesses or investments and is no longer receiving any grants.

There is a massive cash surplus before financing at the end of the years trading of $2300. This is used to buy back equity and repay debt. A process that theoretically could continue until the business finally self liquidates.

This is a typical set of successful decline cash flows. It is included to provide a complete understanding of how the basic patterns of cash flow should appear in the four phases of the life of a successful business. In the real world a declining business rarely displays this sort of cash flow performance. This is discussed in more detail in Chapter 10.

CONCLUSION

We should now have gained an understanding of what we expect the cash flows of business to look like through the four phases of a successful businesses existence. This is summarised in Table 3.5.

Table 3.5   The cash flows through the four phases of a successful business

Summary example Restated cash flows	Start-up $'000	Growth $'000	Mature $'000	Decline $'000
OPERATING CASH MARGIN	−10	1000	3500	7000
(INV)/GEN FROM NET WORKING ASSETS	−200	−400	−600	1000
NET CAPITAL EXPENDITURE	−500	−900	−1000	1500
TAXATION	0	−300	−1000	−3200
CATS FINANCE PROVIDERS	**−710**	**−600**	**900**	**6300**
NET INTEREST	30	−100	−400	−1000
NET DIVIDENDS	0	0	−400	−3000
OTHER NON-OPERATING INC/(EXP)	300	100	0	0
NET CASH GEN/(ABS) BEFORE FINANCING	**−380**	**−600**	**100**	**2300**
Financed by:				
INCREASE/(DECREASE) IN EQUITY	500	300	0	−1000
INCREASE/(DECREASE) IN DEBT	0	210	−100	−1300
(INCREASE)/DECREASE IN CASH	−120	90	0	0
TOTAL CHANGE IN FINANCING	**380**	**600**	**−100**	**−2300**

SUMMARY

The goal of this chapter was to present to the reader a typical set of cash flows for a successful business in the four phases in the life of that business, these being: Start-up, Growth, Mature and Decline. These examples provide a sort of budget or ideal against which we can examine actual cash flows taken from the real world.

It should now be clear that each line of the cash flow template is driven by different cash flow drivers or behaviours. By developing our understanding of these drivers we can improve our ability to evaluate the cash flows of a business when presented in the Jury's Template format.

4

Restating the Cash Flows
of a Real Business

INTRODUCTION

This chapter commences the more detailed part of the book. The following chapters present everything the financial analyst may require to become fully conversant with historic cash flow analysis.

This chapter seeks to present all the information required by an analyst to summarise and restate an indirect cash flow statement into a common format for analysis.

The restatement process that is described is essentially a technical exercise. Accordingly, this chapter is organised to be as user friendly as possible when read for the first time and easily accessible subsequently when used as a technical reference.

OUR OBJECTIVE

We have a cash flow statement to analyse, how do we go about our task?

> There are two possible ways of preparing and presenting a cash flow statement, these are known as the direct method and the indirect method. The first task to ascertain is whether the cash flow is a direct cash flow or an indirect cash flow.

In this chapter we will concentrate on the restatement of indirect cash flows. The reason for this is most of the published cash flows in the world are prepared using the indirect method. Cash flow statements prepared using the direct method are rare. If you wish to know more about direct cash flows at this point Chapter 15 is devoted entirely to direct cash flows.

> A direct cash flow is prepared by taking the cash records of the business, coding each cash transaction during the period into its relevant cash flow constituent and then summarising the resulting information into a cash flow statement.

We can identify whether a cash flow statement is direct or indirect by examining the first few lines of the cash flow statement. In the case of direct cash flow statements instead of starting with a profit value taken from the profit and loss account the cash flow typically starts with receipts from customers and payments to employees and suppliers.

> An indirect cash flow is prepared by identifying the various cash flows required to prepare the cash flow statement from information contained within the profit and loss account and the current and previous balance sheet of the business.

THE IMPLICATION OF DIFFERENT GAAPs

GAAP is an acronym for Generally Accepted Accounting Principles. The next question we need to consider is, under which GAAP rules has the cash flow statement been prepared?

Whilst most countries follow a broadly similar approach to the preparation and presentation of cash flow statements, there are differences in the minutiae of the different GAAP rules. This chapter starts by showing how to summarise cash flows prepared under International Accounting Standards (IAS) GAAP rules.

Once you are familiar with a variety of the cash flow statements from different countries, you will be able to anticipate the typical problems that you will be likely to encounter when restating particular countries cash flows. For this reason, Chapter 5 is devoted to the specific issues involved in analysing the cash flows of entities prepared using US GAAP.

We can now proceed to understanding in detail the restatement process. We will work through this process section by section using the a cash flow statement taken from the accounts of Nokia (the global mobile telephone group) as an initial example. Nokia has been producing IAS accounts for many years.

Arithmetic Signage in the Cash Flows

By *signage* we mean whether a cash flow is positive (an inflow) or negative (an outflow). Generally the treatment of the signage of values contained within a cash flow statement is straightforward. Positive values represent cash inflows and negative values represent cash outflows. All signage should be summarised into Jury's Template as observed.

In the template, brackets are used with certain of the labels to signify the meaning of the signage of the cash flow, in the examples brackets or a minus sign may be used to signify negative cash flows.

The only exception to this rule is the last number in the cash flow statement, which is usually the change in cash, or the change in cash and cash equivalents.

Unless the published cash flow is laid out as a balancing statement the final cash value shown will require its signage reversing to make the restated cash flow template balance. The reasons for this being explained in Chapter 2.

Acronyms

From now on we will start to use the following acronyms to describe certain values. The first time the term is used in the text the acronym will normally follow.

EBIT	Earning before interest and tax
EBITDA	Earnings before interest, tax, depreciation and amortisation
P&L	Profit and loss account
IAS	International Accounting Standard
IFRS	International Financial Reporting Standard
M or m	Million meaning 1 000 000

RESTATING THE CASH FLOWS FROM OPERATING ACTIVITIES

The information in Table 4.1 is taken from the published accounts of Nokia.

Table 4.1 is the *cash flow from operating activities* part of the full IFRS cash flow statement.

Table 4.1 Summary of net cash from operating activities

FINANCIAL YEAR ENDED DECEMBER 31st	Notes	20XX €M
CASH FLOW FROM OPERATING ACTIVITIES		
Profit attributable to equity holders of the parent		3988
Adjustments, total	32	3469
Change in net working capital	32	−2546
Cash generated from operations		**4911**
Interest received		416
Interest paid		−155
Other financial income and expenses, net received		−195
Income taxes paid, net received		−1780
NET CASH FROM OPERATING ACTIVITIES		**3197**

Generally the cash flow from operating activities section of a published cash flow statement contains values relating to the first two lines of the template. It may also contain other values relating to interest and taxation. The persons responsible for the preparation of the cash flow statement can choose to disclose them here. So, in Table 4.2 we are going to extract the values relating to the items shown in bold below.

Table 4.2   Building up the template – dealing with the first two lines

---

OPERATING CASH MARGIN
(INVESTED)/GENERATED FROM NET WORKING ASSETS
NET CAPITAL EXPENDITURE
TAXATION
CASH AVAILABLE TO SATISFY FINANCE PROVIDERS
NET INTEREST
NET DIVIDENDS
OTHER NON-OPERATING INCOME/(EXPENDITURE)
NET CASH GENERATED/(ABSORBED) BEFORE FINANCING
Financed by:
INCREASE/(DECREASE) IN EQUITY
INCREASE/(DECREASE) IN DEBT
(INCREASE)/DECREASE IN CASH
TOTAL CHANGE IN FINANCING

IDENTIFYING THE OPERATING CASH MARGIN

The cash flow statement starts with the value net profit. Where does this come from in the profit and loss account (P&L)?

In Table 4.3, we can see that this is identical to the value of the profit after tax and minority interests (shown as the *Profit attributable to equity holders of the parent* in Table 4.3). In other words the cash flow statement starts with the profit after interest and after tax and minority interests. This means that we will expect to find the following values as add-backs in Note 32 when we examine it.

1. Minority interests
2. Tax
3. Financial income and expenses
4. Share of results of associated companies
5. Depreciation and amortisation
6. Profit and loss on sale of fixed assets
7. Movements on provisions and other non-cash adjustments

Why do I know this before examining the note? The reason is that the first value we require for the template, the OPERATING CASH MARGIN, is typically

Table 4.3   Nokia – Consolidated profit and loss account

FINANCIAL YEAR ENDED DECEMBER 31ˢᵗ	Notes	20XX €M
Net sales		50 710
Cost of sales		−33 337
Gross profit		17 373
Research and development expenses		−5968
Selling and marketing expenses		−4380
Administrative and general expenses		−1284
Other income	6	420
Other expenses	6,7	−1195
Operating profit	2–9,22	4966
Share of results of associated companies	14,31	6
Financial income and expenses	10	−2
Profit before tax		4970
Tax	11	−1081
Profit before minority interests		3889
Minority interests		99
Profit attributable to equity holders of the parent		3988

similar in value to (but not the same as) the profit and loss sub-total known as EBITDA (Earnings before interest, tax depreciation and amortisation). (In Nokia's accounts EBIT is labelled *Operating profit*.) That means that the first five items in the list above must be added back just to get to this value. The reason the EBITDA is not he same as the OPERATING CASH MARGIN is to do with the last two items.

Remember that in the last chapter we learned that the OPERATING CASH MARGIN is actually the cash received from selling goods and services less the cash paid out in creating those same goods and services. Unfortunately the profit and loss account does not disclose these values implicitly. The nearest we get from the Nokia P&L is the first four values shown in the P&L in Table 4.3:

Nokia Consolidated profit and loss accounts, IFRS	20XX €M
Net sales	**50 710**
Cost of sales	−33 337
Research and development expenses	−5968
Selling and marketing expenses	−4380
Administrative and general expenses	−1284
POSSIBLE OPERATING CASH MARGIN	**5741**

Is this the correct answer? Unfortunately it is not! The reason for this is that certain of the expense items above shown contain within them other items which have been recognised as expenses and are non-cash items.

Typically there are three commonly recurring non-cash items included in these expenses.

1. Depreciation and Amortisation

The terms depreciation and amortisation essentially mean the same thing. In certain countries such as the UK it is a convention to use the word depreciation for tangible assets and the word amortisation for intangible assets. In the USA the word amortisation is used for both tangible and intangible assets.

Depreciation was created as a concept a long time ago to make the P&L more meaningful to users. Imagine for a moment a world without depreciation. In periods where a business acquired fixed assets it would show a big loss in the P&L (because buying the asset is simply treated as a cost like any other). In years when little or no asset purchase took place it would show a profit. This would make it very difficult to assess whether the business was in fact consistently successful at generating a profit from its activities.

Even more worrying the asset is still contributing to the generation of profit after the year in which it is shown as a cost. So we have a matching problem, in subsequent periods we have the benefit of the asset (the income generated by the asset) but no corresponding cost of the asset. If there was no concept of depreciation we would be showing all the cost at the beginning of the life of the asset even though we have the benefit of the asset for many accounting periods after this.

So, depreciation was created to spread the cost of assets in the P&L over their estimated useful lives and that is exactly what it does. In order to calculate the periodic depreciation charge on an asset the person responsible for preparing the accounts estimates the assets useful life and residual value at the end of its useful life. The difference between original cost and residual value is then written off over the estimated useful life. This can be expressed as a formula:

$$\text{Periodic depreciation charge} = \frac{\text{Original cost} - \text{Estimated residual value}}{\text{Estimated useful life}}$$

So we now know what depreciation (and amortisation) represents. Why does it appear as an adjustment to net profit in the cash flow statement? This is because it is a non-cash cost. No one writes a cheque for depreciation.

Let us consider what happens in cash terms when we buy and use an asset. There are only two cash transactions involved, buying the asset (known as *capital expenditure* or *capex*) and selling the asset when it has reached the end of its useful life (known as the *proceeds from the sale of fixed assets*). The transactions in the P&L relating to the recognition of depreciation as a cost are not cash flows. So, the amount relating to depreciation and amortisation must be added back to the net profit value to arrive at the correct value for the OPERATING CASH MARGIN.

2. Profit or Loss on the Disposal of Fixed Assets

The label on this adjustment does little to explain the true nature of this item. The profit or loss on the disposal of fixed assets is a non-cash, balancing adjustment to depreciation that arises on disposal. The label itself is misleading; it should be called additional depreciation arising on disposal or, alternatively, reduction in depreciation arising on disposal. What follows is a detailed explanation of how the profit or loss on disposal of fixed assets arises and what it represents.

When a fixed asset is disposed of, various book entries are required in the nominal ledger of the business to complete the bookkeeping relating to the disposal. The most convenient way to explain this is to show the entries required. A disposal account is opened each time an asset is sold or scrapped. The first entry to this account is the proceeds of sale, (which is the cash or consideration we receive when we dispose of the asset when we no longer want it). This is debited to the cashbook and credited to the disposal account. As the fixed asset has now been disposed of, the next thing we need to do is remove the original cost from the nominal ledger of the business. To do this we credit the original cost account and debit the disposal account. We also need to remove the accumulated depreciation on the asset by debiting the accumulated depreciation account and crediting the disposal account, at which point the process of removing the asset appears complete. This is what the disposal account might look like at this point.

Disposal Account – example one

Original cost	20 000	Proceeds of sale	2000
		Accumulated depreciation	14 000

However, there is a problem. As you can see, there is a difference between the two sides of the disposal account. We have to deal with this difference in some way; this is achieved by writing off the difference to the P&L as a profit or loss on disposal of fixed asset. In the example below a loss on disposal of fixed assets arises of 4000.

Disposal Account – example two

Original cost	20 000	Proceeds of sale	2000
		Accumulated depreciation	14 000
		Loss on disposal of fixed asset	4000
Total	20 000	Total	20 000

In the next example the proceeds of sale have been increased to 8000. As a consequence of this we now have a *profit on disposal of fixed assets* of 2000.

Disposal Account – example three

Original cost	20 000	Proceeds of sale	8000
		Accumulated depreciation	14 000
Profit on disposal of fixed assets	2000		
	22 000		22 000

Does this represent a real profit? A little thought should reveal the insight that profit is made when goods and services are sold for more than it costs to produce them. Generally we are not in the business of generating profits from selling our fixed assets, most businesses buy fixed assets such as buildings and plant to assist them in making profits from selling goods and services. Typically we will have sold our fixed asset for a small fraction of what we paid for it as it is obsolete and no longer required. So this is not really profit as such. The key question that finally reveals the nature of this item is: which of the transactions shown above are cash transactions?

Disposal Account – example four

Original cost – CASH	20 000	Proceeds of sale – CASH	2000
		Accumulated depreciation	14 000
		Loss on disposal of fixed asset	4000
	20 000		20 000

The proceeds of sale is a recent cash item and the original cost was a cash item when the asset was originally purchased. The accumulated depreciation is not a cash item and the loss on disposal is not a cash item either. In the above example, what has happened is we have purchased the asset for 20 000, charged depreciation on it of 14 000, and sold it for 2000. In other words we have under-depreciated the asset. The loss on disposal of the fixed asset simply represents additional depreciation that should have been charged over the asset's estimated useful life. It means the original estimate of useful life or residual value was optimistic or the asset has suddenly become surplus due to some other unexpected external change affecting the business.

I am going to take this opportunity to propose that from now on the loss on disposal of fixed assets be renamed 'additional depreciation arising on disposal' because that's what it actually is!

Let us consider the second example.

Disposal Account – example five

Original cost	20 000	Proceeds of sale	8000
		Accumulated depreciation	14 000
Profit on disposal of fixed assets	2000		
	22 000		22 000

Here we bought the asset for 20 000 depreciated it 14 000 and sold it for 8000. This means we have over-depreciated the asset. The profit on disposal isn't a real profit, it represents a reversal of the over-depreciation of the asset.

I am going to take this further opportunity to propose that from now on the profit on disposal of fixed assets be renamed 'reduction of depreciation arising on disposal' because that is what it actually is!

To summarise, the profit or loss on disposal of fixed assets represents a final positive or negative balancing adjustment to depreciation required on disposal to make the carrying value on disposal match the proceeds of sale. As such it is identical in nature to depreciation. It is a non-cash income or expense item charged to the P&L that needs to be adjusted for when identifying the OPERATING CASH MARGIN.

3. Movements in Provisions and Other Adjustments Within the Operating Income and Expenses in the Profit and Loss Account Relating to Non-Cash Items

The third item which is typically disclosed as an adjustment is any movements in provisions charged as operating expenses in the P&L and other adjustments for items which are either non-cash, or belong in another cash flow category such as financing costs.

Let us now look at the note to the cash flow statement from the Nokia accounts and see what items are not yet accounted for in our reconciliation of operating cash margin to net profit (Table 4.4).

Table 4.4   Nokia consolidated accounts note 32

32. Notes to cash flow statement	20XX €M
Adjustments for:	
Depreciation and amortisation (Note 9)	1617
(Profit)/loss on sale of property, plant and equipment and available-for-sale investments	−11
Income taxes (Note 11)	1081
Share of results of associated companies (Note 14)	−6
Minority Interest	−99
Financial income and expenses (Note 10)	2
Impairment charges (Note 7)	149
Retirements (Note 8, 12)	186
Share based compensation (Note 22)	74
Restructuring charges	448
Customer financing impairment charges and reversals	−
Finnish pension settlement (Note 5)	152
Other income and expenses	−124
Adjustments, total	**3469**
Change in net working capital	
Increase in short-term receivables	−534
Decrease(+)/Increase(−) in Inventories	321
Decrease (−)/Increase(+) in interest-free short-term liabilities	−2333
Change in net working capital	**−2546**

Compare this with the profit and loss account shown at Table 4.3, we can immediately match the following four items:

Income taxes	1081
Share of results of associated companies	6
Minority interest	99
Financial income and expenses	2

Depreciation and amortisation is also here as a reversing item as expected. So we are left with the following outstanding items to consider:

(Profit)/loss on sale of property, plant and equipment and available-for-sale investments	−11
Impairment charges	149
Retirements	186
Share based compensation	74
Restructuring charges	448
Customer financing impairment charges and reversals	0
Finnish pension settlement	152
Other income and expenses	−124

Items from the Table Above Representing Movements in Provisions

Impairment charges	149
Retirements	186
Restructuring charges	448
Customer financing impairment charges and reversals	0

These items both relate to movements in provisions for foreseeable losses, or the write-off of assets formerly carried at higher values.

Impairment Charges

Impairment charges could be viewed as an emergency depreciation charge.

IAS 36 – Impairment charges – is the relevant international accounting standard. For a detailed understanding of the accounting GAAP on impairment you should read the standard itself. What follows is a brief précis of the main provisions.

Impairment charges are required whenever an asset or cash-generating unit is being carried in the accounts at more than its recoverable amount. Its recoverable amount is the higher of its fair value less costs to sell and its value in use. Value in use is defined as the present value of the future cash flows expected to be derived from an asset or cash-generating unit.

To summarise, whenever you expect to get less back in the future (adjusted for the time cost of money) than the current carrying value, the asset is considered impaired and IAS 36 requires an impairment charge for the difference to be recognised in the P&L. The impairment charge is, of course, a non-cash item as we have not sold or disposed of the asset or cash-generating unit at this point. Another way of expressing this is that we are recognising in the P&L an unrealised loss. Unrealised means we have not yet sold it, we have just changed our mind about what it's worth! The same logic applies to the reversal of an impairment charge in later periods.

Retirements

Retirements is an unusual heading. Reviewing the accounts of Nokia reveals that most of this relates to the acquisition of Symbian. Symbian is the entity that licences the operating system used in a number of PDA-style mobile phones produced by Nokia and others; during the reporting period Nokia increased its ownership of Symbian from 47.9% to 100%. Nokia wished to establish an open source framework for the operating system and therefore donated the Symbian software and S60 platform software to a foundation set up to licence the Symbian platform. This means that the group has to write off the existing carrying values of the software which are €55 million for the Symbian identifiable intangible assets and €110 million for the value of capitalised S60 development costs. So, in this case, this is similar in nature to an impairment adjustment. As no cash flow is involved this represents another add-back or adjustment required to arrive at the operating cash margin.

Restructuring Charges

Restructuring charges typically represents provisions for restructuring activities within the group, the recognition of such an item as a cost is an application of the prudence concept which obliges the preparers of accounts to provide for losses as soon as they are foreseeable. Again there is no cash outflow until the actual costs of the restructuring are actually incurred in future accounting periods.

Customer Financing Impairment Charges and Reversals

Customer-financing impairment charges and reversals are essentially movements in bad-debt provisions. Customer financing may be provided as trade credit or as a more complex (and usually longer term) lending transaction (this is often referred to as vendor finance). It is normal practice to provide for doubtful debts each year, which are debts where you believe you may not receive payment. Bad debts are already written off in the period to sales. Again we come across the concept of an unrealised and realised loss. The provision for doubtful debts is a provision for an unrealised loss (or a loss that is not yet certain). Realised losses (losses where we are certain we will not get the money back) are recognised in the P&L as expense. So, customer finance impairment charges and reversals are also non-cash movements in provisions for foreseeable losses. As they do not represent cash flows we reverse them out when identifying the operating cash margin.

Other Adjustments Within the Operating Income and Expenses in the Profit and Loss Account Relating to Non-Cash Items

Three items are now left from Note 32. We will deal with each one in turn.

(Profit)/loss on sale of property, plant and equipment and available-for-sale investments	−11

The (profit)/loss on sale of property, plant and equipment is another way of labelling the profit or loss on disposal of fixed assets. The nature of this has already been explained in detail earlier in the chapter. The (profit)/loss on available-for-sale investments is something new. What is this?

First of all we know this represents some sort of unrealised profit or loss, otherwise it would not be shown as an adjusting item. An examination of Nokia's accounting policies reveals that this is the recognition in the P&L of changes to the fair value of a pool of investments that Nokia classifies as available-for-sale.

IAS 39 – Financial instruments – recognition and measurement requires that investments be shown at their fair value each year and the profit or loss be charged to the P&L. This is, of course, an unrealised profit or loss, as we have not sold the investments at this point.

This is another example of a misleading label. The use of the terms profit and loss implies the investments have been disposed of when in fact they haven't. Using the term change in the value of, or recognition of the change in value of available-for-sale investments would be clearer. It would then be more obvious these items do not represent cash flows.

Share based compensation	74

Share-based compensation arises when employees are granted rights over shares in Nokia that can be exercised in the future. They are typically share options. No cash flow arises when they are granted as they represent a right to buy shares at a specified price at some point in the future.

IFRS 2 – Share-based payment – requires that these rights be valued using option-pricing models and the resulting cost be recognised in the P&L as pay. As this is non-cash it needs to be adjusted for in the cash flow statement.

Finnish pension settlement	152

Following a significant re-organisation of the way it recognises and administers its pension obligations Nokia has changed the way it accounts for certain pension liabilities so that they are treated as defined benefit pension liabilities in the accounts.

IAS19 – employee benefits – requires that any deficit be recognised as a liability. However this only represents a change in the value of the liability recognised in the balance sheet and is not a cash flow.

Other income and expenses	−124

This label turns up a lot in accounts! This is extremely annoying for any analyst as it can be used to hide things that should be disclosed. Its use is acceptable where the amounts disclosed are immaterial to the overall analysis (as they are in the Nokia accounts). The comments about materiality above are relevant. Again as Nokia have applied these values as adjustments we will assume they are appropriate and accept them. The notes to the accounts reveal a variety of items some of which constitute this item. Once again this represents non-cash items.

We have now explored much of the minutiae involved in correctly identifying the value of the OPERATING CASH MARGIN when restating cash flows. We will continue this process in a number of further examples. We have now identified the first value in the template (Table 4.5).

Table 4.5   Building up the template – completing line one

OPERATING CASH MARGIN	**7457**
(INVESTED)/GENERATED FROM NET WORKING ASSETS	
NET CAPITAL EXPENDITURE	
TAXATION	
CASH AVAILABLE TO SATISFY FINANCE PROVIDERS	
NET INTEREST	
NET DIVIDENDS	
OTHER NON-OPERATING INCOME/(EXPENDITURE)	
NET CASH GENERATED/(ABSORBED) BEFORE FINANCING	
Financed by:	
INCREASE/(DECREASE) IN EQUITY	
INCREASE/(DECREASE) IN DEBT	
(INCREASE)/DECREASE IN CASH	
TOTAL CHANGE IN FINANCING	

Identifying the Amount (Invested)/Generated from Net Working Assets

Typically, the second part of the cash flow from operating activities section deals with the amount invested or generated from changes in the amounts invested in net working assets.

In the Nokia example the net value has been disclosed as a total in the cash flow statement and an analysis of that value is shown in a note as follows (€M):

Change in net working capital	
Increase in short-term receivables	−534
Decrease(+)/Increase(−) in Inventories	321
Decrease (−)/Increase(+) in interest free short term liabilities	−2333
Change in net working capital	**−2546**

Identifying the changes in the amounts invested in net working assets in this example is therefore straightforward. In future examples we will see that identifying which values to include can sometimes be more difficult. It is quite common to see movements in provisions included as a working asset item (it is, of course, an adjustment to the operating cash margin).

It is tempting to see if these asset change values can be reconciled to relevant changes disclosed in the balance sheet. In a simple business this may be possible, however, for Nokia it is not possible. This is explained in a note directly underneath the cash flow statement.

> The figures in the consolidated cash flow statement cannot be directly traced from the balance sheet without additional information as a result of acquisitions and disposals of subsidiaries and net foreign exchange differences arising on consolidation.

The implications of this will be explained in detail in chapter 16 which deals with the creation of a notional cash flow statement from profit and loss account and balance sheet data.

Identifying the Taxation and Net Interest Values

Again, in the case of Nokia this is relatively straightforward, there is one taxation value disclosed and three values relating to finance costs. Interest received and interest paid are clear and self-explanatory. What do we do with other financial income and expenses, net received?

Finance costs include all costs relating to financing the business using debt instruments, this must include arrangement fees and other income or expenses relating to instruments used to hedge or modify debt such as interest rate and currency swaps and other derivatives forming part of the debt financing of the business. So, it is reasonable to include this item in the NET INTEREST line of the restated cash flows as it is part of the overall financial cost (or income) of Nokia.

We can now complete those elements of Jury's Template that relate to the cash flows from operating activities (Table 4.6).

Table 4.6 Building up the template – Cash flow from operating activity items

OPERATING CASH MARGIN	7457
(INVESTED)/GENERATED FROM NET WORKING ASSETS	−2546
NET CAPITAL EXPENDITURE	
TAXATION	−1780
CASH AVAILABLE TO SATISFY FINANCE PROVIDERS	
NET INTEREST	66
NET DIVIDENDS	
OTHER NON-OPERATING INCOME/(EXPENDITURE)	
NET CASH GENERATED/(ABSORBED) BEFORE FINANCING	
Financed by:	
INCREASE/(DECREASE) IN EQUITY	
INCREASE/(DECREASE) IN DEBT	
(INCREASE)/DECREASE IN CASH	
TOTAL CHANGE IN FINANCING	

Restating the Cash Flows from Investing Activities

The information in Table 4.7 is taken from the published accounts of Nokia (€M)

Table 4.7 Summary of net cash from investing activities

Nokia cash flow statement	
Cash flow from investing activities	
Acquisition of Group companies, net of acquired cash	−5962
Purchase of current available-for sale investments, liquid assets	−669
Purchase of non-current available-for-sale investments	−121
Purchase of shares in associated companies	−24
Additions to capitalised development costs	−131
Long term loans made to customers	−
Proceeds from repayment and sale of long-term loans receivable	129
Recovery of impaired long-term loans made to customers	−
Proceeds from (+)/payment of (−) other long–term receivables	−1
Proceeds from (+)/payment of (−) short–term loans receivable	−15
Capital expenditures	−889
Proceeds from disposal of shares in associated companies	3
Proceed from disposal of businesses	41
Proceeds from maturities and sale of current available-for-sale investments, liquid assets	4664
Proceeds from sale of non-current available-for-sale investments	10
Proceeds from sale of fixed assets	54
Dividends received	6
Net cash from (+)/used in (−) investing activities	**−2905**

Table 4.7 shows the *cash flow from the investing activities* part of the full IFRS cash flow statement.

Generally, the cash flow from investing activities section of a published cash flow statement contains values relating to NET CAPITAL EXPENDITURE and OTHER NON-OPERATING INCOME/(EXPENDITURE) from the template. It may also contain other values relating to interest, taxation or dividends should it be the preferences of the persons responsible for the preparation of the cash flow statement to disclose them here. So, in Table 4.8 we are going to extract the values relating to the items shown in bold.

Table 4.8 Building up the template – Investing cash flow items

OPERATING CASH MARGIN	7457
(INVESTED)/GENERATED FROM NET WORKING ASSETS	−2546
NET CAPITAL EXPENDITURE	
TAXATION	−1780
CASH AVAILABLE TO SATISFY FINANCE PROVIDERS	
NET INTEREST	66
NET DIVIDENDS – the dividend received part of this value	
OTHER NON-OPERATING INCOME/(EXPENDITURE)	
NET CASH GENERATED/(ABSORBED) BEFORE FINANCING	
Financed by:	
INCREASE/(DECREASE) IN EQUITY	
INCREASE/(DECREASE) IN DEBT	
(INCREASE)/DECREASE IN CASH	
TOTAL CHANGE IN FINANCING	

Identifying the Net Capital Expenditure

The number of items disclosed in Nokia's cash flows from investing activities appears extensive. Reading through them reveals that most of the items relate to the purchase or sale of investments or businesses owned by Nokia. Which of the remaining items relate to net capital expenditure?

The two values we expect to see are as follows:

Capital expenditures	−889
Proceeds from sales of fixed assets	54

This is the amount spent on new fixed assets and the cash received on disposing of old, unwanted fixed assets. In this example there is one other value that should be included in the net capital expenditure.

Additions to capitalised development costs	−131

IAS 38 – Intangible Assets – allows businesses to recognise internally created intangible assets in certain circumstances. Essentially, these are cash flows
spent on internal projects that are expected to generate probable future economic
benefits and all the resources are available to complete the project, together with
the intention to use or sell the intangible asset. So, the additions to capitalised
development costs represent investments in intangible fixed assets. They should
be included in capital expenditure as they are intended to contribute to the pool of
assets that generate the businesses operating cash margin. So, the NET CAPITAL
EXPENDITURE is the sum of these three values or −€966 million.

Identifying the Other Non-Operating Income/(Expenditure)

In the Nokia example the other non-operating income/(expenditure) is everything
else in this section other than the value of dividends received at the bottom of the
section.

Careful examination of these items will reveal that they relate to four things:

1. Acquisition and disposal if interests in group companies, (by which I think they
   mean subsidiaries).
2. Purchase or sale of interests in associated companies.
3. Purchase or sale of investments representing the investment of cash surpluses
   in things other than cash equivalents.
4. Vendor-financing activities such as lending or receiving repayment of loans
   to customers and the proceeds of securitising future cash flows due from customers.

In certain circumstances it might be beneficial to disclose some of this sub-analysis
by modifying Jury's Template to accommodate the additional data. This idea will
be explored in later chapters dealing with the specific interests of groups such as
lenders and equity analysts. For the moment we are going to report all these values
as one number in the template.

Identifying the Dividend Received

This is the last number in this section. Its meaning is self-explanatory. So we can
now summarise the investing cash flows into the template (Table 4.9).

We have now sufficient information to identify the cash available to satisfy
finance providers. I have inserted the total, which is €2165 million.

Table 4.9 Building up the template – inserting the investing cash flow items

OPERATING CASH MARGIN	7457
(INVESTED)/GENERATED FROM NET WORKING ASSETS	−2546
NET CAPITAL EXPENDITURE	**−966**
TAXATION	−1780
CASH AVAILABLE TO SATISFY FINANCE PROVIDERS	**2165**
NET INTEREST	66
NET DIVIDENDS – the dividend received part of this value	**6**
OTHER NON-OPERATING INCOME/(EXPENDITURE)	**−1945**
NET CASH GENERATED/(ABSORBED) BEFORE FINANCING	
Financed by:	
INCREASE/(DECREASE) IN EQUITY	
INCREASE/(DECREASE) IN DEBT	
(INCREASE)/DECREASE IN CASH	
TOTAL CHANGE IN FINANCING	

Restating the Cash Flows from Financing Activities

The information below is taken from the published accounts of Nokia.

Nokia cash flow statement	
Cash flows from financing activities	
Proceeds from stock options exercises	53
Purchase of treasury shares	−3121
Proceeds from long-term borrowings	714
Repayment of long-term borrowings	−34
Proceeds from (+)/ repayment of (−) short-term borrowings	2891
Dividends paid	−2048
Net cash used in financing activities	**−1545**

This is *cash flow from financing activities* part of the full IFRS cash flow statement.

Generally, the cash flow from financing activities section of a published cash flow statement contains values relating to the last three lines of the template. It may also contain other values relating to interest, taxation and dividends should it be the preferences of the persons responsible for the preparation of the cash flow statement to disclose them here. So in Table 4.10 we are going to extract the values relating to the items shown in bold below.

Table 4.10   Building up the template – financing cash flow items

OPERATING CASH MARGIN	7457
(INVESTED)/GENERATED FROM NET WORKING ASSETS	−2546
NET CAPITAL EXPENDITURE	−966
TAXATION	−1780
CASH AVAILABLE TO SATISFY FINANCE PROVIDERS	**2165**
NET INTEREST	66
NET DIVIDENDS – the dividend paid part of this value	**6**
OTHER NON-OPERATING INCOME/(EXPENDITURE)	−1945
NET CASH GENERATED/(ABSORBED) BEFORE FINANCING	
Financed by:	
INCREASE/(DECREASE) IN EQUITY	
INCREASE/(DECREASE) IN DEBT	
(INCREASE)/DECREASE IN CASH	
TOTAL CHANGE IN FINANCING	

Identifying the Change in Equity

The first three lines of the cash flow from financing activities section relate to cash equity changes. The *proceeds from stock option exercises* is cash received for new equity issued to employees and directors in respect of stock options. The *purchase of treasury shares* is the cash expended on buying back Nokia's own equity from the stock market. In some countries this is only allowed if the shares are then cancelled; under Finnish company law it appears to be allowed to retain these shares in the company for later re-sale. I know this because the treasury shares appear in the balance sheet as a negative equity item, implying the shares still exist and can be resold.

Identifying the Change in Debt

The next three line items relate to changes in debt. They are all clearly labelled as such and simply require summarising into one value.

Identifying the Dividend Paid

This is the last number in this section. Its meaning is self-explanatory. So we can now summarise the investing cash flows into the template (Table 4.11).

Table 4.11   Building up the template – financing cash flow items

OPERATING CASH MARGIN	7457
(INVESTED)/GENERATED FROM NET WORKING ASSETS	−2546
NET CAPITAL EXPENDITURE	−966
TAXATION	−1780
CASH AVAILABLE TO SATISFY FINANCE PROVIDERS	**2165**
NET INTEREST	66
NET DIVIDENDS	**−2042**
OTHER NON-OPERATING INCOME/(EXPENDITURE)	−1945
NET CASH GENERATED/(ABSORBED) BEFORE FINANCING	**−1756**
Financed by:	
INCREASE/(DECREASE) IN EQUITY	**−3068**
INCREASE/(DECREASE) IN DEBT	**3571**
(INCREASE)/DECREASE IN CASH	
TOTAL CHANGE IN FINANCING	

Identifying the Cash Change Value and Balancing the Template

Our template is almost complete; we now need to input the final values in respect of the movement in cash and cash equivalents to the template in order to complete it.

Foreign exchange adjustment	−49
Net increase (+)/ decrease (−) in cash and cash equivalents	−1302
Cash and cash equivalents at beginning of period	6850
Cash and cash equivalents at end of period	5548

NOTE VALUE CHANGE 6050 BECOMES 6850

To complete the restatement process we need to identify the overall change in cash and cash equivalents. The value required is shown below.

Foreign exchange adjustment	−49
(Increase)/decrease in cash and cash equivalents	1302
(INCREASE)/DECREASE IN CASH	**1253**

Foreign Exchange Adjustment

The foreign exchange adjustment represents the gain or loss on restating the opening cash value of cash held locally or overseas in currencies other than the reporting currency at the rate of exchange used to prepare the accounts at the period end. This adjustment is required as a consequence of consolidation and is necessary or the cash flow statement (and balance sheet) will not reconcile with the previous year.

An example will make this clearer.

A European group has a foreign subsidiary in the US. The group reports in euros, to consolidate the US subsidiary all accounting values are translated at the closing exchange rate at the end of each accounting period. The table below summarises the effect of this process on the cash change value over two years:

	End of period cash dollars	End of period exchange rate $: €	End of period translated € value
31 Dec 20XX	10 000	1 : 0.9	9000
31 Dec 20XY	8000	1 : 1.2	9600
Change	(2000)		600

In dollar terms we see a decrease in cash of 2000. After translation this appears to be an increase in euro currency terms of 600. This means a cash flow statement prepared in dollar terms will appear to be out of balance, when translated, if the opening euro cash value is same as the previous period closing cash value in the cash flow statement. The reason for this is because we take the opening cash value at its value in euros using *last year's* exchange rate (we have to do this to reconcile from one period cash and cash equivalents value to the next). In order for the statements to remain in balance on translation we have to restate last year's opening cash balance using this years closing exchange rate. When this is done all the values disclosed in the cash flow statement remain equivalent on translation.

	End of period cash dollars	End of period exchange rate $: €	End of period translated € value
31 Dec 20XX dollar cash	10 000	1 : 0.9	9000
Foreign exchange adjustment			3000
31 Dec 20XX restated at 20XY rate	10 000	1 : 1.2	12 000
31 Dec 20XY dollar cash	8000	1 : 1.2	9600
Change in dollar cash	(2000)		(2400)

By restating the opening cash value using the closing exchange rate we restore the correct relationship between the dollar and euro exchange rate cash value. Now the change in cash in dollars is equivalent to the change in the same values expressed in euros at the closing exchange rate. To reconcile between the two periods closing cash position we need both the foreign exchange adjustment and the cash change value expressed in the reporting currency.

The foreign exchange adjustment is not a cash flow. It represents the gain or loss in value of the opening cash held in currencies other than the reporting currency due to changes in exchange rates during the accounting period. The need to make this adjustment arises solely as a consequence of consolidation. We have not repatriated the cash or spent it and there has been no real gain or loss because the currency has not actually been converted to euros. The cash is still held in dollars. In that sense the value of the dollars shown at the period end in euro terms is a notional value on that date, (this is the value of the cash if the dollars were converted at the closing exchange rate used to consolidate the rest of the accounts). The day after the accounting period end the notional value of the dollars in euros will have changed again due to exchange rate changes.

(Increase)/Decrease in Cash and Cash Equivalents

The decrease in cash and cash equivalents value in the cash flow statement of Nokia is shown as −€1302 million. It is arrived as follows:

Nokia	20XX
Summary cash flow statement	€ M
Net cash from operating activities	3197
Net cash used in investing activities	−2905
Net cash used in financing activities	−1545
Foreign exchange adjustment	−49
Net increase (+)/decrease (−) in cash and cash equivalents	**−1302**

The value is negative because it is the sum of the items above. This cash flow statement is not laid out as a balancing statement. If we modified the layout to make the total at the bottom zero (this is a balancing layout where the cash inflows precisely equal the cash outflows in the cash flow statement), look at what happens to the signage of the last number.

Nokia	20XX
Summary cash flow statement	€ M
Net cash from operating activities	3197
Net cash used in investing activities	−2905
Net cash used in financing activities	−1545
Foreign exchange adjustment	−49
Net increase (−)/decrease (+) in cash and cash equivalents	1302
Total	**0**

The change in cash and cash equivalents is still a decrease. However, its sign changes to positive to represent a decrease in a balancing layout. In this version the cash flows in precisely equal the cash flows out. This is the form taken in the cash flow template, and this is why it is necessary to change the sign of the last number (in the case of Nokia from negative to positive). This issue is explained in more detail in Chapter 2. When we do this we sum it with the foreign exchange adjustment and enter it into the template; the template cash flows balance (Table 4.12).

Table 4.12 Building up the template – the completed balanced template

OPERATING CASH MARGIN	7457
(INVESTED)/GENERATED FROM NET WORKING ASSETS	−2546
NET CAPITAL EXPENDITURE	−966
TAXATION	−1780
CASH AVAILABLE TO SATISFY FINANCE PROVIDERS	**2165**
NET INTEREST	66
NET DIVIDENDS	**−2042**
OTHER NON-OPERATING INCOME/(EXPENDITURE)	−1945
NET CASH GENERATED/(ABSORBED) BEFORE FINANCING	**−1756**
Financed by:	
INCREASE/(DECREASE) IN EQUITY	**−3068**
INCREASE/(DECREASE) IN DEBT	**3571**
(INCREASE)/DECREASE IN CASH	**1253**
TOTAL CHANGE IN FINANCING	**1756**

CONCLUSION

We have successfully summarised the cash flows of Nokia for the accounting period ending December 31, 20XX into the template and balanced it. We know what the constituents of each value represent and we have created two new totals that do not appear in the published cash flow statement. We are now ready to analyse the resulting data.

5
Restating US GAAP Cash Flows

INTRODUCTION

In the United States all entities subject to the US Securities and Exchange Commission (SEC) control have been required to publish a cash flow statement as part of their statutory disclosure since 1998.

In Chapter 4 we analysed in detail the cash flow statement of Nokia, a business that has been reporting using IAS GAAP for some years.

Rather than repeating in detail the general issues involved in restating the operating, investing and financing cash flows into the recommended template, in this chapter we will look at the essential points of difference between the IAS GAAP restatement and a US GAAP restatement. This approach will also be used in the following chapters when discussing differences between types of GAAP and IAS.

This means if you have started with this chapter because you only wish to analyse a US GAAP cash flow, you should initially read Chapter 4 covering IAS GAAP restatement as well.

THE US GAAP CASH FLOW ANALYSIS PROCESS

We have a US GAAP cash flow statement to analyse, how do we go about our task?

> There are two possible ways of preparing and presenting a cash flow statement, these are known as the direct method and the indirect method. The first task to ascertain is whether the cash flow is a direct cash flow or an indirect cash flow.

FAS 95 – Statement of cash flows – encourages US companies to use the direct method. Despite this guidance from the standard setters I have yet to come across a US GAAP cash flow statement prepared using the direct method. All the US GAAP cash flow statements I have ever seen were prepared using the indirect method.

> A direct cash flow is prepared by taking the cash records of the business, coding each cash transaction during the period into its relevant cash flow constituent and then summarising the resulting information into a cash flow statement.

We can identify whether a cash flow statement is direct or indirect by examining the first few lines of the cash flow statement. In the case of direct cash flow statements instead of starting with a profit value taken from the profit and loss account the cash flow typically starts with receipts from customers and payments to employees and suppliers.

> An indirect cash flow is prepared by identifying the various cash flows required to prepare the cash flow statement from information contained within the profit and loss account and balance sheet of the business. All the US GAAP cash flow statements I have ever analysed were indirect cash flow statements.

We can now proceed to understanding in detail the restatement process for a US GAAP reporting entity. We will deal with this issue section by section using Black & Decker, the US manufacturer of DIY power tools as an example.

Arithmetic Signage in the Cash Flows

By *signage* we mean whether a cash flow is positive (an inflow) or negative (an outflow). Generally the treatment of the signage of values contained within a cash flow statement is straightforward. Positive values represent cash inflows and negative values represent cash outflows. All signage should be summarised into the template as observed.

In the template, brackets are used with certain of the labels to signify the meaning of the signage of the cash flow, in the examples brackets or a minus sign may be used to signify negative cash flows.

The only exception to this rule is the last number in the cash flow statement, which is usually the change in cash, or the change in cash and cash equivalents. Unless the published cash flow is laid out as a balancing statement the final cash value shown will require its signage reversing to make the restated cash flow template balance. The reasons for this are explained in Chapter 3.

Acronyms

From now on we will start to use the following acronyms to describe certain values. The first time the term is used in the text the acronym will normally follow.

EBIT	Earning before interest and tax
EBITDA	Earnings before interest, tax, depreciation and amortisation
P&L	Profit and loss account
IAS	International accounting standard
IFRS	International financial reporting standard
M or m	Million meaning 1 000 000

SOURCES OF CASH FLOW DATA

All filings of businesses listed on US stock markets are available online at www.sec.gov/edgar.shtml.

Domestic US entities file a Form 10-K. Overseas entities file a Form 20-F. These forms are the regulatory equivalents of annual reports, they contain the same information, but in a highly organised regulatory format, with much additional disclosure required by US regulators. Many larger companies also issue a glossy annual report and accounts, which is typically available as a pdf file download from the group's corporate web site.

The Major Differences Between US GAAP Cash Flows and IAS GAAP Cash Flows

Firstly, indirect US GAAP cash flows start with the value *net income* or *net earnings*. This is the profit value from the P&L that represents the equity providers' earnings. It is the value of profit after interest, tax and minority interests. As a consequence of this we expect to see a significant number of add-backs in the operating cash flow section of the cash flow statement in order to arrive at the OPERATING CASH MARGIN.

Secondly, we do not find the values relating to interest-paid or taxation-paid in the cash flow. As a consequence if we restate all of the numbers in a US GAAP cash flow into the template we have no entries for interest or taxation in the template and the resulting OPERATING CASH MARGIN value at the top of the template is actually the operating cash margin *after interest and taxes*.

The good news is that the values of interest and tax paid are usually disclosed elsewhere in the 10-K Form. In the case of Black & Decker the interest payments are shown in Note 8 to the accounts and the taxation payments are shown in Note 11. Sometimes these values are disclosed in a note referring to cash flows; sometimes they are shown as additional information directly underneath the cash flow statement.

RESTATING THE CASH FLOWS FROM OPERATING ACTIVITIES

The information in Table 5.1 is taken from the form 10-K of Black & Decker for a sample year.

This is *cash flow from the operating activities* part of the full 10-K cash flow statement.

Generally the cash flow from operating activities section of a published cash flow statement contains values relating to the first two lines of the template. Because of the omission of interest and taxation information from the published

Table 5.1 Consolidated statement of cash flows, the Black & Decker Corporation and subsidiaries (millions of dollars)

YEAR ENDED DECEMBER 31st	
OPERATING ACTIVITIES	
Net earnings	**$518.1**
Adjustments to reconcile net earnings to cash flow	
from operating activities of continuing operations:	
Loss from discontinued operations	–
Non-cash charges and credits:	
Depreciation and amortisation	**143.4**
Stock-based compensation	**25.9**
Amortization of actuarial losses and prior service costs	**25.7**
Tax settlement	**(153.4)**
Restructuring and exit costs	**19.0**
Other	**.5**
Changes in selected working capital items	
(net of effects of businesses acquired or divested):	
Trade receivables	**99.4**
Inventories	**(32.0)**
Trade accounts payable	**32.6**
Other current liabilities	**33.3**
Restructuring spending	**(1.0)**
Other assets and liabilities	**14.4**
CASH FLOW FROM OPERATING ACTIVITIES **OF CONTINUING OPERATIONS**	**725.9**
CASH FLOW FROM OPERATING ACTIVITIES **OF DISCONTINUED OPERATIONS**	–
CASH FLOW FROM OPERATING ACTIVITIES	**725.9**

cash flow there will be no reference to either value in the cash flow statement itself.

How then do we analyse the cash flows of a US entity reporting under US GAAP?

Our strategy is to first complete Jury's Template without the interest or taxation values inserted and make it balance, so confirming that we have avoided arithmetic errors in our extraction and summarising of the cash flow statement. In this form the template will be incomplete.

The most important thing to remember is that without the interest and tax values inserted the top line does not represent the operating cash margin, it represents the operating cash margin after interest and tax payments.

Table 5.2 Building up the template – dealing with the first two lines

---

BLACK & DECKER – Summary cash flow template

OPERATING CASH MARGIN (after interest and tax payments)
(INVESTED)/GENERATED FROM NET WORKING ASSETS
NET CAPITAL EXPENDITURE
TAXATION
CASH AVAILABLE TO SATISFY FINANCE PROVIDERS
NET INTEREST
NET DIVIDENDS
OTHER NON-OPERATING INCOME/(EXPENDITURE)
NET CASH GENERATED/(ABSORBED) BEFORE FINANCING
Financed by:
INCREASE/(DECREASE) IN EQUITY
INCREASE/(DECREASE) IN DEBT
(INCREASE)/DECREASE IN CASH
TOTAL CHANGE IN FINANCING

Once we have summarised all three sections into the template and made it balance we will then add the interest and tax values and adjust the operating cash margin value accordingly. This is an important step that should not be omitted, the reason for this is that it changes the CASH AVAILABLE TO SATISFY FINANCE PROVIDERS to the correct value. Without the interest and tax values inserted this value is incorrect and the template is incomplete.

IDENTIFYING THE OPERATING CASH MARGIN (AFTER INTEREST AND TAX PAYMENTS)

The cash flow statement starts with the value net earnings/(loss). Where does this come from in the profit and loss account (P&L)? The full P&L is shown in Table 5.3, from this it can be seen that it is identical to the net earnings value in the P&L, which is the share of profit 'owned' by the equity providers. In US GAAP it is also the value on which the net earnings per common share is calculated.

The second line of the cash flow then explains that the next few items are 'adjustments to reconcile net earnings to cash flow from operating activities'. These are the add-backs (or reversals) required in order to identify the operating cash margin after interest and taxes. Once again we have a misleading label in the US GAAP cash flow, the item referred to as cash flow from operating activities, is actually the cash flow from operating activities after interest and taxation.

Table 5.3 Consolidated statement of earnings, the Black & Decker Corporation and subsidiaries (dollars in millions except per share data)

YEAR ENDED DECEMBER 31st	
SALES	**$6563.2**
Cost of goods sold	**4336.2**
Selling, general, and administrative expenses	**1625.8**
Restructuring and exit costs	**19.0**
OPERATING INCOME	**582.2**
Interest expense (net of interest income of	
$19.8 for 2007, $29.6 for 2006, and $36.5 for 2005)	**82.3**
Other expense (income)	**2.3**
EARNINGS FROM CONTINUING OPERATIONS	
BEFORE INCOME TAXES	**497.6**
Income taxes (benefit)	**(20.5)**
NET EARNINGS FROM CONTINUING OPERATIONS	**518.1**
Loss from discontinued operations (net of income taxes)	–
NET EARNINGS	**518.1**
BASIC EARNINGS PER COMMON SHARE	
Continuing operations	**8.06**
Discontinued operations	–
NET EARNINGS PER COMMON SHARE – BASIC	**8.06**
DILUTED EARNINGS PER COMMON SHARE	
Continuing operations	**7.85**
Discontinued operations	–
NET EARNINGS PER COMMON SHARE –	
ASSUMING DILUTION	**7.85**

See Notes to Consolidated Financial Statements.

The *adjustments to reconcile net earnings to cash flow from operating assets* from the cash flow statement of Black and Decker are listed below:

- Loss from discontinued operations
- Non-cash charges and credits:
    Depreciation and amortisation
    Stock-based compensation
    Amortisation of actuarial losses and prior service costs
    Tax settlement
    Restructuring and exit costs
    Other

The loss from discontinued operation is split out because cash flows relating to discontinued operations are disclosed separately in the cash flow statement.

The nature of depreciation and amortisation has been adequately covered in the previous chapter. However, there are a number of items we have not come across earlier.

Stock-Based Compensation

Stock-based compensation is the removal of the recognition as a cost of the value of employee compensation in the form of stock options or similar arrangements. From June 2005 FASB Statement 123R – Share Based Payment – requires the recognition of share options or other forms of deferred equity reward to be recognised as a cost at their value when granted. We are adding this back because there is no cash flow at the time the share option is awarded to the employee.

Amortisation of Actuarial Losses and Prior Service Costs

Amortisation of actuarial losses and prior service costs relates to the writing off through the P&L of liabilities recognised in respect of pension plans operated by the company for its employees. Again there is no cash flow associated with this charge so it is added back.

Tax Settlement

Tax settlement is an unusual item, examination of the notes reveals this is result of settling litigation between Black & Decker and the US government on this year's taxes of reinstating capital losses originally disallowed in previous years. We remove this in the cash flow because it is essentially a prior-year adjustment. It saves cash in the current year but relates to matters arising in previous years.

Restructuring and Exit Costs

Restructuring and exit costs is likely to be a provision or accrual and hence non-cash.

Other

'Other' is not helpful as a label for the analyst, but can be forgiven, as the amounts involved are immaterial.

Whilst it is useful to understand what these add-backs relate to, it is not essential as the cash flow statement tells us these are all adjustments to reconcile net earnings to cash flow from operating activities. As long as we are comfortable that the cash flow has been properly prepared we can normally accept these items at face value.

Working Capital Items

The second element in the operating activities section is headed 'Changes in selected working asset items'. This is where we expect to find the changes in inventory, debtors and creditors and, indeed, we do!

The only item that appears out of place is 'restructuring spending', if this label is correct I consider it should be treated as an operating cost rather than a working asset change item. So, in my answer, I have classified this item as part of the operating cash margin.

We have now explored the major point of difference between this cash flow and the earlier example involved in correctly identifying the value of the OPERATING CASH MARGIN and the amount (INVESTED)/GENERATED FROM NET WORKING ASSETS when restating cash flows. We have now identified the first two values in Jury's Template (Table 5.4).

Table 5.4   Building up the template – competing the first two lines

BLACK & DECKER – Summary cash flow template	
OPERATING CASH MARGIN (after interest and tax payments)	578.2
(INVESTED)/GENERATED FROM NET WORKING ASSETS	147.7
NET CAPITAL EXPENDITURE	
TAXATION	
CASH AVAILABLE TO SATISFY FINANCE PROVIDERS	
NET INTEREST	
NET DIVIDENDS	
OTHER NON-OPERATING INCOME/(EXPENDITURE)	
NET CASH GENERATED/(ABSORBED) BEFORE FINANCING	
Financed by:	
INCREASE/(DECREASE) IN EQUITY	
INCREASE/(DECREASE) IN DEBT	
(INCREASE)/DECREASE IN CASH	
TOTAL CHANGE IN FINANCING	

RESTATING THE CASH FLOWS FROM INVESTING ACTIVITIES

The information in Table 5.5 is taken from the Form 10-K of Black & Decker.

Generally the cash flow from investing activities section of a US GAAP cash flow statement contains values relating to NET CAPITAL EXPENDITURE and OTHER NON OPERATING INCOME/(EXPENDITURE). So in this example we are going to extract the values relating to the items shown in bold in Table 5.6.

Table 5.5 Consolidated statement of cash flows, the Black & Decker Corporation and subsidiaries (millions of dollars)

YEAR ENDED DECEMBER 31ˢᵗ	
INVESTING ACTIVITIES	
Capital expenditures	**(116.4)**
Proceeds from disposal of assets	**13.0**
Purchase of business, net of cash acquired	–
Reduction in purchase price of previously acquired business	–
Proceeds from sale of business, net of cash transferred	–
Proceeds from sale of discontinued operations, net of cash transferred	–
Cash inflow from hedging activities	**2.0**
Cash outflow from hedging activities	**(47.4)**
Other investing activities, net	**(1.0)**
CASH FLOW FROM INVESTING ACTIVITIES	**(149.8)**

See Notes to Consolidated Financial Statements.

Table 5.6 Building up the template – Investing cash flow items

BLACK & DECKER – Summary cash flow template	
OPERATING CASH MARGIN (after interest and tax payments)	5193
(INVESTED)/GENERATED FROM NET WORKING ASSETS	299
NET CAPITAL EXPENDITURE	
TAXATION	−1368
CASH AVAILABLE TO SATISFY FINANCE PROVIDERS	
NET INTEREST	219
NET DIVIDENDS	
OTHER NON-OPERATING INCOME/(EXPENDITURE)	
NET CASH GENERATED/(ABSORBED) BEFORE FINANCING	
Financed by:	
INCREASE/(DECREASE) IN EQUITY	
INCREASE/(DECREASE) IN DEBT	
(INCREASE)/DECREASE IN CASH	
TOTAL CHANGE IN FINANCING	

Identifying the Net Capital Expenditure

There are nine items disclosed in the cash flows from investing activities of Black & Decker. Reading through them reveals that many of the items relate to the purchase or sale of investments or businesses owned by Black & Decker. We also have cash flow relating to hedging activities to consider. Which of the remaining items relate to net capital expenditure?

The two values we expect to see are as follows:

Capital expenditures	−116.4
Proceeds from disposal of assets	13.0

This is the amount spent on new fixed assets and the cash received on disposing of old, unwanted fixed assets. So, the NET CAPITAL EXPENDITURE is the sum of these two values or −$103.4 million.

Identifying the Other Non-Operating Income/(Expenditure)

In the Black & Decker example, the other non-operating income/(expenditure) is everything else in this section other than the two cash flows relating to hedging activities.

This consists of:

Purchase of business, net of cash acquired
Reduction in purchase price of previously acquired business
Proceeds from the sale of business, net of cash transferred
Proceeds from sales of discontinued operations, net of cash transferred
Other investing activities, net

The first four headings all relate to the purchase or sale of businesses, the last one is ambiguous and immaterial so we will include it here. There is little point in spending any significant time on non-material items with unhelpful labels such as 'Other'. This is because, irrespective of where you put them in the template, they will not affect the resulting value significantly, or alter your analysis of the resulting template summary.

The Cash Flows Relating to Hedging Activities

These cash flows almost certainly relate to financial hedging activities such as swapping fixed and floating interest rates and possibly different currencies to reduce risk. Accordingly they represent part of the finance costs of the business and therefore will be shown in the template in the net interest line. So we can now summarise the investing cash flows into the template (Table 5.7).

We now have all the information we are able to get from the cash flow statement to identify the cash available to satisfy finance providers. I have inserted the total, which is $622.5 million.

Table 5.7   Building up the template – inserting the investing cash flow items

BLACK & DECKER – Summary cash flow template	
OPERATING CASH MARGIN (after interest and tax payments)	578.2
(INVESTED)/GENERATED FROM NET WORKING ASSETS	147.7
NET CAPITAL EXPENDITURE	**−103.4**
TAXATION	
CASH AVAILABLE TO SATISFY FINANCE PROVIDERS	**622.5**
NET INTEREST	**−45.4**
NET DIVIDENDS	
OTHER NON-OPERATING INCOME/(EXPENDITURE)	**−1**
NET CASH GENERATED/(ABSORBED) BEFORE FINANCING	
Financed by:	
INCREASE/(DECREASE) IN EQUITY	
INCREASE/(DECREASE) IN DEBT	
(INCREASE)/DECREASE IN CASH	
TOTAL CHANGE IN FINANCING	

RESTATING THE CASH FLOWS FROM FINANCING ACTIVITIES AND DEALING WITH THE FINAL CASH BALANCE

The information in Table 5.8 is taken from the form 10-K of Black & Decker

Generally, the cash flow from the financing activities section of a published cash flow statement contains values relating to the last three lines of the template. As in this case it may also contain other values relating to dividends. So, in this example, we are going to extract the values relating to the items shown in bold in Table 5.9. When this is completed correctly the template should balance.

Identifying the Change in Equity

The change in equity consists of three things. The *purchase and issuance of common stock* represents cash changes to the common equity of the business. The *repayment of preferred stock of subsidiary* also represents a cash change to the

Table 5.8 Consolidated statement of cash flows, the Black & Decker Corporation and subsidiaries (millions of dollars)

YEAR ENDED DECEMBER 31st	
FINANCING ACTIVITIES	
Net increase (decrease) in short-term borrowings	**68.8**
Proceeds from issuance of long-term debt (net of debt issue cost of $2.4 for 2006)	–
Payments on long-term debt	**(150.3)**
Repayment of preferred stock of subsidiary	–
Purchase of common stock	**(461.4)**
Issuance of common stock	**83.3**
Cash dividends	**(108.6)**
CASH FLOW FROM FINANCING ACTIVITIES	**(568.2)**
Effect of exchange rate changes on cash	**13.5**
INCREASE (DECREASE) IN CASH AND CASH EQUIVALENTS	**21.4**
Cash and cash equivalents at beginning of year	**233.3**
CASH AND CASH EQUIVALENTS AT END OF YEAR	**254.7**

See Notes to Consolidated Financial Statements.

Table 5.9 Building up the template – financing cash flow items

BLACK & DECKER – Summary cash flow template	
OPERATING CASH MARGIN (after interest and tax payments)	578.2
(INVESTED)/GENERATED FROM NET WORKING ASSETS	147.7
NET CAPITAL EXPENDITURE	−103.4
TAXATION	
CASH AVAILABLE TO SATISFY FINANCE PROVIDERS	622.5
NET INTEREST	−45.4
NET DIVIDENDS	
OTHER NON-OPERATING INCOME/(EXPENDITURE)	−1
NET CASH GENERATED/(ABSORBED) BEFORE FINANCING	
Financed by:	
INCREASE/(DECREASE) IN EQUITY	
INCREASE/(DECREASE) IN DEBT	
(INCREASE)/DECREASE IN CASH	
TOTAL CHANGE IN FINANCING	

total equity employed by the group and so must also be included in the equity change value.

Identifying the Change in Debt

The first three line items in the cash flows from financing activities section relate to changes in debt. They are all clearly labelled as such and simply require summarising into one value.

Identifying the Dividend Paid

This is the last number in this section. Its meaning is self-explanatory. So we can now summarise the investing cash flows into the template (Table 5.10).

Table 5.10   Building up the template – inserting the financing cash flows

BLACK & DECKER – Summary cash flow template	
OPERATING CASH MARGIN (after interest and tax payments)	578.2
(INVESTED)/GENERATED FROM NET WORKING ASSETS	147.7
NET CAPITAL EXPENDITURE	−103.4
TAXATION	
CASH AVAILABLE TO SATISFY FINANCE PROVIDERS	622.5
NET INTEREST	−45.4
NET DIVIDENDS	**−108.6**
OTHER NON-OPERATING INCOME/(EXPENDITURE)	−1
NET CASH GENERATED/(ABSORBED) BEFORE FINANCING	467.5
Financed by:	
INCREASE/(DECREASE) IN EQUITY	**−378.1**
INCREASE/(DECREASE) IN DEBT	**−81.5**
(INCREASE)/DECREASE IN CASH	
TOTAL CHANGE IN FINANCING	

Identifying the Cash Change Value and Balancing the Template

Our template is almost complete. We now need to input the final values in respect of the movement in cash and cash equivalents to the template in order to complete it.

To complete the restatement process we need to identify the overall change in cash and cash equivalents. The value required is shown in the following.

Effect of exchange rate changes on cash	13.5
(Increase)/decrease in cash and cash equivalents	−21.4
(INCREASE)/DECREASE IN CASH	**-7.9**

Notice that I have once again reversed the signage of the last cash flow value only. The value still represents an increase as it did in the original cash flow statement. Its signage is reversed to allow the template to show two balancing values, which, when summed, equal zero.

The need for the signage reversal is explained in detail in Chapter 2. The reason for the recognition of the effect of exchange rate changes on cash is explained in detail in Chapter 4.

We have now completed summarising all the cash flows shown in the cash flow statement of Black & Decker into the template (Table 5.11). The good news is that the template balanced as predicted, so reassuring us that we have avoided any errors relating to incorrect values being inserted in the template.

It is still possible to make errors of classification, for example, by putting values under the wrong heading. Indeed, you may not necessarily agree with the decisions I have made about where things go in the template. Whatever you consider to be appropriate remember that if the value is small it is unlikely to have much impact on the outcome of your analysis; the most important values to get right are the large ones!

Table 5.11   Building up the template – the completed balanced template

BLACK & DECKER – Summary cash flow template	
OPERATING CASH MARGIN (after interest and tax payments)	578.2
(INVESTED)/GENERATED FROM NET WORKING ASSETS	147.7
NET CAPITAL EXPENDITURE	−103.4
TAXATION	
CASH AVAILABLE TO SATISFY FINANCE PROVIDERS	622.5
NET INTEREST	−45.4
NET DIVIDENDS	**−108.6**
OTHER NON-OPERATING INCOME/(EXPENDITURE)	−1
NET CASH GENERATED/(ABSORBED) BEFORE FINANCING	**467.5**
Financed by:	
INCREASE/(DECREASE) IN EQUITY	**−378.1**
INCREASE/(DECREASE) IN DEBT	**−81.5**
(INCREASE)/DECREASE IN CASH	**−7.9**
TOTAL CHANGE IN FINANCING	**−467.5**

Remember also that we have not yet completed the task of summarising the cash flows of Black & Decker. We still have no values for interest or taxation in the template. Remember the −45.1 shown earlier in the template related to hedging activities. It is now time to introduce them.

INTRODUCING THE INTEREST AND TAXATION CASH FLOWS TO A US GAAP CASH FLOW TEMPLATE

The numbers, which are taken from the notes in the Form 10-K are shown below:

Information from the notes ($ millions)	
Interest payments – Note 8	−104.3
Taxation payments – Note 11	−139.5

We can now introduce these values to the template. Having brought them into the interest and taxation lines we must also add the same value to the OPERATING CASH MARGIN line in order for the template to be correct. This will also change the value of the CASH AVAILABLE TO SATISFY FINANCE PROVIDERS total (Table 5.12).

Table 5.12 Building up the template – the completed template with interest and taxes included

BLACK & DECKER – Summary cash flow template	
OPERATING CASH MARGIN	**822.0**
(INVESTED)/GENERATED FROM NET WORKING ASSETS	147.7
NET CAPITAL EXPENDITURE	−103.4
TAXATION	**−139.5**
CASH AVAILABLE TO SATISFY FINANCE PROVIDERS	**726.8**
NET INTEREST	**−149.7**
NET DIVIDENDS	−108.6
OTHER NON-OPERATING INCOME/(EXPENDITURE)	−1
NET CASH GENERATED/(ABSORBED) BEFORE FINANCING	**467.5**
Financed by:	
INCREASE/(DECREASE) IN EQUITY	−378.1
INCREASE/(DECREASE) IN DEBT	−81.5
(INCREASE)/DECREASE IN CASH	−7.9
TOTAL CHANGE IN FINANCING	**−467.5**

CONCLUSION

We have successfully summarised the cash flows of Black & Decker into Jury's Template, we know what the constituents of each value represent and we have created two new totals that do not appear in the published cash flow statement. We are now ready to analyse the resulting data to gain insights about the performance and cash flow behaviour of the business.

Notice that we have taken a complicated looking document (the published cash flow statement) and simplified it considerably, it is now simpler and clearer, this will assist us when we interpret the values.

6

Analysing the Cash Flows of Mature Businesses

In Chapter 3, covering *Start-up, Growth, Mature, Decline* we introduced the typical cash flow patterns to be observed in successful businesses in the four phases of the life of a business. The purpose of this was to develop an understanding of what the cash flows should look like in the four phases and to introduce some of the drivers of each line of the cash flow. The word 'driver' being used to denote the fundamental economic and market forces or management decisions that causes cash flows to change.

In this chapter we are going to go into more detail about what we mean by the word 'mature' when used in this context. We will also look at what constitutes success from a cash flow point of view when managing a mature company and finally examine the cash flows of a number of real-world, mature businesses taken from different countries around the world.

WHAT DO WE MEAN BY 'MATURE'?

Earlier in the book I made the point that all businesses want to grow and that generally a mature business is no longer growing the volume of its output significantly and hence has reduced investment needs compared to a growth business. However, these insights, whilst useful, are insufficient if we are seeking to understand the cash flows of mature businesses properly.

THE FIRST PROBLEM: *INFLATION*

Table 6.1 has been assembled from data sets maintained by the International Labour Organisation in Geneva. I am indebted to them for this dataset. It shows the inflation in consumer prices including housing costs over the year 2005–2006. This period has been chosen because it was the moment when inflation in Zimbabwe was getting out of control.

The data has been sorted to display lowest to highest inflation. Where a country has been omitted, it is because the data for 2006 was not present in the sample.

Table 6.1 A snapshot of global country inflation rates

INTERNATIONAL LABOUR ORGANISATION Geneva
LABORSTA Labour Statistics Database Consumer price inflation for one year 2005 to 2006
Copyright International Labour Organisation 1998–2010

COUNTRY	INFLATION	COUNTRY	INFLATION	COUNTRY	INFLATION
Kiribati	−1.52%	French Guiana	2.09%	New Caledonia	2.88%
India	−0.40%	Hong Kong,	2.09%	Jersey	2.94%
Seychelles	−0.37%	China		American	2.99%
Niger	0.08%	San Marino	2.10%	Samoa	
Brunei	0.20%	Vanuatu	2.11%	Isle of Man	3.01%
Darussalam		Senegal	2.16%	Bermuda	3.03%
Japan	0.30%	Israel	2.17%	Kuwait	3.03%
Taiwan, China	0.60%	Korea,	2.20%	Saint Vincent	3.05%
Kosovo (Serbia)	0.61%	Republic of		and the	
Cayman Islands	0.77%	Saudi Arabia	2.21%	Grenadines	
Switzerland	0.98%	Togo	2.25%	Oman	3.09%
Singapore	1.00%	Norway	2.26%	Portugal	3.15%
Poland	1.03%	Niue	2.31%	Macedonia,	3.19%
Netherlands	1.15%	Saint Lucia	2.35%	The former	
Sweden	1.36%	Papua New	2.36%	Yugoslav	
China	1.40%	Guinea		Rep. of	
Maldives	1.43%	Burkina Faso	2.36%	United	3.19%
Austria	1.50%	Albania	2.37%	Kingdom	
Faeroe Islands	1.53%	Martinique	2.39%	Croatia	3.20%
Mali	1.56%	Côte d'Ivoire	2.43%	Greece	3.20%
Finland	1.60%	Slovenia	2.46%	Andorra	3.20%
Germany	1.66%	Cyprus	2.49%	United States	3.23%
France	1.68%	Panama	2.51%	Netherlands	3.25%
Tuvalu	1.73%	Fiji	2.54%	Antilles	
Belgium	1.79%	Réunion	2.56%	Ecuador	3.30%
Algeria	1.80%	Greenland	2.56%	Morocco	3.32%
Bahamas	1.83%	Czech	2.58%	New Zealand	3.34%
Denmark	1.91%	Republic		Cook Islands	3.36%
Guinea-Bissau	1.97%	Dominica	2.62%	Chile	3.39%
Peru	2.00%	Gibraltar	2.64%	Oman	3.44%
Gambia	2.04%	Burundi	2.67%	Armenia	3.51%
Canada	2.04%	Luxembourg	2.67%	Spain	3.52%
Guadeloupe	2.04%	Malta	2.72%	Australia	3.55%
Italy	2.05%	French	2.74%	Malaysia	3.60%
Bahrain	2.05%	Polynesia		Mexico	3.63%

(Continued)

Table 6.1   *(Continued)*

INTERNATIONAL LABOUR ORGANISATION Geneva
LABORSTA Labour Statistics Database Consumer price inflation for one year 2005 to 2006
Copyright International Labour Organisation 1998–2010

COUNTRY	INFLATION	COUNTRY	INFLATION	COUNTRY	INFLATION
Aruba	3.64%	Macau, China	5.15%	Bulgaria	7.26%
Lithuania	3.74%	Swaziland	5.29%	Barbados	7.31%
Benin	3.75%	Cape Verde	5.39%	Uganda	7.38%
West Bank and	3.76%	Kyrgyzstan	5.55%	Norfolk	7.41%
Gaza Strip		Honduras	5.62%	Island	
Samoa	3.83%	Lesotho	5.94%	Dominican	7.55%
Hungary	3.90%	India	5.99%	Republic	
Ireland	3.95%	Bosnia and	6.12%	Nepal	7.61%
Colombia	3.97%	Herzegovina		Egypt	7.65%
Gabon	4.03%	Mauritania	6.24%	Pakistan	7.92%
El Salvador	4.04%	Philippines	6.24%	Solomon	8.02%
Brazil	4.18%	Jordan	6.26%	Islands	
Saint Helena	4.25%	Viet Nam	6.33%	Sierra Leone	8.06%
Bolivia	4.28%	Uruguay	6.41%	Anguilla	8.10%
Marshall	4.35%	Congo	6.52%	Chad	8.21%
Islands		Guatemala	6.56%	Nigeria	8.24%
Slovakia	4.44%	Romania	6.56%	Trinidad and	8.33%
Tunisia	4.46%	Latvia	6.56%	Tobago	
Belize	4.46%	Central African	6.59%	Azerbaijan	8.33%
Estonia	4.48%	Republic		Kazakhstan	8.57%
Thailand	4.67%	Lebanon	6.62%	Jamaica	8.62%
South Africa	4.69%	Guyana	6.69%	Rwanda	8.84%
Cambodia	4.77%	Iceland	6.76%	Mauritius	8.92%
Northern	4.89%	Bangladesh	6.77%	Zambia	9.02%
Mariana		Lao People's	6.79%	Ukraine	9.08%
Islands		Dem. Rep.		Nicaragua	9.16%
Bhutan	5.00%	India	6.90%	Georgia	9.16%
Namibia	5.04%	Belarus	7.00%	United Arab	9.29%
India	5.10%	Tonga	7.19%	Emirates	
Cuba	5.11%	Tanzania	7.20%	Sierra Leone	9.54%
Cameroon	5.14%	(Tanganyika)		Turkey	9.60%

(Continued)

Table 6.1   (*Continued*)

INTERNATIONAL LABOUR ORGANISATION Geneva
LABORSTA Labour Statistics Database Consumer price inflation for one year 2005 to 2006
Copyright International Labour Organisation 1998–2010

COUNTRY	INFLATION	COUNTRY	INFLATION	COUNTRY	INFLATION
Russian	9.67%	Iran, Islamic	11.93%	Malawi	13.90%
Federation		Rep. of		Ethiopia	13.98%
Syrian Arab	10.03%	Haiti	12.33%	Puerto Rico	14.66%
Republic		Moldova,	12.78%	Kenya	19.56%
Paraguay	10.58%	Republic of		Myanmar	20.00%
Madagascar	10.73%	Indonesia	13.10%	Yemen	21.31%
Ghana	10.87%	Mozambique	13.25%	Sao Tome and	23.07%
Argentina	10.90%	Angola	13.31%	Principe	
Suriname	11.27%	Ethiopia	13.50%	Guinea	34.69%
Costa Rica	11.46%	Mozambique	13.58%	Iraq	53.23%
Botswana	11.56%	Venezuela,	13.66%	Zimbabwe	1016.68%
Guam	11.58%	Bolivarian			
Serbia	11.70%	Rep. of			
Qatar	11.84%	Sri Lanka	13.69%		

Some countries appear more than once due to data being sourced from different agencies within the country.

Table 6.1 provides an overview of consumer price inflation from a worldwide perspective and demonstrates that inflation is still a significant issue in many countries.

In 2006 the United Kingdom was experiencing retail price inflation at about 3%, India was at about 6%, Indonesia 13% and Zimbabwe 1016%. Zimbabwe was experiencing runaway inflation. Inflation is still a significant global problem and there are many commentators who think it may become a much more serious problem in the next decade. Why is inflation important?

If we make the assumption that our mature company is not going to expand geographically or invest significantly to increase the volume of its output the first thing a mature business must do is make sure its sales match the rate of inflation in nominal turnover terms. This means its turnover will represent the same volume of output as it enjoyed in the previous year.

So, if a business faces 6% inflation in its market, it must increase its prices by 6% a year at a constant volume of output (with all other things being equal) in order to be in the same position at the end of the year as it was in the beginning.

We use the term 'nominal' to denote the values we observe in annual reports. In most countries the monetary values shown in accounts are *after* the effects of inflation, unless they originate from countries that adjust for inflation each year, a practice known as current purchasing parity (CPP) accounting. We use the term 'real' to denote what is actually happening, to show the performance of the business *before* the effects of inflation on the monetary values.

This means that, unless we are in a zero inflation economy (such as Japan), we expect all mature companies to increase their turnover year on year in nominal terms, however, this does not necessarily mean they have increased their output! Indeed, it may have dropped in real terms!

THE SECOND PROBLEM: *THE MARKET GROWTH RATE*

Mature companies produce most of the products that we see in a modern supermarket. For many of the segments served demand is driven mainly by demography. The market for food products is large, as everyone in the entire population is a potential consumer. However, the growth rate of the market is very small. It grows at less than 1% a year (this due to population change). Within this market each individual product faces competition from similar versions produced by competitors and the supermarkets themselves. Some segments achieve growth rates greater than the whole market due to changes in consumer preferences. For example, there has been a trend towards convenience for some years, consumers preferring to purchase partly prepared or fully prepared meals instead of purchasing raw ingredients and preparing the whole meal themselves. Businesses focused on this market may have growth rates in double digits as the market abandons more traditional products in favour of convenience foods.

So, the second thing a mature company must do in order to be in the same situation as it was in the previous year is to match the market growth rate. This may be negligible or it may be 15% or more if there is significant change in the mature segment served by the business.

So, mature businesses must match both inflation and the market growth rate of the segments they serve, in order to stand still in real terms relative to their competitors. If the market growth rate is say 2% and inflation 3% this means a 5% increase in turnover and profits each year is equivalent to standing still. Less than this and the business is in decline *relative to competitors*. Another way of looking at this is to say the business must maintain its market share in nominal turnover terms each year.

THE THIRD PROBLEM: *DO WE REALLY MEAN 'MATURE' COMPANY?*

When we talk about a mature company in an analysis context what we actually mean is a company operating in a mature market. As I have mentioned already all companies want to grow if they can.

So, why does competing in a mature market result in many companies achieving low or zero growth?

In most mature markets adoption took place decades or centuries ago. By adoption we are referring to consumers adopting the use of the product for the first time. Adoption of foods such as rice as a staple food goes back to the very origins of agriculture. Tea, coffee, beer and milk have been around for centuries! This means that the businesses competing in these markets have been around a very long time. These industries have spent hundreds of years improving the way things are done and reducing unit costs. They are, in many ways, hyper-efficient producers. They have had a lot of time to think about it.

How then do businesses grow in these markets? Occasionally, small shifts in consumer preferences offer opportunities to grow market share. Whilst the product is usually a commodity there may be opportunities in repackaging or repositioning the product to better satisfy sub-groups of consumers. Müller have reinvented the yoghurt concept with a double product where the consumer mixes the two items just before consumption. This is a good example from the dairy industry. Cans are a relatively recent innovation in the brewing industry; prior to the use of cans, beer was only available in draught form or in bottles.

However, growth in mature markets is different to growth in growth markets. In a growth market all participants can grow in a given year. In a mature market if one participant grows more than the market growth rate in one year it follows that its direct competitors have lost market share and hence sales. The market itself is effectively a zero sum game. Generally, competitors respond aggressively to any innovation that results in lost sales to a competitor, the usual response is to copy the innovation and reflect it in their own products and business so negating the advantage over time and returning to some sort of equilibrium.

Other growth options are to acquire your competitors or to expand the markets in which you operate. The result of this over time is very large companies! Anheuser-Busch Inc, InBev, Nestlé and Unilever all had their corporate origins over 100 years ago.

- Anheuser-Busch Inc has it roots in 1852 in a Bavarian brewery.
- Inbev has its roots in Den Horen in Leuven, Belgium. It began making beer in 1366.
- In 1866, Henry Nestlé developed a food for babies who were unable to breastfeed.
- In 1890, William Lever, founder of Lever brothers, wrote down his ideas for Sunlight soap.

So, when we talk about a mature company we usually mean a business operating in a mature market. The business itself may be experiencing zero, negative or positive growth in any given measurement period depending on sector conditions. It is a consequence of the nature of mature markets that it is very difficult to grow a successful mature business consistently.

THE FOURTH PROBLEM: *WHERE MATURE BUSINESSES COMPETE*

Having defined a mature business as a business operating in a mature market, the final issue is location. All of the above discussion about the meaning of mature is relative to where a business chooses to compete.

The business may compete in a single town, or in a county, state or province or it may be regional or national, or it may be transnational, operating in a number of countries, or it may be a multinational operating across whole continents.

The point being that the market may be mature in one location, but growth in another! So the market for after-market replacement exhaust systems in the UK is mature (a little further explanation may help here for some readers, after-market means an exhaust or muffler produced by a supplier other than the original supplied by the car manufacturer). There are dozens of companies in the UK listed in national directories all competing fiercely to supply wholesalers and retailers. As a consequence margins for producers are tiny. When I visited Egypt in the 1990s there were two manufacturing businesses operating in this market, one being dominant. Competition was minimal and huge growth opportunities were available. Many markets that are mature in developed nations are in the growth phase in emerging market countries.

So, it is the market conditions in the *location* where the business chooses to operate that define whether we should treat the business as mature or not for the purpose of analysing its cash flows.

IN CASH FLOW TERMS, WHAT CONSTITUTES SUCCESS FOR MATURE COMPANIES?

The analysis of the cash flows of a mature business can be summed up in one sentence.

> In the long run, mature businesses must generate sufficient Cash Available to Satisfy Finance Providers to cover interest, dividends and scheduled debt repayment.

In order to develop our understanding of the sentence let us start by looking at an example of a really successful mature business. Here is the Jury's Template version of the cash flows of Coca-Cola taken from a recent Form 10-K and summarised into the recommended format. This is one of the most successful mature businesses in the world. The cash flow available to satisfy finance providers has averaged $5397 million over the three years shown in Table 6.2!

Table 6.2   An example of the cash flows of a successful mature company

COCA COLA Summary Cash Flows	20XX $millions	20XW $millions	20XV $millions
Cash from operations	8909	8182	7667
Change in NWA	6	−615	430
Net Capex	−1409	−1295	−811
Cash taxes	−1596	−1601	−1676
CASH FLOW AVAILABLE TO SATISFY CAPITAL PROVIDERS	**5910**	**4671**	**5610**
Net interest	−169	−9	2
Net dividends	−3149	−2911	−2678
Other	−5310	−405	−685
NET CASH INFLOW/(OUTFLOW)	**−2718**	**1346**	**2249**
Inc/(Dec) in equity	−219	−2268	−1825
Inc/(Dec) in debt	4341	−1404	−2282
(Inc)/Dec in cash	−1404	2326	1858
FINANCING CASH FLOW	**2718**	**−1346**	**−2249**

Note – Interest received value taken from P&L

Really successful mature businesses may generate substantial surpluses of cash after their interest, dividend and debt repayment needs. Businesses that are capable of this usually have significant competitive advantages not generally available to their competitors or new entrants.

THE CONSEQUENCES OF FAILURE TO GENERATE SUFFICIENT CASH FLOW

However, to understand the sentence better let us consider what happens to mature companies when they fail to achieve the equilibrium state summarised above. To do this we will use a fictional example.

Let us assume we are analysing a medium sized manufacturing group whose products are widely used by a variety of other industries. The business is listed on a stock exchange and has recently seen a fall in performance. Demand for the core products is falling due to changes in technology and fashion. A failure to innovate at the same speed as competitors has reduced financial performance. At the end of the year the cash available to satisfy finance providers is insufficient to cover interest and dividends. What actions do the senior managers typically take at this point in time?

Observation of a number of early distress business scenarios has revealed the usual response of managers at this point is to borrow. Whether the business can borrow is largely determined by the existing leverage. If the business has low or negligible net debt it is normally easy to borrow substantial sums without problems. The business is well established with mature products selling to thousands of customers in markets with good geographic spread, the balance sheet is strong at this point with substantial fixed assets to provide asset backing for the lenders. Even if the business has typical levels of leverage it is still likely to be feasible to borrow more money.

Managers rarely take more vigorous action at this point; they still believe that the factors causing underperformance are either outside their control or temporary in nature.

Let us assume that despite the signals from the business of continuing underperformance the managers again fail to take sufficiently robust action. Another six months of underperformance ensues. What actions would the senior managers now take at this point? Observation of real businesses in this condition reveals the usual response is to borrow even more money!

In one sense they have no choice; the business requires cash to operate and this has to come from somewhere, if the operating cash margin is falling, the only other quick source of cash is by borrowing. Banks will be more wary at this point, only providing further funds against better security, documentation and at a higher interest rate (due to the existing leverage and increasing credit risk). The business may now be reaching the limits of the leverage available to it.

Eventually, perhaps in the following six months, there will come the point at which more radical actions will have to be taken. In markets more wedded to aggressive styles of capitalism this will involve early management change, with the chairman, chief executive and possibly the finance director all being vulnerable to replacement. Job losses (redundancies), cost reduction and restructuring all commence. The disposal of non-core businesses, or secondary elements of the core business may be considered.

It may also be necessary at this point to reduce or eliminate the dividend temporarily. Mature businesses are always reluctant to mess with the dividend because any negative announcement regarding dividends will have a negative impact on the share price. By maintaining the dividend in the early stages of what has now developed into a crisis the managers are signalling that the problems are considered to be temporary. Managers will do this even if they are paying an uncovered dividend. (An uncovered dividend is a dividend not paid for out of the current period's profits. This means the business may have to borrow, or use cash generated in previous years, to pay the dividend.) Disturbing announcements regarding dividends occur late in the succession of adverse events. The same logic applies to raising further equity capital; announcements of the intention to raise new equity will normally adversely affect the stock price. Moreover, the additional equity means the business has to generate even more returns to provide the same reward per share as it achieved before the cash flow problems arose.

So what eventually emerges from this process is a smaller, more focused, mature business whose Cash Available to Satisfy Finance Providers is greater than or equal to its need to pay interest, dividends and any scheduled debt repayment. It is rare for listed groups of mature businesses to fail completely; they usually go through this restructuring and divestment process until they recover their ability to perform. Takeover by a larger competitor is also a possibility at this point.

So, to summarise, in the long run mature businesses must generate sufficient Cash Available to Satisfy Finance Providers to cover interest, dividends and scheduled debt repayment. In the short run (by which I mean six months to three years) they may fail to do so, surviving on historic surpluses and leverage. However, time is running out in this scenario and at some point action has to be taken to rectify the underperformance. If managers fail to act, external forces on the business will typically force the issue.

Invensys

Invensys is a good example of the above. Between 1960 and 1998 this business, formerly known as Siebe, had developed, through acquisition and organic growth, from a small UK-based safety business to being a multinational engineering group with sales of £3900 million focused on control systems. In 1999, one year after new CEO Allan Yurko was appointed, the group acquired a number of companies including BTR, a large UK-based industrial and engineering conglomerate, and changed its name to Invensys. As a consequence, the groups leverage increased significantly. 1999 marked the start of a significant global recession that hit the group hard. Despite this they continued acquiring companies, particularly in industrial software and services. One of these was the Dutch software company Baan (purchased for $700m in June 2000).

In October 2001 the leadership changed again. A new CEO, Rick Haythorn-thwaite, was appointed. By this time Invensys had reduced its workforce by 23 000, the share price had dropped from 195p to 27p, and the group had over £3500 million of debt. The debt was so large that disposing of significant parts of the group was the only option. Over the next five years the group made a number of significant disposals one of which was the sale in June 2003 of Baan to SSA Global technologies for $135m – a loss of $565m.

The cash flows of Invensys for the 10 years to 2008 summarised into the template are shown in Table 6.3.

The cash flow generally exhibits the behaviour outlined in the earlier fictional example used to illustrate our summarising sentence (in the long run, mature businesses must generate sufficient Cash Available to Satisfy Finance Providers to cover interest, dividends and scheduled debt repayment). The operating cash margin was in decline from 1999. By 2001 the group is unable to service interest and dividends from current-period cash generation and debt increases by £605 million in this year. In 2002 the company is unable to increase debt further because it is not available on reasonable terms.

It achieves debt service by cutting Capex (depreciation in this year being £260 million), by recovering money invested in net working assets and business disposal. In 2003 the group starts selling significant parts of the group raising £1473 million from disposals, which is used to service and reduce outstanding debt. This process continues for the next five years. The group is cash negative from 2001 until 2007 when once again the cash available to satisfy finance providers is sufficient to cover interest and dividends. In 2007 and 2008 business disposal and debt reduction is still continuing.

Notice that, despite problems being evident from 2001, the dividend is not eliminated until 2004, when the company also raises new equity because it has no other acceptable options.

What we end up with is a smaller, mature engineering group, which is generating sufficient cash available to satisfy finance providers to cover interest, dividends and scheduled debt repayment.

Let us now look at a number of examples of other mature businesses.

Table 6.3   An example of the cash flows of an underperforming mature business

INVENSYS PLC

SUMMARY CASH FLOW £ millions	2008	2007	2006	2005	2004	2003	2002	2001	2000	1999
OPERATING CASH MARGIN	205	274	102	80	5	315	446	883	1239	1370
INV/(GEN)FROM NET WORKING ASSETS	−45	27	10	30	−212	−105	90	−560	−171	−135
NET CAPITAL EXPENDITURE	−57	−71	−66	−74	−122	−103	−98	−236	−458	−580
TAXATION	−37	−23	−25	−76	−73	−62	−43	−135	−60	−292
CASH FLOW AVAILABLE TO SATISFY FINANCE PROVIDERS	**66**	**207**	**21**	**−40**	**−402**	**45**	**395**	**−48**	**550**	**363**
NET INTEREST	−57	−112	−110	−113	−119	−113	−167	−210	−174	−208
NET DIVIDENDS	−1	−3	0	0	−2	−73	−220	−276	−331	−451
OTHER NON-OPERATING INC/(EXP)	264	162	179	347	493	1473	178	−298	903	3050
NET CASH IN/(OUT) BEFORE FINANCING	**272**	**254**	**90**	**194**	**−30**	**1332**	**186**	**−832**	**948**	**2754**
Financed by:										
CHANGE IN EQUITY INCREASE/(DECREASE)	−13	323	0	0	448	0	0	4	−990	−1596
CHANGE IN DEBT INCREASE/(DECREASE)	−363	−697	−305	−111	−165	−1417	0	605	−117	−1639
CHANGE IN CASH (INCREASE)/DECREASE	104	120	215	−83	−253	85	−186	223	159	481
TOTAL CHANGE IN FINANCING	**−272**	**−254**	**−90**	**−194**	**30**	**−1332**	**−186**	**832**	**−948**	**−2754**

Black & Decker

The Black & Decker Corporation, is a leading global manufacturer and marketer of power tools and accessories, hardware and home improvement products, and technology-based fastening systems. With products and services marketed in over 100 countries, the corporation enjoys worldwide recognition of its strong brand names and a superior reputation for quality, design, innovation, and value. The corporation is one of the world's leading producers of power tools, power tool accessories, and residential security hardware, and the corporation's product lines hold leading market share positions in these industries. The corporation is also a major global supplier of engineered fastening and assembly systems.

The above paragraph is extracted from the most recent Form 10-K filing for Black & Decker. The markets in which it operates are mature and fiercely competitive. There are numerous other manufacturers of similar products to those produced by Black & Decker.

I am now going to illustrate a cash flow centric analysis exercise. That is to say I start with cash flow data and pull in other data as I require it.

Table 6.4 shows a sample six years' cash flows of Black & Decker summarised in Jury's Template form. What do they tell us?

In each of the six years, the cash flow to satisfy finance providers has exceeded the value spent on net interest and net dividends by a factor of two or three. In five of the six years the business has achieved a cash surplus at the net cash inflow/(outflow) line. In 20X4 the only time the business failed to generate a surplus at the net cash inflow/(outflow) line the group made a major acquisition (Other non-operating income/(expenditure) line −727.10). This was financed in that year by the residual cash flow generated in that year plus an increase in equity and debt.

The business has repaid debt in four of the six years illustrated. In the two years where debt increased 20X4 was the year of the acquisition mentioned above. In the other year (20X5) the business added leverage by increasing debt and using this to reduce equity, so improving the return to shareholders.

Already it should be clear this is a good set of cash flows. From the template I can deduce much of what has been changing in the business. Whilst it is always useful to read the financial report in full I can use the template to monitor performance very effectively without looking at any other data. Indeed, with experience, once the cash flows have been summarised in this way, they can be assessed in seconds. This time saving for the analyst can be invaluable. It is one of the most powerful aspects of this style of analysis.

Let us review the business year on year. All the insights below come directly from Jury's Template alone. If we wish to be more specific about the cause of any particular movement or change in the cash flow values we can, of course, look at all the other information disclosed in the Form 10-K filed by Black & Decker:

Table 6.4 Six years cash flows for Black and Decker

BLACK AND DECKER	20X7 $m	20X6 $m	20X5 $m	20X4 $m	20X3 $m	20X2 $m
Cash from operations	822.00	1018.00	981.20	728.10	574.70	513.10
Change in Net Working Assets	147.70	−75.60	−107.00	57.70	158.20	86.30
Net Capex	−103.40	−89.90	−98.40	−91.80	−87.50	−89.70
Cash taxes	−139.50	−221.70	−165.80	−89.50	−82.00	−47.00
CASH FLOW AVAILABLE TO SATISFY CAPITAL PROVIDERS	726.80	630.80	610.00	604.50	563.40	462.70
Net interest	−149.70	−111.40	−91.80	−77.90	−80.30	−100.80
Net dividends	−108.60	−109.10	−88.60	−67.50	−44.30	−38.60
Other	−1.00	−137.70	61.30	−727.10	−280.60	−0.90
NET CASH INFLOW/(OUTFLOW)	467.50	272.60	490.90	−268.00	158.20	322.40
Inc/(Dec) in equity	−378.10	−847.80	−591.80	168.00	−65.90	−22.30
Inc/(Dec) in debt	−81.50	−168.00	565.10	291.40	−315.50	−41.10
(Inc)/Dec in cash	−7.90	743.20	−464.20	−191.40	223.20	−259.00
FINANCING CASH FLOW	−467.50	−272.60	−490.90	268.00	−158.20	−322.40

In 20X2 the major issues were:

- A healthy operating cash margin.
- A reduction in the amount invested in net working assets. This implies a reduction in debtors and/or inventory and/or an increase in the operating creditors.
- The resulting cash surplus being used to reduce debt and equity and increase closing cash by $259 million.

In 20X3 the major issues were:

- A healthy operating cash margin.
- A further reduction in the amount invested in net working assets.
- There was net acquisition activity costing $280 million.
- The business generated a cash surplus that was used to reduce debt and equity.
- Closing cash was reduced by $223 million.

In 20X4 the major issues were:

- An impressive increase in operating cash margin.
- A further reduction in the amount invested in net working assets.
- A major net acquisition costing $727 million. This being financed from the year's cash flow surplus and a modest increase in debt and equity.
- Closing cash increased by $191 million.

In 20X5 the major issues were:

- A further increase in operating cash margin.
- An increase in the amount invested in net working assets.
- Some modest business level disposals.
- A healthy cash surplus on the year.
- A reduction in equity financed largely by an increase in debt.
- Closing cash increased by $464 million.

In 20X6 the major issues were:

- A modest increase in operating cash margin.
- A modest increase in the amount invested in net working assets.
- Some acquisition activity.
- A major reduction in equity financed by the surplus on cash for the year.
- An increase in debt.
- A major reduction in the cash surplus built up over previous years of $743 million.

In 20X7 the major issues were:

- A reduction in the operating cash margin of about 20%.
- This was partially offset by a reduction in the amount invested in net working assets.

- The business was still generating a healthy net cash surplus.
- The cash surplus was used to reduce equity and debt.

The big question that now arises is: is the reduction in the operating cash margin a serious problem?

Notice how the template tells us a story about the business in each of the years in question. We can deduce many of the major initiatives taken by the business without actually reading anything else in the accounts!

From the six years' cash flow summarised into the template we can observe the following:

- Emphasis on operating cash margin improvement.
- Good working asset control.
- Significant acquisition activity in two of the years.
- A decision taken in 2005 to reduce equity and increase the leverage used by the group to improve equity performance.

Notice also I have not commented significantly about capital expenditure, taxes, interest or dividends. This is because none of these numbers stand out as particularly exceptional or unusual in this example.

What is particularly impressive about Black & Decker is the consistency of their performance. They operate in highly competitive markets. They have reduced their exposure to cyclical effects by operating on a global basis where possible. They acquire other companies in complimentary areas of their business where they see opportunities for further growth or value generation.

There are other things we can do to further assess performance. At this point, whilst our tentative conclusion is that all is well, we are not certain that the operating cash margin performance is as good as it looks because the business may have been recovering from a very poor performance at the beginning of the sample period. Maybe the operating cash margin should be higher. What can we do to examine this?

Table 6.5 shows the sales, operating cash margin and other non-operating cash income and expenditure line from the cash flow, together with some percentage change data.

Firstly, we can see that when the sales grew substantially there was significant acquisition activity in the previous year. It is probable that much of the sales increase can be attributed to the acquisitions.

Reviewing the Form 10-K confirms this. In the last three years sales have been flat, this being classic behaviour for a mature business operating in a mature market.

Secondly, the operating cash flow margin as a percentage of sales is remarkably consistent at 13%. In 20X5 and 20X6 it exceeded this level, possibly due to the benefits of the previous acquisition activity and/or beneficial sector conditions or

Table 6.5 Six years sales data for Black and Decker

BLACK & DECKER	20X7 $m	20X6 $m	20X5 $m	20X4 $m	20X3 $m	20X2 $m
Sales	6563.2	6447.3	6523.7	5398.4	4482.7	4291.8
Sales increase/ (decrease) year %	**1.80%**	**−1.17%**	**20.85%**	**20.43%**	**4.45%**	
Cash from operations	822.00	1018.00	981.20	728.10	574.70	513.10
Cash operations/ Sales %	**12.5%**	**15.8%**	**15.0%**	**13.4%**	**12.8%**	**12.0%**
Other non-operating inc/(exp)	−1.00	−137.70	61.30	−727.10	−280.60	−0.90

currency movements. This sample of performance suggests that Black & Decker is capable of sustaining this margin in normal economic and sector conditions. It also means that the fall observed in the most recent years' performance may not be due to management failure.

By comparing the operating cash flow margin data with sales we are able to satisfy ourselves that the operating cash values are not distorted by a previous period of underperformance. We can, of course, compare this data with other similar companies within the hand tool sector and elsewhere. This would give us further evidence for over or underperformance.

There is one other exercise we can perform at this point to satisfy ourselves that all is well with Black & Decker. Another reason they may be generating such healthy net cash surpluses from their business is they may be underinvesting, running down their capital assets and harvesting the resulting cash flow. This approach can lead to disaster when our ageing capital assets are no longer efficient or in extreme cases fail completely. What can we do to examine this issue?

Table 6.6 shows the depreciation and amortisation values from the Form 10-K. For the most recent three years we have the depreciation value only. The net Capex is from the cash flow.

Before we can interpret this data there are a number of issues that must be considered. The depreciation and amortisation value includes an element of amortisation of intangible assets. Examination of Form 10-K reveals that this amortisation is in relation to customer relationships, technology and patents and trademarks and trade names. The depreciation value alone is quoted in Form 10-K for 20X7 as relating solely to tangible assets. For this reason I have calculated the ratio for the last three years only.

When Black & Decker acquires a business the cash expended in acquiring the business is in the cash flow template on the other non-operating

Table 6.6   Six years depreciation and capex data for Black and Decker

BLACK & DECKER	20X7 $m	20X6 $m	20X5 $m	20X4 $m	20X3 $m	20X2 $m
Depreciation & amortisation	143.4	154.9	150.6	142.5	133.4	122.4
Depreciation	132.65	146.2	146			
Capital expenditures	−116.4	−104.6	−111.1	−117.80	−102.50	−94.30
Proceeds from disposal of assets	13	14.7	12.7	26.00	15.00	4.60
Net Capex	−103.40	−89.90	−98.40	−91.80	−87.50	−89.70
New Capex/ Depreciation %	−88%	−72%	−76%			

income/(expenditure) line. What Black & Decker recognises in its balance sheet in exchange for this is the net assets of the business together with excess paid which is treated as goodwill. This means that when acquisitions are made, fixed assets arrive in the balance sheet which have not appeared as Capex in the cash flow. What net Capex represents in the cash flow is the net value spent by the group on fixed assets other than those acquired in the same period as part of a business. The same logic applies in reverse when the group makes material disposal of entire businesses by sale of their equity. This means the ratio above will not be meaningful in any year where there is material acquisition (or disposal) of businesses from the group.

However, the cash flow template shows us there was no material acquisition or disposal activity in 20X7. In this year Black & Decker invested in new Capex at a rate 88% of its depreciation charge. This appears to be low.

Given that the apparent trend over the six years looks similar there may be reasons why this particular sector has unusually low investment needs going forward, compared to its historic investment rate. It could be that the cost of new machinery is lower for the same output than was the case historically (meaning that there could be price deflation in the machinery used by the sector). It could be there has been little technological change in the last few years compared to earlier periods thus requiring much less investment. It could be that, as a mature group with numerous manufacturing units all over the world, investment needs are limited to maintenance asset replacement of computer, machines and transport only. It could be that the group over depreciates its assets by writing them off before their useful life is in fact over. It is not clear whether this pattern of apparent underinvestment is sustainable or not.

Finally, there is a reasonable contribution to cash flow from proceeds of disposal of fixed assets. It could be that the group has been steadily concentrating production in fewer and fewer low cost centres thus slowly realising its older, less efficient manufacturing facilities back to cash.

Comparing the charge for depreciation with the level of Capex can give us insights about the level of investment taking place in a business. It can be a useful addition to the examination of the cash flows in the template form. Bear in mind that it is not a particularly exact relationship; it is affected by inflation, acquisitions and disposals, technology change, and demand supply change in the markets for capital assets themselves. Generally we expect the Capex of a mature business to be similar to fixed asset depreciation (when the depreciation is calculated in accordance with IAS standards by writing off the asset over its estimated useful life to an estimate of its residual value) because the business has no growth investment needs. It is merely maintaining its output, replacing machinery and other assets, as required.

Black & Decker is a good example of a successful mature business operating in mature markets. Let us now consider the cash flows of another mature business.

Dairy Crest

The main activity of Dairy Crest Group plc is the manufacture and trading of milk and dairy products. The Group's strategy continues to be focused on growing its branded business together with the value added elements of its key retailer relationships. The group is one the leading national milk processing groups in the UK.

Table 6.7 is a sample of the cash flows of Dairy Crest, summarised in Jury's Template form.

The operating cash margin peaked in 20X4 and has been falling since then. In four of the six years the cash flow to satisfy finance providers has exceeded the value spent on net interest and net dividends. In two of the six years the business has achieved a cash surplus at the net cash inflow/(outflow) line. The group made major acquisitions in 20X3, 20X6 and 20X7. A brief examination of the template data suggests this is a less attractive business from a cash flow point of view than Black & Decker.

Let us review the business year on year.

In 20X2 the major issues were:

- A reasonable operating cash margin.
- What looks like a big increase in the amount invested in net working assets, (which implies an increase in debtors and/or inventory and/or a decrease in the operating creditors).

Table 6.7   A further sample of the cash flows of a mature business

DAIRY CREST PLC
TEMPLATE SUMMARY CASH FLOWS

	20X7 £m	20X6 £m	20X5 £m	20X4 £m	20X3 £m	20X2 £m
Operating cash margin	97.0	89.7	122.4	126.4	111.0	100.6
Change in NWA	−2.8	−16.3	20.6	10.2	−6.1	−52.1
Net Capex	−26.6	−34.6	−29.5	−29.7	−27.0	−52.3
Cash taxes	−6.1	−15.5	−12.6	−8.7	−4.1	−5.3
CASH FLOW AVAILABLE TO SATISFY CAPITAL PROVIDERS	**61.5**	**23.3**	**100.9**	**98.2**	**73.8**	**−9.1**
Net interest	−15.3	−16.4	−17.7	−20.6	−22.0	−18.7
Net dividends	−18.8	−16.6	−23.9	−19.9	−17.4	−15.9
Other	−235.0	−43.7	−9.7	6.6	−93.4	1.1
NET CASH INFLOW/(OUTFLOW)	**−207.6**	**−53.4**	**49.6**	**64.3**	**−59.0**	**−42.6**
Inc/(Dec) in equity	39.7	0.7	3.6	0.2	1.0	4.4
Inc/(Dec) in debt	178.4	39.9	−42.6	−57.7	65.2	35.9
(Inc)/Dec in cash	−10.5	12.8	−10.6	−6.8	−7.2	2.3
FINANCING CASH FLOW	**207.6**	**53.4**	**−49.6**	**−64.3**	**59.0**	**42.6**

- This, together with extremely high net Capex, resulted in a negative cash flow to satisfy finance providers and indicates a negative net cash flow performance.
- The year results in a cash deficit of £42.6 million, which is financed largely by an increase in debt.

In 20X3 the major issues were:

- The operating cash margin increases by 11%.
- There is a further small increase in the amount invested in net working assets.
- Net Capex is much reduced at £27 million.
- The cash flow available to satisfy finance providers is now positive and sufficient to cover interest and dividend service.
- The business spent £93.4 million on acquisitions.
- This resulted in a net cash outflow for the year £59 million, which was again financed largely by an increase in debt.

In 20X4 the major issues were:

- The operating cash margin increases by 13%.
- The amount invested in net working assets reduces by £10.2 million.
- The cash flow available to satisfy finance providers is improved and is sufficient to cover interest and dividend service by a factor of more than two.

- The resulting net cash inflow of £64.3 million is used mainly to reduce debt.
- This is the peak year for cash flow performance.

In 20X5 the major issues were:

- The operating cash margin is starting to decline compared to the previous year.
- There is a reduction in the amount invested in net working assets of £20.6 million.
- The cash flow available to satisfy finance providers is further improved and sufficient to cover interest and dividend service by a factor of over two.
- The resulting cash surplus of £49.6 million is used to reduce debt and increase cash.

In 20X6 the major issues were:

- Operating cash margin continuing to decline (with a drop of 25%).
- An increase in the amount invested in net working assets of £16.3 million.
- The cash flow available to satisfy finance providers is dramatically reduced and is insufficient to cover interest and dividend service.
- There is a deficit before acquisition activity of £9.7 million.
- After acquisitions of £43.7 million the resulting net cash outflow of £53.4 million is financed by an increase in debt and utilising cash reserves from previous years.

In 20X7 the major issues were:

- A increase in the operating cash margin of about 8%, but still well below the peak of 20X4.
- There is a small increase in the amount invested in net working assets.
- The cash flow available to satisfy finance providers is adequate to cover interest and dividend service leaving a modest surplus before acquisition activity.
- There is major acquisition activity of £235 million.
- The deficit for the year of £207.6 million being financed by some equity, a large increase in debt and some of the existing cash surplus.

Notice how the template tells us a story about the business in each of the years in question. We can deduce many of the major initiatives taken by the business without actually reading anything else in the accounts!

From the six years' cash flow summarised into the template we can observe the following:

- A variable operating cash margin which appears to be in decline.
- Significant variation in working asset investment with increases in the years when cash available to satisfy is inadequate to cover interest and dividends.
- Significant acquisition activity in three of the years.
- Significant reliance on debt.

Notice also I have not said much about taxes, interest or dividends. This is because none of these numbers stand out as particularly exceptional or unusual in this example.

The cash flows of Dairy Crest are not as good as those of Black & Decker. They show a lot more variability, a significant reliance on debt for financing as required and mediocre operating cash margin performance.

Some of this is likely to be attributable to the nature of the market in which Dairy Crest operates (analysts generally refer to this as *sector risk*). The basic business of milk processing is brutally competitive and distribution to consumers is via the major supermarket groups who often regard milk merely as a major traffic builder for their stores (and therefore seek to offer it a cheaply as possible). There is huge low cost emphasis throughout the value chain. The sector itself has gone through a series of step changes in the last decade as the delivery model moved from home delivery in glass bottles to supermarket purchase in plastic containers. There has been massive consolidation in the processing and distribution of milk.

The farmer has also been affected. The minimum economic size of a primary milk producer has increased to the point where super farms are now being created to capture the necessary economies of scale required to keep milk production a viable business.

Dairy Crest is aware of these fundamentals. It is seeking to move into areas where it can generate more value added and hence cash flow for itself from the products it produces. As the managing director points out in a recent report the group's strategy continues to be focused on growing its branded business together with the value added elements of its key retailer relationships.

What this means is moving towards branded products where better retail margins are available for producers and only working with supermarkets whenever there is an adequate return. The group is expanding in cheese and spreads, products with more potential to add value for the producer.

Notice that, whilst I am still stressing a cash-centric approach, some sector knowledge is invaluable for putting the numbers onto context whenever the analysts seeks to understand business performance through cash flows. As in the last example it would seem sensible to examine the operating cash margin relationship to sales (Table 6.8).

Given that we have inflation at about 2% the first five years sales performance is average at best. The business is losing turnover in real terms. Let us look at this in more detail. Table 6.9 uses the data from Table 6.8 with an inflation adjustment added.

Before continuing let me note that there are many potential pitfalls for the analyst in adjusting data for inflation. Some of the problems are:

• Selecting an index which has a meaningful relationship with the dataset to be adjusted (to do this well can take a significant amount of time).

Table 6.8   Six years sales data for Diary Crest

DAIRY CREST	20X7 £m	20X6 £m	20X5 £m	20X4 £m	20X3 £m	20X2 £m
Sales	1309.3	1161.0	1348.8	1361.8	1326.1	1366.7
Sales increase/ (decrease) year %	12.8%	−13.9%	−1.0%	2.7%	−3.0%	
Cash from operations	97.0	89.7	122.4	126.4	111.0	100.6
Cash operations/ Sales %	7.4%	7.7%	9.1%	9.3%	8.4%	7.4%
Other non-operating inc/(exp)	−235.0	−43.7	−9.7	6.6	−93.4	1.1

- Identifying the correct values to be used (it's easier to work with the index series data rather than the percentage change data).
- Avoiding errors in setting up the spreadsheet formulae.
- Recognising that the outcome of the exercise is not correct in any sense unless the index used has constituents that match the constituents of turnover in the business. The result is an approximation.

Table 6.9   Six years inflation adjusted sales data for Diary Crest

DAIRY CREST	20X7 £m	20X6 £m	20X5 £m	20X4 £m	20X3 £m	20X2 £m
Sales	1309.3	1161.0	1348.8	1361.8	1326.1	1366.7
Nominal sales inc/ (dec) year %	12.8%	−13.9%	−1.0%	2.7%	−3.0%	
Inflation UK RPI excluding housing	2.70%	2.60%	1.60%	1.20%	1.70%	1.40%
Index 13 January 1987 = 100	183.2	178.3	173.7	170.9	168.9	166.0
Real sales inc/(dec) year in 20X7 money	1309.3	1192.9	1422.6	1459.8	1438.4	1508.3
Real sales inc/(dec) year %	9.8%	−16.1%	−2.6%	1.5%	−4.6%	
Cash from operations	97.0	89.7	122.4	126.4	111.0	100.6
Cash operations/ Sales %	7.4%	7.7%	9.1%	9.3%	8.4%	7.4%
Other non-operating inc/(exp)	−235.0	−43.7	−9.7	6.6	−93.4	1.1

When we see the adjusted data it is clear that the business is failing to grow at all in real terms. The increase in turnover in the most recent period is likely to be largely due to the acquisition of two businesses in France and Italy during the financial year. Segment analysis reveals the majority of the group's turnover (70%) is still in the lower value-added milk-processing area with the remaining 30% in foods.

So we can see that the business is still dealing with the step changes in its traditional market. The milk business is being steadily rationalised and consolidated to reduce costs and attain greater economies of scale. To use a military metaphor, this is a little like a rearguard action, seeking to preserve as much profitable business as possible whilst managing the transitions. The group sees its future in branded foods and is steadily moving in this direction to improve its return on investment.

Finally, let us examine the relationships between Capex and depreciation (Table 6.10).

Table 6.10 Six years depreciation and capex data for Dairy Crest

DAIRY CREST	20X7 £m	20X6 £m	20X5 £m	20X4 £m	20X3 £m	20X2 £m
Depreciation	40.6	38.3	34.4	36	35.8	37
Payment to acquire Property Plant and Equipment	−37.4	−44.3	−37.7	−41.7	−61.6	−60.2
Grant received	1.1	0.3				
Proceeds from disposal	9.7	9.4	8.2	12	34.6	7.9
Net Capex	−26.60	−34.60	−29.50	−29.70	−27.00	−52.30
New Capex/Depreciation %	92%	116%	110%	116%	172%	163%

Dairy Crest has a net Capex below depreciation in the last five years of the sample. Investigation of this reveals that the proceeds of sale from the steady rationalisation of the historic investment in milk processing is offsetting the new Capex. The level of investment in new Capex is above depreciation in every year except 20X7. New Capex in 20X2 and 20X3 was considerably above depreciation. This could be due to changes in health regulations, technological change or it could be due to investment needed to create new facilities at the size required to capture economies of scale.

Dairy Crest is a mature business operating in a low value-added mature market undergoing fundamental sector change. It appears to be in the latter stages of a business transformation designed to optimise the returns from the historic business (milk) and move the business into products related to its historic core business (milk based) with higher potential value-added available to the group. Cash flows are volatile and there is evidence of gradual decline in performance. It may be that the move to higher value added markets is not taking place fast enough to offset the decline.

Fiat Group

Our next example is taken from Europe. Fiat Group is a diversified industrial group involved in car, truck, bus, agricultural and construction equipment manufacture.

All the markets in which the group operates are mature, many facing intense competition on a global basis. Sectors such as cars, trucks and agricultural products have seen steady rationalisation and consolidation over the last few years. At this point Fiat controls the following car brands, Fiat, Lancia, Alfa Romeo, Maserati and Ferrari.

The cash flows of the group for the sample seven years chosen are shown in Table 6.11.

Before we commence our analysis of the seven years of Fiat performance the first thing we should notice is that the template has changed. A new line item '(Increase)/Decrease in vendor financed assets' and a further sub-total have been added. I will briefly discuss the variation between this template and the earlier versions of the template.

The Issue of Vendor Financing

Over the last 50 years or so it has become more and more common for sellers of capital goods in particular not only to sell the product, but also provide a loan, deferred purchase arrangement or lease arrangement to the customer which is then paid off from the cash flows generated by using the product, directly or indirectly. For example Ford Motor Credit, the original finance business of the Ford Motor Company, was founded in 1959. FCE Bank plc, the European arm of Ford's vendor financing activities, was founded in 1964.

This approach to selling capital goods is common not only for vehicles but also for most moveable plant and machinery. The technique has also been extended to include assets such as immovable plant and machinery, power stations, bridges, pipelines and mobile phone networks, where it is more normally known as project financing or non-recourse project financing. In these larger projects both the vendors in house finance operation and external finance providers will be involved.

The provision of a loan to a customer is a banking activity. The risks inherent in such a loan are identical to those taken by any banking institution that lends money to a customer to buy a vehicle.

For this reason it is preferable for us to keep the cash flows associated with the financing of customers (other than typical trade credit) separate from the cash flows of the rest of the business. This separation means that we can assess the

Table 6.11 Seven years cash flows for Fiat Group

FIAT GROUP - SEVEN YEAR SUMMARY

FIAT GROUP	2007	2006	2005	2004	2003	2002	2001
Operating cash margin	5637	4864	4817	617	−232	−511	339
(Inv)/Gen from net working assets	1588	812	114	−609	−1282	2016	2388
Net Capital expenditure	−3726	−3402	−2625	−1754	2156	460	−786
Taxation paid in period estimate	−833	−551	−419	−292	−132	−660	−660
CATS (before investment in leased assets)	**2666**	**1723**	**1887**	**−2038**	**510**	**1305**	**1281**
(Increase)/Decrease in vendor financed assets	−1032	−876	−251	2976	1146	2456	−189
Cash Available To Satisfy Finance Providers	**1634**	**847**	**1636**	**938**	**1656**	**3761**	**1092**
Net interest paid estimate	−564	−576	−843	−74	−301	208	368
Net dividends	−229	46	18	165	−15	−228	−380
Other	220	2665	2500	−45	2660	−645	−2027
Net cash	**1061**	**2982**	**3311**	**984**	**4000**	**3096**	**−947**
Increase/(Decrease) in equity	−390	22	0	20	1842	1138	−266
Increase/(Decrease) in debt	−1675	−1730	−2839	−2735	−3055	−2703	1364
Decrease/(Increase) in cash	1004	−1274	−472	1731	−2787	−1531	−151
	−1061	**−2982**	**−3311**	**−984**	**−4000**	**−3096**	**947**

CATS is an abbreviation of Cash Available To Satisfy (Finance Providers)
All amounts € millions

performance of the businesses business activities separate from the businesses banking activities!

Whilst it is my preference to keep Jury's Template absolutely standard and to deal with variations due to sector differences by way of explanation, it is clear to me that an exception should be made in the case of vendor financing. I have introduced a new line to deal with the vendor financing activities of a business after the Cash available to Satisfy Finance Providers value (CATS) and before the Net interest paid. After inserting the movement in Vendor Financed Assets I have created a second Cash Available to Satisfy Finance Providers Total after Vendor Financing. This has the effect of separating the cash flow related to vendor financing, and so on from the remaining cash flows of the business.

Bear in mind that in larger groups the financing subsidiary itself may raise finance directly from capital markets to engage in its chosen activities. These loans will end up being consolidated as part of the group debt. This means that the change in debt value in the group cash flow statement will include both finance raised to invest in the manufacturing and other business activities of the group and finance raised for vendor financing purposes.

The Use of Estimates for Interest and Taxation

In the case of Fiat the original cash flow statements from which Jury's Cash Flow Template was prepared contain no interest or taxation numbers. This is because the commencing profit value is the net result (this being the profit after interest and taxation from the P&L).

To complete the template I have used the values of net interest and taxation taken from the notes to the annual report and accounts. Where a taxation or net interest paid value has been disclosed I have used it. I have adjusted the taxation value to remove the change in the deferred tax provision, which is not a cash flow. I have assumed the remaining taxes disclosed are cash taxes paid in the period in which they are disclosed. It is unlikely that the cash net interest value is materially different from the P&L value; this is because the only differences should be for opening and closing accruals of interest due but not yet paid, and any interest recognised in the P&L on deep discount bonds and other debt instruments that do not require any cash interest service during the life of the loan.

Taxation may be distorted if the taxes recognised in the current period P&L are paid over in the following year. I do not know whether this is the case for Fiat or not.

Note that to change our perception of the performance of the Fiat Group business from a cash flow point of view the estimation error on these values would have to be large. The magnitude of the net interest and taxation values used is small relative to the other values in Jury's Template.

I have chosen Fiat Group to illustrate what a worrying set of mature company cash flows look like. It is public knowledge that the Fiat Group has gone through a sustained period of underperformance. In the period 2001 to 2004 the operating cash margin was wholly inadequate to sustain the group and in 2002 and 2003 it was negative! Since 2005 the top line performance has improved to a point where, in 2008, the group is trying to expand its sales with important new model launches.

Let us review the business year on year.

In 2001 the major issues were:

- Severely inadequate operating cash margin.
- €2.3 billion recovered from a reduction in the amount invested in working assets.
- Massively reduced Capex.
- Positive CATS Finance Providers of €1.2 billion.
- A small increase in vendor financed assets.
- Net interest receivable – this includes the interest earned on vendor financing receivables.
- Major acquisition activity of €2 billion resulting in a negative net cash position of just under €1 billion.
- The deficit on the year being financed by an increase in debt of €1.4 billion with a reduction in equity and an increase in cash.

In 2002 the major issues were:

- A negative operating cash margin, this means that overall the business spent more cash on the expenses of its operating business than it generated from customers, a very worrying result.
- The amount invested in net working assets reduces by a further €2 billion, which is the main reason the business has a positive CATS Finance Providers.
- The net Capex is a positive value implying significant fixed assets disposal during the year.
- The decrease in vendor assets of €2.4 billion is the other major contributor to cash.
- The net cash surplus of €3.1 billion is used to repay debt of €2.7 billion.
- A share issue raises €1.1 billion and cash has increased by €1.5 billion.

In 2003 the major issues were:

- Another year of negative operating cash margin.
- The investment in net working assets now increases by €1.2 billion.
- The net Capex is a positive value implying substantial assets disposal in the year.
- Dividend payments cease. Notice how late this action occurs in the process of recovering performance.
- There is a further decrease in vendor assets of €1.1 billion.

- This, together with net business disposals of €2.7 billion, generates sufficient cash to repay €3.1 billion of debt.
- There is a further equity issue raising €1.8 billion.
- Cash increases by €2.7 billion.

In 2004 the major issues were:

- A modest improvement in operating cash margin; however, it is still significantly below the sort of value needed to sustain the group.
- Investment in net Capex recommences.
- There is another huge reduction in vendor receivables of €3.0 billion.
- This allows the business to finish with a cash surplus of €1.0 billion.
- Debt reduces by a further €2.7 billion, with €1.7 billion of this coming from cash.

In 2005 the major issues were:

- A significant recovery of performance at the operating cash margin.
- Control of working asset investment looks good.
- Net Capex returning to more normal levels.
- Vendor financed assets now start to increase.
- Interest paid has increased.
- There is significant business disposal raising €2.5 billion.
- Debt reduces again, by €2.8 billion.

In 2006 the numbers all start to look as they should in a successful mature business:

- Investment in working assets further reduces.
- Major business disposals raise €2.7 billion.
- Debt is reduced again by €1.7 billion with a cash increase of €1.3 billion.

In 2007:

- The operating cash margin appears healthy with further net working asset reduction.
- Vendor financing activities are increasing and absorb €1 billion.
- Dividend payment is resumed.
- Debt is reduced again by €1.7 billion.
- Equity is reduced, cash reduces by €1 billion.

This is the third example we have considered. By now you should be starting to become familiar with the process. The template tells us a story about what is going on in the business. In the first four years of the time line we can see a seriously underperforming mature business. The effect of this on the business is to cause the finance providers (mainly debt providers), to lose faith in the company, which results in the need for constant debt reduction over the ensuing few years.

Fiat Group becomes unable to access the short-term credit market directly. This means the business is then unable to offer its own vendor finance. Fiat has to enter into joint ventures with other banks in order to continue to provide vendor finance to its customers, this also means sharing the rewards of such business with third parties so reducing the financial benefit flowing to the group.

In order to survive the complete loss of operating cash margin (mainly due to losses in the car business) the group sells off fixed assets and recovers the amount invested in historic vendor finance transactions as the customers repay their loans without new loans being added and sells interests in a number of businesses. Over the six years 2002 to 2007 the group has reduced debt by €14.7 billion.

A review of the annual reports and the group's Form 20-F reveals that the group is an industrial engineering conglomerate involved in hundreds of business around the world. The recovery story is a classic one of asset and business disposal, cost reduction and business reinvention. Notice that it took at least five years before the business entered the recovery phase in cash flow terms. Notice also that despite being recognised as a seriously damaged business it never entered any formal insolvency process. Recovery was achieved by refocussing the business.

Let us see how this compares with the cash margin to sales data (Table 6.12).

Table 6.12   Seven years sales data for Fiat Group

FIAT GROUP	2007 €M	2006 €M	2005 €M	2004 €M	2003 €M	2002 €M	2001 €M
Sales	58 529	51 832	46 544	45 637	48 346	55 427	57 525
Sales increase/ (decrease) year %	**12.9%**	**11.4%**	**2.0%**	**−5.6%**	**−12.8%**	**−3.6%**	
Cash from operations	5637	4864	4817	617	−232	−511	339
Cash operations/ Sales %	**10%**	**9%**	**10%**	**1%**	**0%**	**−1%**	**1%**
Other non-operating inc/(exp)	220	2665	2550	−45	2660	−645	−2027

Notice both the falling turnover and negligible margin in the first four years. The group is downsizing, concentrating on the most profitable parts of the business, and dropping those that are less profitable. When we take inflation into account turnover does not begin to increase until 2006. During the period 2003 to 2007 the group has disposed of about €8 billion of business interests.

Once again let us examine the relationships between Capex and depreciation (Table 6.13).

Table 6.13 Seven years depreciation and capex data for Fiat Group

FIAT GROUP	2007 €m	2006 €m	2005 €m	2004 €m	2003 €m	2002 €m	2001 €m
Depreciation	2738	2969	2590	2168	2269	2614	2880
Investments in Fixed Assets	−3985	−3789	−3052	−2112	−2011	−2771	−3438
Proceeds from disposal	259	387	427	358	4167	3231	2652
Net Capex	−3726	−3402	−2625	−1754	2156	460	−786
New Capex/Depreciation %	146%	128%	118%	97%	89%	106%	119%
Net Capex/Depreciation %	136%	115%	101%	81%	Neg	Neg	27%

Notice first that the depreciation charge itself falls then rises through time; the business is contracting from 2001 to 2004. The same pattern can be seen in the new Capex where there are two years where new Capex is lower than depreciation. The proceeds from disposal show us there were substantial disposals of fixed assets in 2001 to 2003. Once again the data appears consistent with the portrait of a poorly performing mature business group engaged in a prolonged period of restructuring and business reinvention.

As expected, this additional analysis essentially confirms what we have already deduced from the template cash flows themselves, the business has been through four years of losses followed by three years of recovery, which is ongoing.

ISSUES RELATED TO MATURE BUSINESS DIVERSITY

All three examples we have looked at are groups of businesses. The first two are groups which have a relatively narrow strategic and market focus: Black & Decker (various tools containing small electric motors); and Dairy Crest (milk processing distribution and derivative products).

Fiat has a broader strategic focus. The 2007 annual report lists the reporting segments as follows:

- Automobiles.
- Agricultural and construction equipment.
- Trucks and commercial vehicles.
- Components and production systems (virtually all vehicle related).
- Other businesses (publishing and group services).

Again, all these segments are essentially mature markets. This is why the example fits for the purpose for which it has been designed. However, groups are not always this homogeneous.

When I commenced writing this chapter I spent some time trying to develop an example of a mature market around the market for televisions. Having written half a page or so I realised this is not suitable, the reason being that elements of the market for television were not mature. The market for televisions based on cathode ray tube technology is in terminal decline. The market for plasma and LCD based screens is a growth market. In most developed economies the market for televisions themselves as a category is a mature market (initial adoption of the product having taken place 40 years ago), with the overall market going through an important step change to a new delivery technology. In emerging markets the market for televisions is a growth market with fundamental technology change taking place. Finally, the products themselves are produced by very large mature groups (Sony, Panasonic, Toshiba, Samsung Phillips and LG, for example).

So, when we discuss 'mature' in the context of a group we need to be careful. As you can see from the above examples this works if the group has a narrow focus, it also works if most of the businesses in a group serve mature markets. It does not work if the group consists of a mix of mature businesses, growth businesses, decline businesses and possibly even start-up businesses.

This does not mean it is pointless to analyse the group cash flows of such an entity, the exercise will still reveal much about the performance, cash efficiency and investment pattern of the group. It will be difficult or impossible, however, to relate this to particular external drivers of change other than the most basic macro economic changes. In order to do this for a group it will be necessary to disaggregate its activities into elements that are more amenable to in-depth analysis, and then analyse the cash flows of each one.

It may be possible to disaggregate the activities by reporting by segment, sector or market. Alternatively, it may be possible to group mature segments and growth segments separately. Every group is different, it is this important point that makes analysis both challenging and interesting. Making elegant decisions about how to go about identifying the true performance of a business entity is the essence of good analysis practice.

ISSUES RELATED TO BUSINESS SIZE

Earlier in this chapter I presented the idea of a sort of mature business, cash flow break-even point as follows. I said that the analysis of the cash flows of a mature business could be encapsulated in one sentence:

> In the long run, mature businesses must generate sufficient Cash Available to Satisfy Finance Providers to cover interest, dividends and scheduled debt repayment.

To apply this in the real world we need to break this down further, into large, medium and small examples. What do I mean by this?

The Large Business

A large business will almost certainly be a group. It is often a business sufficiently large that it is essentially immune to problems involving the raising of finance. It can raise debt or equity at any time should it wish to do so. It does not need banks as lenders as it is sufficiently large that it can issue bonds, medium-term notes and commercial paper directly into capital markets in a variety of geographic locations.

Most businesses of this type are publicly listed entities with their shares traded on one or more major stock markets. There is a small group of large private companies that also qualifies – examples are the Mars Group (a confectionery and pet food producer) and Maersk (the Danish shipping group).

Such businesses usually have permanent leverage. If you look in their accounts you will find both short- and long-term debt items. However, when these are due for renewal they are rolled over into whatever debt instrument is most cost effective at the time. They fund themselves as cheaply as possible in any currency using a variety of sophisticated financing techniques to do so (using, for example, swaps, options, derivatives). Unless they have made fundamental management errors they are unlikely ever to be in a situation where they are faced with the need to repay all their debt quickly.

Where such a large mature group has 'normal' leverage the sentence can be restated as follows:

In the long run, large mature businesses must generate sufficient Cash Available to Satisfy Finance Providers to cover interest and dividends.

For large listed entities the dividend is as important as interest service. This is because the share price will drop rapidly if the business announces dividend reduction or omission. Senior managers are largely rewarded on stock price performance, so paying the dividend is to them as important as interest service despite not being a contractual obligation.

If the group has 'abnormal' leverage then the situation is as stated in the original version of the one sentence, in addition to interest and dividend service, debt repayment may be required. The typical scenario where this may occur is where large amounts of debt finance have been raised to make a substantial acquisition. As a result the group's leverage is significantly above a level that would be regarded as normal or sustainable. Large groups in this position will normally place significant emphasis on debt repayment until their leverage is once more at a level considered 'normal' for their sector after which they will resume the pattern of rolling over debt into whatever instrument is most suitable at the time.

The Small Business

A small business is typically a private company or sole trader. Access to debt is almost exclusively via banks and other debt finance providers, which act as intermediaries between the business and capital markets. Small businesses are therefore vulnerable to banking cycles, event risk that affects debt markets, and fashion in banks, which can result in the withdrawal of liquidity at quite short notice. Unlike large businesses, small businesses cannot assume that they can refinance on demand. This means they should always seek to generate sufficient Cash Available To Satisfy Finance Providers to be able repay scheduled debt obligations without refinancing or replacing them.

However, small businesses do not need to pay dividends, and many do not. Dividend payment is largely a decision driven by tax considerations. If paying a dividend is the most tax effective way of extracting cash from a small business then the business may pay a dividend. However, there are no negative consequences in not paying a dividend, the dividend is truly discretionary. So we can exclude dividends from the sentence for small businesses. It now becomes:

> In the long run, small mature businesses must generate sufficient Cash Available to Satisfy Finance Providers to cover interest and scheduled debt repayment.

The Medium-Sized Business

We are now left with the remainder – medium-sized businesses. They may be small- and medium-sized listed groups, or medium and large private businesses. Businesses in this group may have the need to service dividend and may also be too small to guarantee access to refinancing as required. For them the original sentence still stands:

> In the long run, medium-sized mature businesses must generate sufficient Cash Available to Satisfy Finance Providers to cover interest, dividends and scheduled debt repayment.

So, a business that is able to comply with the one sentence test is performing in a cash flow sense.

If a business passes the test consistently this tells us its cash flows are sufficient for the business to sustain itself. The most successful businesses from a cash flow point of view are those that generate vast amounts of surplus cash, this can be paid out as dividend, used to reduce equity or debt, or retained for future investment.

SUMMARY

This chapter has covered much of the knowledge of cash flows required to assess whether a mature business is performing or not. Additional insights, which are also relevant to mature business analysis, are contained in the following chapters on growth, decline and start-up.

Summarising reported cash flows into Jury's Cash Flow Template and analysing them is an efficient and powerful method of analysis that avoids many of the problems of seeking to evaluate performance from the P&L.

7

Analysing the Cash Flows of Growth Businesses

In Chapter 3 on *Start-up, Growth, Mature, Decline* we introduced the typical cash flow patterns to be observed in successful businesses in the four phases of the life of a business. The purpose of this was to develop an understanding of what the cash flows should look like in the four phases and to introduce some of the drivers of each line of the cash flow. The word 'driver' being used to denote the fundamental economic and market forces or management decisions that cause cash flows to change.

In this chapter we are going to go into more detail about what we mean by the word 'growth' when used in this context. We will also look at what constitutes success from a cash flow point of view when managing a growth company and, finally, examine the cash flows of a number of real growth businesses taken from different countries around the world. As some of the commentary assumes knowledge of the previous chapter, this chapter should be read in conjunction with the previous chapter discussing the analysis of mature businesses.

WHAT DO WE MEAN BY 'GROWTH'?

When we talk about a growth business what we usually mean is a business operating in a growth market. A growth market is a market where adoption of new products or services is taking place for the first time. Some of the big growth markets of the last 25 years have been mobile phones, computers and freight containerisation.

Growth markets are different to mature markets. In a growth market all the businesses participating in the market can grow at the market rate. If a market is expanding at say 40% a year this means all the businesses involved can also grow at 40% a year on average. This makes such markets very attractive places to invest. Once a new growth market is recognised as such – and assuming there are no unusual barriers to entry – we can expect many new entrants in the early growth phase. Typically, these will be existing businesses that have the knowledge and expertise to supply the new growth product or service.

As the new market becomes established and develops, those participants who can capture market share faster than their competitors will start to enjoy any economies of scale that are available earlier than their competitors, so leading to a cost advantage for them over time. In the latter stages of the development of the new market the growth rate starts to reduce year on year. In this latter part of the growth phase (which is sometimes referred to as 'shake-out') we expect to see the gradual consolidation of the numerous competitors as they get taken over, merge or exit leaving a handful of large players in an increasingly static market structure. Over the last decade Dell and HP Compaq have been the dominant players in desktop computers and Nokia was the clear leader in mobile phones although this is rapidly changing.

It follows from this that once a growth market has been identified as such and the decision is made to enter, strategy is usually all about gaining market share. The more the better! So, what are the problems of growth?

IRRATIONAL INVESTOR BEHAVIOUR

Growth markets are so attractive that investors will invest in them at almost any price. This can result in extreme and absurd outcomes. The most recent example of this was the dot-com boom. In 1990, Tim Berners-Lee started developing a GUI browser at CERN. He made up WorldWideWeb as a name for the program and World Wide Web as a name for the project, which was initially an internal CERN initiative. By 1994 the load on the first web server (info.cern.ch) was 1000 times what it had been three years earlier. On 1 October 1994 the world wide web consortium (W3C) was founded. Over the next five years, knowledge of this new platform became widely disseminated. Once the significance of the browser/web combination was recognised this resulted in a frenzy of web site development to exploit this new way of interacting with potential consumers.

The term Silicon Valley came into use to describe the concentration of new IT companies in the Santa Clara Valley outside San Francisco. Here could be found young entrepreneurs busy developing concepts for consumer web sites. These businesses were able to raise millions of dollars from venture capitalists or IPO on NASDAQ, to spend on web site development. Many of these businesses regarded their project as successful if they generated thousands of hits a day, meaning their site was been surfed by thousands of users a day. Share prices valued these companies in the millions and values often rocketed.

However, a web site is not a business. In the introductory chapter on start-ups I pointed out that my definition for a business (as opposed to a charity) is one where products or services are being supplied to customers in exchange for cash. In other words there is cash flow from customers. This in turn implies that the product or service has some economic value to the consumer. Many of these web sites were proud to inform investors that it was too early to get users to subscribe for or otherwise pay for content, the argument being that building a user base (measured in hits) or developing markets share was more important. The flaw in this argument is that the service may have no real economic value when a charge is made, with consumers simply identifying a cheaper or free substitute, or abandoning the service altogether because they do not really need it.

Whilst a small number of these companies went on to success in the late 1990s, most collapsed spectacularly. History now recognises this as the dot-com bubble. The term 'bubble' referring to the collective hysteria that results in stock prices in such companies rising to levels that bear no relationship with reality. This has happened many times before in many different markets – Europe has lived through the Dutch tulip bulb bubble (difficult to pronounce!) and the South-Sea Company bubble hundreds of years ago.

So, my first observation about the nature of growth is that attractive new growth markets can lead to irrational investor behaviour and a general delusion about the real cash flow potential of the new growth market.

NEGATIVE CASH FLOWS

The second problem with growth companies is that they require investment in order to grow. Going back to my definition of a growth business as one that has already demonstrated the viability of its offer by gaining real sales from customers, the next problem for the business is to build the necessary infrastructure to produce and sell the product to the target customer group. This can involve so much investment that the net cash flow is negative for years.

Even though a successful growth company may be earning a healthy margin from its existing customers, the need to invest in working assets, and new factories, distribution facilities and possibly retail outlets typically results in a negative value for Cash Flow Available to Satisfy Finance Providers and Net Cash Inflow/(Outflow). Cash may also be consumed in the late growth phase acquiring the businesses and/or assets of former competitors.

So, my second observation about growth is that we expect the net cash flows of many successful growth businesses to be negative!

CORPORATE COLLAPSE

Over the previous decade we have observed the failure of a number of large listed businesses. The most high profile of these was Enron, others were Worldcom and Global Crossing. All of these businesses were exploiting growth markets. In the rest of the world we have seen the failure of Daiwoo and Parmalat.

It is striking how many of these business are growth businesses or, in the case of business failures involving fraud, seeking to give the impression that they are growth businesses. The reason they collapse is that they run out of cash and there are no other cash generative businesses available within the group to offset this. It is far less likely for large mature businesses to collapse in this way for the reasons already stated in the previous chapter.

In the early 1990s there were two large growth business failures in the United Kingdom – these were Tiphook and Brent Walker. When Brent Walker collapsed there were 65 banks that had lent money to various parts of the group. This means that 65 different credit functions had looked at the credit risk inherent in their exposure to the group and decided that the risks involved were acceptable. This implies to me some sort of systemic failure. It implies that identifying whether growth companies are in fact viable business entities is a challenging and difficult problem. It implies the performance of growth businesses is difficult to analyse.

So, my third observation about growth is that we expect growth companies to be cash negative, even if seeking equity or debt for investment. It appears there is a self-fulfilling prophesy at work.

We are growing, so we are cash negative, therefore we need funds.
This accords with investor's perceptions, so they provide finance, even though in some cases the growth is false (not real) in some way. This false growth only becoming apparent to many investors after the businesses collapse. To make this even more obvious I could restate the above statement as:

We are running a fraud, so we are cash negative, therefore we need funds.
   or, if not a fraud:

We are spending lots of money on something that might or might not be successful in the future, so we are cash negative, therefore we need funds.

TO SUMMARISE THIS INTRODUCTION

- New growth markets may be so attractive that this leads to irrational investor behaviour and a general delusion about the real business potential of the new growth market.
- We expect the cash flows of many successful growth businesses to be negative.
- Growth companies justify their need for funds by using a circular argument. We are growing, so we are cash negative, therefore we need funds. Unfortunately, the only growth business worth funding in the long run is a growth business that results in a sustainable, cash generative mature business. During the market growth phase it is extremely difficult to predict whether this will be the eventual outcome for a growth market business.

IN CASH FLOW TERMS, WHAT CONSTITUTES SUCCESS FOR GROWTH BUSINESSES?

There are a wide variety of patterns that we can encounter when looking at growth company cash flows. We can usefully characterise these as follows:

1. The success – a self financing growth company.
2. The investor – a growth company investing in more operating assets each year to expand output.
3. The acquirer – a growth company acquiring other growth companies to achieve apparent or real strategic benefits.
4. The investor/acquirer – a growth company both investing and acquiring.
5. The aspirant – a growth company yet to properly validate its growth model as viable in the long term.

Let us introduce the profile of each one in turn.

The Success

The success is a business that is growing and generating sufficient operating cash margin from the sale of its goods and/or services to provide for all of its investment needs. The investment needs being the investment required to maintain and expand market share in its chosen markets (generally known as research and developments costs) and the expenditure in fixed assets and net working assets needed to grow its output.

Generally, research and development (R&D) costs are absorbed as part of the cash costs put against sales in identifying the operating cash margin, as a result we do not see them identified separately in Jury's Template. Working asset expenditure and capital expenditure (Capex) appear in the template as separate items.

Such a business will generate a surplus at both the Cash Available To Satisfy Finance Providers line and the Net Cash Inflow/(Outflow) line. I have labelled this type of business 'The success' because it is entirely self-financing and is likely to achieve a very high valuation if offered for sale. Its destiny is entirely in the hands of its owners and managers, as it does not require further investment from equity or debt providers. It can move forward irrespective of any disruption or fashion issues that may be affecting the availability of capital from capital markets.

The Investor

The 'investor' is a business that has demonstrated to investors and customers it has a viable long-term business model and is growing its output. It is not able to do this entirely from internally generated cash flow. In order to grow its output the business requires investment in working assets and Capex. This investment may

Table 7.1   Illustration of the patterns in growth cash flows

	Growth Example 1 £'000	Growth Example 2 £'000	Growth Example 3 £'000	Growth Example 4 £'000
OPERATING CASH MARGIN	5500	4000	2500	1000
(INV)/GEN FROM NWA	−500	−500	−500	−500
NET CAPITAL EXPENDITURE	−2000	−2000	−2000	−2000
TAXATION	−1200	−700	−400	−200
CATS Finance Providers	**1800**	**800**	**−400**	**−1700**
NET INTEREST	−1000	−1000	−1000	−1000
NET DIVIDENDS	−400	−200	0	0
OTHER NON-OP INC/(EXP)	0	0	0	0
NET CASH GENERATED/ (ABSORBED) BEFORE FINANCING	**400**	**−400**	**−1400**	**−2700**
Financed by:				
CHANGE IN EQUITY – INC/(DEC)		100	650	1200
CHANGE IN DEBT – INC/(DEC)		200	650	1300
CHANGE IN CASH – (INC)/DEC	−400	100	100	100
TOTAL CHANGE IN FINANCING	**−400**	**400**	**1400**	**2600**

or may not be financed from operating cash flow. This can result in a variety of cash flow outcomes as shown in Table 7.1.

In Example 1 we see the business has generated sufficient cash flow to cover all its investment needs, taxes and interest costs. Only the dividend payment results in a deficit, which is financed from existing cash reserves. This business is still in the well performing category.

In Example 2 the business is generating sufficient cash flow to cover all its investment needs and pay taxes. It does not have sufficient cash to cover all its interest and dividend payments. Unless this cash deficit can be financed from existing cash reserves it will require further equity or debt finance to continue to trade.

In Example 3 we see the business not generating sufficient cash flow to cover its investment needs and taxes. It has a deficit at the CATS Finance Providers line and a larger deficit at the net cash inflow/(outflow) level. Unless the business has considerable cash reserves it will require further equity or debt finance to continue to trade.

In Example 4 we see the business is only generating a modest proportion of the cash required to finance its investment needs and taxes. It has a substantial deficit at the CATS Finance Providers line and a larger deficit at the net cash inflow/(outflow) level. Unless the business has considerable cash reserves it will require substantial injections of further equity or debt finance to continue to trade.

In Examples 2, 3 and 4 the business is vulnerable to financing risk, the possibility that investors will not wish to invest more in the business. Their willingness to do so will be determined by their view of the effect on future periods cash flow of the investment in increased output. Will it increase the operating cash margin sufficiently for the business to be cash generative in the future?

In other words, in these examples the business is more sensitive to investors future expectations about the cash flows of the business. In turn these expectations change with external economic conditions.

It should also be clear from these examples that, in general, default risk (credit risk) is increasing as we move from left to right across the cases illustrated.

We know that Examples 1 and 2 are probably fine in terms of their viability as businesses, because they are generating a surplus CATS Finance Providers after investing to grow their output. Even if Example 2 has too much leverage, new investors might purchase the business from old investors because it is likely to continue to be cash generative and hence has a positive value.

Examples 3 and 4 are more difficult to test because the key numbers are negative. The management will be justifying their current cash flow position by claiming that the investment in working assets and Capex in this year will increase the operating cash margin generated in future years, so tipping the cash flows back to positive sometime in the future. The problem for the analyst is identifying whether this is a likely outcome or not. Remember the self-fulfilling prophecy I mentioned earlier. The management says, 'We are a growth company, we are cash negative, therefore we need funds for investment'. The investor (lender or equity provider) says, 'Of course, you are a growth company, therefore you are cash negative'. In normal market conditions the investor will most likely then invest.

The real issue, however, is whether the growth business will ever reach the point of cash flow break even (or cash neutrality). The eventual outcome being affected by both management actions (internal factors) and equity and debt market conditions, sovereign and sector risk and market, technology and competitor behaviour (external factors).

The Acquirer

At certain point in their development, growth businesses may acquire other business. This may be for offensive or defensive reasons. If the business is a market leader, acquiring similar businesses in adjacent territories to those the business is already operating in may save years of start-up time. These businesses may then be re-branded and integrated into the existing operations of the growth company.

Other offensive reasons for acquisition activity might be to acquire brands, market share, technology or even customers.

Defensive reasons for acquisitions are likely to be market share related, in the shake-out phase of a growth market when increasing consolidation takes place. For example, at the beginning of the shake-out phase there may be 100 companies. Later, the market may end up with just 15. Four of these are large and the rest niche specialists. Number three may acquire number four to become number two, particularly if there are material economies of scale involved in the industry. In the last decade we have seen this type of acquisition activity in personal computers (e.g. HP/Compaq) and in aluminium producers (e.g. Rio Tinto/Alcan).

The examples identified above represent reasons for acquisitions that appear strategically sound. Managers may also make acquisitions for many reasons that are not necessarily strategically sound. Advisers may approach companies seeking to initiate both sales and purchases. Companies may underperform to the extent they become vulnerable to acquisition.

Finally, there is a substantial academic literature that concludes 50% of all acquisitions fail in terms of delivering the expected outcome (wealth, success, value) to the acquirer. The failure rate rises to 75% when the acquisition is an unrelated industry or sector.

Whilst the consolidated P&L of the acquirer will have more turnover and profit in it at the end of a year involving acquisitions, the acquisitions themselves do not represent any growth in *value* for the acquirer. This is because the company has paid to purchase the business what it considers to be the present value of the future cash flows of the business acquired. We have not added value, we have merely exchanged cash or shares or both for the future cash flows of a business.

The added value comes when additional benefits in economies of scale, market share, technology and cost savings are achieved. Collectively these things are known as synergies, these being benefits that will typically arise by taking management action after the acquisition. It is common for sellers to demand a share of the present value of the planned synergies in the purchase price. If the acquiring managers give away too much at this point the transaction may destroy value in the medium term rather than adding it. It is common knowledge that gaining the financial benefit of the synergies in the post acquisition phase may be difficult, or indeed, may never be achieved. The purported synergies may not in fact exist! Many acquisitions fail for these kind of reasons.

Finally, we have problems with information asymmetry. The seller knows all about the business being sold, the buyer knows far less. Buyers try to compensate for this by carrying out a due diligence process. This means checking that everything offered is in fact bona fide. This process can never deliver 100% certainty and every year there are stories of acquisitions of companies that turn out to be carrying substantial undisclosed liabilities. In extreme cases this has resulted in bankruptcy for the acquirer.

So, when growth companies make acquisitions, they are considerably increasing their business risk in the short term. Until the acquisition is properly digested into the acquiring group, the extra burden of managing two businesses at the same time may cause more problems than the acquisition was meant to solve.

In cash flow terms, the success of an acquisition cannot usually be measured for two years. This is because in the year after acquisition we usually see the one-off costs associated with redundancies, plant closures and other reorganisation and restructuring. It is only after these costs have passed that we can look at the operating cash margin and assess whether it has increased sufficiently to justify the earlier acquisition cost.

When analysing the cash flows of an entity, if we find evidence of acquisition activity in a business we should consider the following:

- The size of the acquisition relative to the present business of the acquirer. How material is the transaction?
- The leverage and cash position after the transaction. Does the business have a cushion of surplus cash or debt facilities to deal with any unexpected costs or losses in the post acquisition phase?
- The strength and sustainability of the operating cash flow margin of the existing business. Is it resilient or is it vulnerable to known cycle or sector risks?
- The managements track record of managing acquisition activity in the past. Have they successfully completed and integrated acquisitions in the past?
- The strategic logic underpinning the acquisition activity. Does it make sense?

The Investor/Acquirer

In this scenario we have a business that is both investing in operating assets at a rate ahead of its ability to generate operating cash margin and acquiring other businesses.

It should be obvious from my earlier observations that this is a high-risk combination. The metaphor that springs to mind is that of tightrope walking. For the managers pursuing such a strategy there is no margin for error. The amount of change that is being managed is immense. As well as opening new factories/outlets and managing the changes associated with rapid growth, they also have the burden of integrating newly acquired businesses.

In very attractive growth markets there may be periods where taking such risks is justified, the result being a bigger market share and lower costs than competitors. For this strategy to be justified the potential benefits should bear some relationship to the risks involved. In the last few years we have seen a spate of ill-advised takeovers in the banking industry in the UK and Holland which have effectively ruined the businesses of the acquirers, all of whom have required state assistance to survive. For the acquiring group these transactions appear to be more about getting bigger than adding value.

The Aspirant

The aspirant is a business that is selling its product for a reasonable margin and is growing its turnover. However, it has not yet reached a point where it is cash positive at the Net Cash Inflow/(Outflow) Total. The usual reason for this is because adoption is not taking place at the rate foreseen when the decision to invest was taken. The business has not yet reached the size necessary to establish itself as a long-term member of the sector in which it operates. The junior stock markets of those nations that have them are full of such companies. These businesses have not yet demonstrated that they have a viable long-term cash generative business. Turnover is small but growing, they may or may not be profitable; cash flow is not yet adequate to be self-sustaining.

Whilst we may be confident about our predictive abilities, as analysts we should not anticipate whether the business will or will not make it to viability. All we can do is assess the significance of the principle factors that will affect the outcome, and express an opinion about our view of the likelihood of success. This is essentially a forecasting exercise. Forecasting cash flow is dealt with as a separate subject in section two of this book.

What we can look at is the resources available to support the business until its viability is properly secured and demonstrated. This is represented by the cash and banking facilities that are in place for the business to draw on in the short- and medium-term. These can be compared to the rate at which cash is being consumed, which is why a focus on cash flow is essential for those running the business and for those seeking to analyse it. From this we can estimate how many months or years the business can continue assuming there are no changes to the business.

When developing your analysis, making any assumption is dangerous. We may fail to recognise threats and weaknesses that cause a more rapid business decline than history suggests is likely. In general, however, the *no change* assumption is generally a conservative assumption.

Managers are there to manage change, so, if we assume competence in management, we normally expect to observe a succession of beneficial changes in the business. In other words, in most cases, there will be a general bias in management actions towards positive change. In a few cases there will be adverse events, which make the effects of change negative, this will of course accelerate the speed at which the business proceeds towards bankruptcy unless there are later positive changes.

We are using this assumption because it enables us to develop a useful measure. Lets call this measure the *no-change time to default*. If we are looking at default risk in particular, for example, we may be comfortable if this measure reveals the business has three years' worth of finance but less happy if this measure is only six months of finance.

Having reviewed the different profiles of growth companies let us consider a number of examples.

GROWTH CASH FLOW EXAMPLES: THE SUCCESS

Nokia is a good example of a successful growth company from the last decade. Table 7.2 shows the cash flows for a recent six year period.

In each of the six years Nokia has generated a surplus at both the Cash Available to Satisfy Finance Providers line and for five years at the Net Cash Inflow/(Outflow) line. In all years the Cash Available to Satisfy Finance Providers has been more than sufficient to cover interest and dividends. The only reason the Net Cash before Financing was negative in 2008 was due to two major acquisitions for Nokia. They purchased Navtec, a US-based GPS and mapping specialist and they increased their remaining ownership of Symbian from 47.5% to 100%. At this point in time, this is, by any standards, a very successful business having evolved to become the world's number one supplier of mobile phones.

Table 7.2

Nokia Summary group cash flow statement Year ended 31ˢᵗ December	20X8 €m	20X7 €m	20X6 €m	20X5 €m	20X4 €m	20X3 €m
OPERATING CASH MARGIN	7457	8474	6163	5390	5193	6545
(INV)/GEN FROM NET WORKING ASSETS	−2546	605	−793	−366	299	−194
NET CAPITAL EXPENDITURE	−966	−800	−748	−593	−643	−631
TAXATION	−1780	−1457	−1163	−1254	−1368	−1440
CASH FLOW AVAILABLE TO SATISFY FINANCE PROVIDERS	**2165**	**6822**	**3459**	**3177**	**3481**	**4280**
NET INTEREST	66	260	271	374	219	341
NET DIVIDENDS	−2042	−1748	−1553	−1530	−1391	−1354
OTHER NON-OPERATING INC/(EXP)	−1945	78	1754	2436	292	−2608
NET CASH GEN/(ABS) BEFORE FINANCING	**−1756**	**5412**	**3931**	**4457**	**2601**	**659**
Financed by: INCREASE/(DECREASE) IN EQUITY	−3068	−2832	−3325	−4256	−2648	−1332
INCREASE/(DECREASE) IN DEBT	3571	760	−88	217	−257	−70
(INCREASE)/DECREASE IN CASH	1253	−3340	−518	−418	304	743
TOTAL CHANGE IN FINANCING	**1756**	**−5412**	**−3931**	**−4457**	**−2601**	**−659**

There is not a lot more to say, the Jury's Cash Flow Template is eloquent in illustrating the cash flow consequences of success.

GROWTH CASH FLOW EXAMPLES: THE INVESTOR

Vestas (a Danish company) is at this point in time the worlds leading supplier of wind turbines for electricity production with a market share of 23% in 20X7. In 20X4 it acquired NEG Micon to become the market-leading business in wind power. In Table 7.3 we can see some examples of the typical growth pattern cash flows over the past six years.

Table 7.3   Six years cash flows for Vestas

VESTAS Summary group cash flow statement Year ended 31st December	20X7 €m	20X6 €m	20X5 €m	20X4 €m	20X3 €m	20X2 €m
OPERATING CASH MARGIN	639	353	44.1	36.5	171.9	145.6
(INV)/GEN FROM NET WORKING ASSETS	190	376	186.8	−15.5	11.2	−244.4
NET CAPITAL EXPENDITURE	−317	−168	−126.6	−118.4	−111.1	−136
TAXATION	−128	−91	−40.6	−10.3	−8.6	−13.3
CASH FLOW AVAILABLE TO SATISFY FINANCE PROVIDERS	**384**	**470**	**63.7**	**−107.7**	**63.4**	**−248.1**
NET INTEREST	0	−40	−42.4	−40.5	−21.4	−13.9
NET DIVIDENDS	0	0	0	0	−10.6	−21.2
OTHER NON-OPERATING INC/(EXP)	0	24	−10.2	−82.2	−7.4	139
NET CASH INFLOW/(OUTFLOW)	**384**	**454**	**11.1**	**−230.4**	**24**	**−144.2**
Financed by: INCREASE/(DECREASE) IN EQUITY	−30	183	0	283.1	0	1.8
INCREASE/(DECREASE) IN DEBT	−24	−284	−46.3	174.4	−9	36.3
(INCREASE)/DECREASE IN CASH	−330	−353	35.2	−227.1	−15	106.1
TOTAL CHANGE IN FINANCING	**−384**	**−454**	**−11.1**	**230.4**	**−24**	**144.2**

In 20X2:

- The group was substantially negative at both the Cash Available to Satisfy Finance Providers and Net Cash Inflow/(Outflow).

- This appears to be due to large investments in Net Working Assets and Capex.
- This was financed by using existing cash reserves and increasing debt.

In 20X3:

- The cash flow performance looked healthy although the business was still investing substantially in fixed assets.

In 20X4:

- The group had both negative Cash Available to Satisfy Finance Providers and Net Cash Inflow/(Outflow).
- This appears to be due to the large investment in Capex.
- This was financed by an increase in equity and debt.

In 20X5:

- The situation in 20X5 would have been the same were it not for the reduction in the amount invested in Net Working Assets of €186.8 million, which resulted in a small surplus at the Net Cash inflow/(Outflow) total.

In 20X6 and 20X7 the cash flow performance has been spectacular:

This was partly due to a substantial contribution to the cash flows from a reduction in the amount invested in Net Working Assets. This benefit to the cash flows has arisen due to a reduction in inventories and an increase in prepayments received from customers. While the business remains in the growth phase the prepayments from customers may increase year on year, however, the reduction in inventory is unlikely to be sustained, and will at some point in the future revert to its normal behaviour in the growth phase, a year on year increase.

Table 7.4 shows the revenue growth over the same period.

Table 7.4   Six years sales data for Vestas

VESTAS Revenue Summary	20X7 €m	20X6 €m	20X5 €m	20X4 €m	20X3 €m	20X2 €m
Group revenue	4861	3854	3583	2363	1653	1394
Growth in Sales %	**26%**	**8%**	**52%**	**43%**	**19%**	
Operating cash margin	639.0	353.0	44.1	36.5	171.9	145.6
Cash operations/Sales %	**13%**	**9%**	**1%**	**2%**	**10%**	**10%**

Revenue is doubling approximately every three years – this is impressive growth! Notice how the operating cash margin is much more volatile than in our examples of mature companies. This is because growth equals change. Everything continues to change in a growth market faster than in a mature market where there is comparative stability. Not only must the business add capacity fast enough to satisfy demand and maintain market share, it must also invest sufficiently in research and product development to maintain its position. In addition there are the small matters of creating a worldwide distribution and service network and developing and maintaining systems to control everything! This is a significant management challenge.

Not only is the operating cash margin more variable, so is the investment in net working assets, as this is also difficult to manage in the growth phase. In a growth company we would normally expect a significant net investment each year as inventory and debtors grow with turnover. We do not see this in Vestas for reasons explained further down the page.

In Chapter 6 on mature businesses we looked at the relationship between depreciation and Capex, let us see how this changes when we examine the cash flows of a growth company once again using Vestas as our example (Table 7.5).

Table 7.5   Six years of depreciation and Capex data for Vestas

VESTAS Depreciation to Capex analysis	20X7 $m	20X6 $m	20X5 $m	20X4 $m	20X3 $m	20X2 $m
Depreciation & amortisation	136	128	125.1	112.6	68.1	50.8
Capital expenditures	−347	−188	−144.8	−127.30	−112.80	−138.00
Proceeds from disposal of assets	30	20	18.2	26.00	8.90	2.00
Net Capex	−317.00	−168.00	−126.60	−101.30	−103.90	−136.00
New Capex/ Depreciation %	255%	147%	116%	113%	166%	272%
Net Capex/ Depreciation %	233%	131%	101%	90%	153%	268%

As you can see, there is a marked difference when this is compared with, say, Black & Decker in the previous chapter. Here we see investment in Capex is way ahead of depreciation. In three of the years the Capex is more than two times depreciation. This is because the business has to put in place the factories, plant and equipment to increase its output. If turnover is doubling approximately every three years the capacity of the group's manufacturing facilities needs to match it.

We would normally expect to see the same sort of cash flow behaviour in the Net Working Assets investment. We do not see this here for a number of reasons unique to this business. Firstly, the group adopted a policy of holding inventory in the early years to try to smooth fluctuations in demand and get better utilisation of its manufacturing facilities. As the business has grown, both in volume and geographic spread the problem of a lumpy order flow has reduced significantly so they have been able to reduce the investment in inventory. Secondly, demand for wind turbines has resulted in the group being able to get advances from customers in order to reserve production. In this market customers are subsidising the need for working asset investment in the growth phase. When the market for wind turbines starts to mature, which could be many years in the future, I would expect this subsidy effect to disappear.

CASH FLOW GROWTH EXAMPLES: THE ACQUIRER

TomTom is at this point in time the worlds leading provider of navigation solutions and digital maps. It sells a variety of GPS solutions throughout the world. Formerly known as Palmtop, it evolved from a software house specialising in applications for the Symbian platform. Over the last five years its success has been spectacular (See Table 7.6 overleaf).

In 20X7 TomTom moved to acquire its mapping provider buying 29.9% of Tele Atlas for €816 million. In 20X8 TomTom purchased the remaining shares expending a further €1833 million. TomTom did this because it realised, following other major companies such as Nokia buying mapping companies, that it might be vulnerable to losing its most important resource. This was a defensive acquisition, securing for the group the resource on which most of its products are based. It eliminated the possibility that a competitor might at some future date acquire their mapping supplier so putting them at a competitive disadvantage. This appears to be an example of a strategically sound acquisition, which adds to the competitive advantages of the whole group. It was, however, expensive, requiring the formerly debt-free group to take on €1387 million of debt.

Looking at the levels of Cash Available to Satisfy Finance Providers it should be possible, if the company wishes, to clear the debt in about five years.

CASH FLOW GROWTH EXAMPLES: THE ASPIRANT

Torotrak is the world leader in full-toroidal traction-drive transmission technology, focused on the development of IVT (InfinitelyVariable Transmission) and TCVT (Toroidal Continuously Variable Transmission) systems which deliver outstanding levels of performance, functionality and commercial advantage in automotive, truck, bus, outdoor power equipment, agricultural and off highway applications.

This introduction is taken from Torotrac's most recent annual report.

Essentially the business owns the intellectual property associated with a new form of transmission for wheeled vehicles, which has a number of superior features relative to the existing solution (manual or automatic gearboxes). It does not intend to manufacture the product. It seeks to licence it to others for use in wheeled vehicles generally. The company joined the stock market in 1998 and has spent the last 10 years attempting to get adoption of the new technology. This has proved difficult. However, in the last two years, more significant progress has been made towards cash break-even.

The cash flows of Torotrak in Jury's Template format are shown in Table 7.7.

The business has spent the last decade steadily developing its transmission product, spending significant amounts on research and patenting each year. In 20X8 the

Table 7.6 Five years cash flows for TomTom

TomTom
Summary group cash flow statement

Year ended 31st December	20X8 €'000	20X7 €'000	20X6 €'000	20X5 €'000	20X4 €'000
OPERATING CASH MARGIN	407 074	506 442	382 136	236 966	46 949
(INV)/GEN FROM NET WORKING ASSETS	55 705	28 957	9982	−134 564	−2485
NET CAPITAL EXPENDITURE	−69 638	−50 537	−28 570	−21 421	−2974
TAXATION	−79 214	−113 407	−110 011	−62 528	−8387
CASH FLOW AVAILABLE TO SATISFY FINANCE PROVIDERS	**313 927**	**371 455**	**253 537**	**18 453**	**33 103**
NET INTEREST	−29 462	19 121	9400	3136	169
NET DIVIDENDS	0	0	0	0	0
OTHER NON-OPERATING INC/(EXP)	−1 833 792	−816 030	0	0	0
NET CASH GEN/(ABS) BEFORE FINANCING	**−1 549 327**	**−425 454**	**262 937**	**21 589**	**33 272**
Financed by:					
INCREASE/(DECREASE) IN EQUITY	20 378	453 417	1113	116 546	0
INCREASE/(DECREASE) IN DEBT	1 387 137	0	0	0	0
(INCREASE)/DECREASE IN CASH	141 812	−27 963	−264 050	−138 135	−33 272
TOTAL CHANGE IN FINANCING	**1 549 327**	**425 454**	**−262 937**	**−21 589**	**−33 272**

Table 7.7 Six years cash flows for Torotrac

TOROTRAC
SUMMARY CASH FLOW

£ millions	20X8	20X7	20X6	20X5	20X4	20X3
OPERATING CASH MARGIN	−2063	−3470	−4260	−5544	−6613	−6151
(INV)/GEN FROM NET WORKING ASSETS	2589	−674	−198	23	−182	−119
NET CAPITAL EXPENDITURE	−404	−688	3010	−276	−316	−411
TAXATION	0	629	749	876	2016	1447
CASH FLOW AVAILABLE TO SATISFY FINANCE PROVIDERS	**122**	**−4203**	**−699**	**−4921**	**−5095**	**−5234**
NET INTEREST	381	266	304	487	505	836
NET DIVIDENDS	0	0	0	0	0	0
OTHER NON-OPERATING INC/(EXP)	0	0	−6	0	0	0
NET CASH IN/(OUT) BEFORE FINANCING	**503**	**−3937**	**−401**	**−4434**	**−4590**	**−4398**
Financed by:						
CHANGE IN EQUITY INCREASE/(DECREASE)	6741	805	550	23	0	0
CHANGE IN DEBT INCREASE/(DECREASE)	0	0	0	0	0	0
CHANGE IN CASH (INCREASE)/DECREASE	−7244	3132	−149	4411	4590	4398
TOTAL CHANGE IN FINANCING	**−503**	**3937**	**401**	**4434**	**4590**	**4398**

Table 7.8   Six years of sales data for Torotrac

TOROTRAK SUMMARY OF TURNOVER £ million	20X8	20X7	20X6	20X5	20X4	20X3
Revenue	3.7	2.7	2.1	0.5	0.2	0.1
% annual increase	37%	29%	320%	150%	100%	

company achieved a significant breakthrough. A major European manufacturer of trucks and buses signed licence agreements and development contracts valued at some £7 million over the next four years. Tata Motors also completed a licence for the technology in 20X8. Torotrac is cash positive because the European company has advanced a significant sum to the company during the year.

So the group has reached a situation where it is a classic aspirant. It is licensing its technology successfully and growing turnover. It achieved cash break-even in 2008 but only because of an advance from a customer (it is not yet positive at the operating cash margin).

The business has £11.5 million available which gives it at least another four-year window to achieve cash break-even if we make the no change time to default assumption.

SUMMARY

Analysing growth businesses with a view to assessing their medium-term viability is one of the most difficult analytical exercises to attempt. The general attractiveness of growth markets to investors and others tends to skew the judgement of market stakeholders towards rampant optimism. Outcomes are rarely as attractive as those forecasted due to unforeseen factors negatively impacting the growth market over time.

Whilst a successful growth business may, in the short term, experience periods of spectacular results, the overwhelming need to retain cost efficiency, competitor response and the demand from consumers for low-cost products and services tends to remove the opportunity to make exceptional levels of profit or cash flow generation in the medium and long term.

This chapter has covered much of the knowledge of cash flows required to assess whether a growth business is performing satisfactorily or not. The next chapter looks at further matters relevant to both mature and growth businesses.

Summarising reported cash flows into the Jury's Cash Flow Template and analysing them is an efficient and powerful method of analysis that avoids many of the problems of seeking to evaluate performance from the P&L.

8

Growth and Mature – Further Analysis Issues

Those readers who are employed as professional analysts typically spend most of their time analysing growth and mature businesses simply because they represent the majority of the business entities out there!

For this reason we will now introduce certain other cash flow analysis techniques of importance when looking at these types of business. These are the nature of net working assets and their behaviour, and the restatement of the Jury's Template cash flows on a no-growth basis.

Understanding both these concepts provides analysts and others with further tools to aid comprehension of the performance of the growth and mature businesses being analysed.

ANALYSING NET WORKING ASSETS FROM A CASH FLOW VIEWPOINT

The periodic changes in the amounts invested in net working assets can provide much useful information to the analyst. This is because the control of net working assets is one of the most important challenges for the management of any business.

Secondly, different sectors of the economy enjoy completely different patterns of working asset investment. In Chapter 1 we contrasted the major supermarket group Tesco with civil aircraft manufacturer Airbus Industrie to illustrate this.

The Supermarket

Let us consider this further. Table 8.1 shows the cash flows of Tesco plc for a six year period summarised in Jury's Cash Flow Template format.

Tesco's overall cash flow performance is spectacular, with the operating cash margin increasing steadily year on year. Cash Flow Available to Satisfy Finance Providers is significantly ahead of interest and dividend service every year except 20X3. Why are successful supermarket groups so cash generative?

The change in net working asset value in the template is positive (representing a cash inflow) in all the years observed. Why is this? Supermarket businesses are in a segment of the retailing industry known as FMCG (fast moving consumer

Table 8.1 Six years cash flows for Tesco

TESCO PLC SUMMARY CASH FLOW	20X8 £m	20X7 £m	20X6 £m	20X5 £m	20X4 £m	20X3 £m
OPERATING CASH MARGIN	3905	3521	3173	2571	2547	2097
(INV)/GEN FROM NET WORKING ASSETS	194	11	239	438	455	289
NET CAPITAL EXPENDITURE	−2386	−2043	−1897	−1374	−2177	−2000
TAXATION	−346	−545	−429	−483	−326	−366
CASH FLOW AVAILABLE TO SATISFY FINANCE PROVIDERS	**1367**	**944**	**1086**	**1152**	**499**	**20**
NET INTEREST	−282	−294	−268	−267	−61	−218
NET DIVIDENDS	−706	−343	−359	−313	−303	−368
OTHER NON-OPERATING INC/(EXP)	−784	−506	−243	−345	−272	−436
NET CASH IN/(OUT) BEFORE FINANCING	**−405**	**−199**	**216**	**227**	**−137**	**−1002**
Financed by:						
CHANGE IN EQUITY INCREASE/(DECREASE)	−621	−334	64	3	817	21
CHANGE IN DEBT INCREASE/(DECREASE)	1827	268	−115	−206	−178	950
CHANGE IN CASH (INCREASE)/DECREASE	−801	265	−165	−24	−502	31
TOTAL CHANGE IN FINANCING	**405**	**199**	**−216**	**−227**	**137**	**1002**

goods) and understanding what this means is the key to this segments fantastic cash flow performance. It also explains why this retailing segment is so attractive and why as a consequence it is so competitive.

Supermarket groups are only interested in offering goods which turn over quickly in the store. They do not want to offer anything that may sit on the shelf for weeks or months before being sold. Amongst other things this strategy avoids problems with obsolescence, fashion and freshness. There are also massive benefits in working capital terms.

Consider what happens when a supermarket buys product from its supplier. The product is ordered and delivered to store in two or three days, it then sells within a week for cash, the business then enjoys the benefit of the cash for the remainder of the supplier credit period at which time the products are paid for. The supermarket does not do this just once; it is doing this continually. The result is that there is a significant contribution to the capital employed by the supermarket business from

Table 8.2   Six years of net working asset data for Tesco

TESCO PLC SUMMARY OF NET WORKING ASSETS	20X8 £m	20X7 £m	20X6 £m	20X5 £m	20X4 £m	20X3 £m
Inventories	2430	1931	1464	1309	1199	1140
Trade and other receivables	1311	1079	892	769	840	662
Trade and other payables	−7177	−6046	−5083	−4974	−2434	−2196
TOTAL NET WORKING ASSETS	**−3436**	**−3036**	**−2727**	**−2896**	**−395**	**−394**

its suppliers, who are essentially granting permanent short-term interest free loans to the supermarket whist they continue to trade with it.

Supermarket groups have no significant trade debtors/receivables; although they accept credit cards they are essentially cash businesses. Despite the value shown in Table 8.2 for trade debtors/receivables appearing quite large it represents just ten days of sales in 20X8. Four days of this relates to prepayments and accrued income and amounts owed by joint ventures and associates leaving the true trade debtor at about six days of sales. Some of this probably relates to debtors arising on asset disposal and the two or three days outstanding on credit card transactions. Goods are sold for cash or for tender in debit or credit cards, which become cash for the retailer typically within one to three days.

Because the goods they sell turn over so quickly they do not carry much inventory. In 20X8 Tesco inventory was about 19 days of sales in its supply chain. Remember that many products sold by Tesco are first delivered to large central distribution warehouses before being delivered by Tesco to their own supermarkets. Some suppliers may deliver bulky items, such as bread and milk, directly to the stores. The trade credit it can obtain from its suppliers is on average about 45 days in the UK (this varies dramatically internationally depending on local conditions, I have heard of 100 days' credit being expected in some overseas markets). This means Tesco enjoys a cash subsidy to its business from suppliers of about one month of turnover all the time. In 20X8 the Tesco trade creditor represented about 55 days of sales. This is a huge sum of money once a supermarket group is large – for Tesco the value in 20X8 was £7277 million.

This also means that Tesco effectively has no money of its own invested in net working assets. Indeed, when we add up the three values of debtors, inventory and creditors we get a negative value as you can see in Table 8.2. This is why analysts refer to supermarkets as having *negative net working assets.*

There are other business segments that enjoy this attractive working asset behaviour. Mail order companies receive orders for goods in their catalogues, which are paid for by cash or credit card; generally they do not hold much inventory themselves. Rather, they send an instruction to the supplier to despatch goods to the customer, only then being billed by the supplier. The result of this is that they also enjoy a negative net working asset behaviour.

Similarly, package holiday companies, usually require payment for holidays some weeks before departure and as a result they receive payment from customers weeks or months before incurring the costs of flights and hotels. This also results in them enjoying negative net working asset behaviour.

Generally business that sell their goods for cash or receive payments in advance, whilst buying their inputs on credit, will have a negative net working asset position.

In contrast, let us look at the net working assets of a typical manufacturing entity.

The Manufacturer

Intimas plc is a supplier of ladies clothing. It manufactures and sells ranges of lingerie and swimwear to retailers. Table 8.3 shows a summary of its net working assets over a sample six year period.

Table 8.3   Six years of net working asset data for Intimas

INTIMAS GROUP PLC SUMMARY OF NET WORKING ASSETS	20X7 £'000	20X6 £'000	20X5 £'000	20X4 £'000	20X3 £'000	20X2 £'000
Inventories	5372	5005	4268	4712	6420	6910
Trade & other receivables	5267	6258	4656	4967	5136	8003
Trade & other payables	−3655	−5703	−2420	−2134	−3132	−2946
TOTAL NET WORKING ASSETS	**6984**	**5560**	**6504**	**7545**	**8424**	**11 967**

The investment in inventory and debtors is substantial. The credit provided by suppliers is insufficient to offset the trade debtors and inventory has to be financed in addition. This means the net amount invested in net working assets is positive. Unlike supermarkets, this requires financing by the business as part of its operating assets.

The riskiness of the amounts invested in working assets is also higher. The customers of the business expect to be offered a credit period, they are in a strong bargaining position and can demand this as a normal element of their trading relationship. This exposes manufacturers to default risk on their debtors. Should customers have a grievance about the quality or performance of a product or a dispute about returned goods they are likely to withhold payment for all the goods being purchased by them. Should a customer get into trading difficulties or become bankrupt, there is a risk of non-payment of the whole debtor. Cash flow management of the business is more demanding, as customers may not necessarily pay when they are supposed to.

Inventory is also riskier. The inventory of a manufacturer typically consists of raw material, work-in-progress and finished goods. Raw materials are the items used to produce the finished products of the business. Ideally, the manufacturer does not want to hold any inventory if it is possible to operate the business in this way. Some industries, such as the car industry, come close to achieving this by using just-in-time and other techniques developed after the Second World War by Japanese manufacturers to minimise inventory. Nevertheless, many businesses do hold significant amounts of raw materials.

This may be for a variety of reasons. It may be necessary to buy in bulk to achieve a sufficiently low price; there may be minimum order quantities from suppliers. It may be important to hold inventory to optimise the efficiency of the manufacturing process so production does not cease due to lack of raw material. Customer demand may vary in unpredictable ways, so requiring buffer inventory to smooth fluctuations.

Work-in-progress represents the value of inventory of partly built products moving through the factory. Again, it may be necessary to build up work-in-progress at certain points in the manufacturing process due to the nature of the process used to create the product. For example many manufacturers produce their product in batches, particularly if there is a significant variation in the products produced on a daily or weekly basis.

Finished goods are the completed products awaiting delivery. Again this may be a significant value because customers demand is uncertain, or because it is the policy of the business to deliver from inventory, rather than make to order. Finished goods are vulnerable to the risks of ageing. Many products have a shelf life. They may deteriorate if kept too long. Clothing and personal apparel are fashion products, finished goods may become unsellable due to changes in consumer fashion preferences. Finally, electrical and IT products are vulnerable to technological obsolescence, newer goods may be cheaper or have more features for the same price.

All inventory is also vulnerable to theft and damage. It needs to be stored in a secure place and properly protected from weather and environmentally related risks. Management error or incompetence can also reduce the value of inventory or render inventory worthless. Manufacturing a product incorrectly so that it is defective or to the wrong specification, for example, or contaminating a product with a dangerous substance (a major risk in the food industry).

By now it should be clear that there are a whole host of potential risks associated with inventory. This is why in the last 50 years so much effort has gone into developing ways of manufacturing that reduce or eliminate much of the inventory from the manufacturing process. Managing inventory is one of the key challenges of any manufacturing business.

So, manufacturers face risks in working assets that are far less significant for retailers. Retailers typically buy finished goods only, in perfect condition, and sell them to consumers as fast as they can. They should be carrying only the inventory they need to hold.

INTERPRETING THE MOVEMENT IN NET WORKING ASSETS

Each year we expect movements in the net working assets due to known factors. The main two, which have already been mentioned, are the effects of inflation and the growth in output. The net working asset investment may also move due to other known factors such as a change in the pattern of trade, seasonality or the mix of product sold.

There may also be unexpected changes in the net working assets, let us consider what these might be for each of the three components of the net working assets – debtors, inventory and creditors.

Changes to Debtors

Generally, inflationary economic conditions imply that the business will be raising prices each year. If the market in which the business operates is suffering inflation at say 5% then we expect, in general, output prices will be increased by at least 5% during the year.

This is not because the management want to raise their prices; it is because the business is suffering the same inflation effect on its inputs, which typically consist of raw materials, overheads and labour. In order to stand still, or keep the effects of inflation neutral for the business, sales prices will have to rise 5%. It follows that debtors will also have to rise by 5% at the same level of output. As this represents an increase in the interest-free loan made to customers this is a cash outflow from the business.

If output is increasing this will also cause an increase in debtors (more sales equals more debtors at a given price). We expect these effects and we can relate any movement in these values in a business to data about inflation and the real growth in sales of the same business.

Unexpected changes to debtors arise when the business has problems. If debtors have increased suddenly for reasons that have nothing to do with growth or inflation, this is usually a bad sign. What could cause such an outcome?

There can be two possible explanations. Either customers are not paying, or the business is not collecting the debtors.

Customers may not be paying for a variety of reasons:

- They cannot – they are distressed. This reason represents a credit control failure of the business selling the goods. It is always important to check that the customer has the ability to pay before trading on credit with them. If there is doubt about this, only cash terms should be offered or deposits taken when accepting the order.
- They can but they do not want to – usually because of some sort of dispute. The dispute may be for valid reason or be a front to attempt to defer payment. If there are no grounds for a dispute then the business should proceed with collection aggressively. If there are grounds for a dispute such as non-delivery, substandard goods, goods damaged on arrival, goods not to specification, or goods inadequately packed or labelled, then the businesses management should resolve the dispute as rapidly as possible by doing whatever is necessary to rectify the situation or concede some value to the customer to resolve the dispute and settle the matter.

To reduce the scope for this problem, competent management will ensure there is documentation to support the fact that a contract exists between the customer and the business. Typically this is in the form of an order confirmation sent by the business. The goal being to avoid the need to litigate about the nature of the contract itself, any dispute arising should only be about whether the contract is satisfied or not.

The business is not collecting its customer debts.

The other reason for an unexpected increase in debtors is the business may not be collecting the debt. Unfortunately, this is not a passive process. Despite that fact that customers know they have an obligation to pay many will not do so unless constantly reminded by letter, fax, e-mail and telephone contact. In larger businesses a separate function called credit control is usually responsible for cash collection. If this is under resourced or neglected the collection period will lengthen.

More serious causes may be to do with failures in the invoicing and record keeping process, IT failures, loss of the relevant accounting data and loss of key employees. Collectively these are known as failures in the financial control of the business.

It should be clear from the above that a sudden unexpected increase in debtors represents a failure of management one way or another. It is the responsibility of management to manage the risks outlined above so that cash flow is not disrupted or lost due to these factors. Analysts should be very interested in any sudden unexpected increase in debtors as this is likely to be for negative, rather than positive reasons.

Changes to Inventories

Much of the same logic applies to inventory. Again, we expect inflation and changes in output to reflect in inventory to some degree. In low inflation countries, good management practice is typically to minimise inventory. In high inflation countries, inventory may be used as a place to hold the cash surpluses of the business, particularly if the inventory does not deteriorate over time. This is because real assets hold their intrinsic value but cash does not. Inflation leads to a fall in the value of cash over time; the inventory, however, is increasing in nominal currency value over time.

Where inventory is falling for other reasons it is typically because management is finding ways to operate with less and less inventory. I mentioned earlier that much of the world has now adopted practices to minimise inventory pioneered in Japan after the Second World War, such as business process re-engineering (BPR) and just-in-time (JIT) systems. Occasionally inventory may fall due to supply shortages, which are typically temporary effects.

When inventory is rising for unexpected reasons it is, once again, usually a bad sign. In many situations inventory rises suddenly because production continues when demand has fallen for the product produced. It may be necessary to produce the product in consistent daily volumes in order to capture economies of scale. The car industry is a good example of this, producers will park up thousands of unsold cars, filling entire airfields with them rather than cut production because there are substantial one-off costs associated with changing the rate of production or ceasing production temporarily. Similarly, the production of iron and steel is a continuous process, which must continue whether or not the business can sell the resulting product profitably or not.

Inventory may also rise because it is less saleable than it was earlier. Again, demand may be falling for reasons to do with fashion, technological obsolescence, competitor initiatives and changes to legislation and regulation. Internal reasons for inventory increase may be to do with bad resource allocation and management decision making about priorities, putting too much effort into the wrong products and neglecting products for which there is substantial untapped demand. The issue of where to focus management resources and effort is a difficult one when the business produces five thousand different products from one factory!

Changes to Creditors

The expected changes to creditors also arise for the same reasons as for debtors and inventory. The effects of inflation and changes to the volume of output will affect the amount of the outstanding creditors in predictable ways. Again, these changes can be compared with inflation data and real volume change data from the business.

There may be other reasons for creditor increase that are less welcome for the business! Most consumer products are sold together with some sort of warranty or guarantee; in financial terms these represent contingent liabilities. Should there be some underlying defect in the product that causes it to fail, the manufacturer suddenly has a substantial cost to incur in rectifying it, which was not planned for. Expensive product recalls occur in the car industry and in the consumer electronics market. Toyota and many other car manufacturers have had to do product recalls on thousands of vehicles to remedy manufacturing design failures. In the recent past Sony and Dell have had to recall lithium batteries due to safety issues. All product-based markets are vulnerable to this problem.

In other business such as those that supply capital goods and in contracting, additional liabilities may arise due to the need to rectify and repair defective machinery, buildings and other capital goods produced for customers.

Creditors can rise for other reasons to do with the business itself. It may be that the business is not settling its liabilities as quickly as it used to. This could be because it doesn't want to or because it cannot do so!

The business itself may have disputes with its suppliers over problems with their supplies. For example, withholding payment is one way to put pressure on a supplier to conform with the wishes of the business.

The business may not be able to pay, because it has some sort of liquidity problem. This may be for reasons which are understandable like a major customer failing to pay when due, or it may be because of persistent underperformance, failure to forecast and manage cash flows, or failure to finance the business properly from debt and equity markets. Collectively, these problems represent failures in financial control.

Once again, these causes of unexpected movements in creditors represent failures of management, who are supposed to be there to anticipate these negative scenarios well before they arise and avoid them.

Decreases in creditors are generally good; it means we have fewer liabilities to others. However, we don't expect creditors to be paid off over time in most cash generative businesses. In developed countries management practice is to take as much supplier credit as the market will tolerate because this represents a cheap form of finance for the business. Careful examination of the value chains of particular industries often reveals that the larger, more profitable business in the chain often provide working capital to those in the more marginal and less profitable parts of the chain.

For example, painting contractors will usually buy the paint and other materials required for a particular contract, do the job, receive payment from the customer and then pay for the paint! For one-off jobs this is essentially the normal working capital behaviour for this particular market. Many other tradesmen adopt this approach to financing their work in progress.

MOVEMENTS IN NET WORKING ASSETS – CONCLUSIONS

When analysing the amount (invested in)/generated from net working assets in Jury's Cash Flow Template, in a well-run business we expect changes consistent with the effects of inflation and growth on the business. Other movements require further analysis to determine their cause. It may be necessary to disaggregate the change into its debtor, inventory and creditor components to properly assimilate what is occurring in the business. Generally, unexpected increases in any of the three elements are likely to be a bad sign. Thus, it is reasonable to conclude that working asset behaviour tells us much about management quality. If we see regular substantial unexpected increases in any of the elements this implies inadequate management performance.

RESTATEMENT OF THE TEMPLATE CASH FLOWS ON A NO-GROWTH BASIS

Earlier in the book we considered the cash flows of mature and growth business and came up with certain rules for their analysis. We also began to consider the use of scenarios to evaluate the condition of a business when we introduced the idea in Chapter 7 of the *no-change time to default*.

We are now going to look at the development of another scenario that is useful for extending our understanding of a businesses performance. I have entitled this *the restatement of the cash flows on a no-growth basis*. This means restating the template cash flows as if the business had not invested in any new capacity during the period. In other words its volume output had remained constant (not grown) in the reporting period.

Why do I want to restate the cash flow of a business on a no-growth basis? When I have adjusted the cash flows of a business to reflect this scenario they represent approximately what the business cash flows would look like if the business had not grown in the period being examined. In other words they reflect what the business would look like if it was mature. We can then apply the logic introduced in the chapter on mature to the resulting values namely:

In the long run, mature businesses must generate sufficient Cash Available to Satisfy Finance Providers to cover interest, dividends and scheduled debt repayment.

In other words, once we have restated the cash flows on a no-growth basis, if the cash available to satisfy finance providers is insufficient to cover interest, dividends and scheduled debt repayment, we have an underperforming business.

This is a very powerful analytical technique, because we can perform this analysis on growth companies and then come to some preliminary conclusions about their medium-term viability, even though their current template cash flow generation is typically negative.

It is also useful to perform this restatement on mature companies, because they are rarely growing at a zero rate. They usually have some positive growth, which distorts the analysis a little unless the cash flows are restated.

WHAT DOES NO-GROWTH MEAN?

In the cash flow template we are seeking to capture what the cash flows would look like if the operating assets of the business did not grow at all in the period being examined. How does this affect the cash flows?

Let us start by saying growth equals investment. In order to grow our business we need first of all additional manufacturing capacity (or in the case of service businesses, outlets). Once that capacity is in place we need the net working assets to operate it so we also expect increases in debtors, inventory and creditors if a business is growing.

To examine this in more detail we will consider each heading from Jury's Cash Flow Template separately.

The Operating Cash Margin

This represents the cash difference between the cash costs of production less the cash received from customers. If the business has added output during the year we would expect this to increase. If the business we are analysing is large, we would not expect this to be much, it might be as little as 1% to 3%. Bear in mind that the new capacity is only going to be available for part of the financial year. Having commissioned the new investment, there may still be a period where performance is built up to a point where it makes a positive cash return. In other words, for everything but small, early growth stage businesses, the contribution to operating cash margin from new investment in the financial period is likely to be small, the major benefit coming from increases in later years.

The Amount (Invested in)/Generated from Net Working Assets

Any change in the value invested in net working assets is typically driven by two things: the effects of inflation, and the additional working capital needed when capacity is increased. The inflation effects have been explained earlier in this chapter. If we invest in a new factory (or indeed a number of new outlets) we need the inventory necessary to operate these, additional creditors will be created, also additional debtors will be created if we trade on credit with our customers.

The Net Capital Expenditure (Capex)

The amount invested in Capex is driven by two things. The amount invested in maintenance Capex and the amount invested in growth or new Capex. Maintenance Capex is the Capex required to maintain the viability of our existing operating assets. Machines, trucks and other vehicles wear out, computers and customer-facing technology requires constant renewal. We have to make these investments even if the business is not growing (mature). Growth Capex is the investment in fixed assets to increase output, new factories, machines, distribution, additional outlets, fixtures and so on. This outlay is required only if we decide to increase capacity in some way.

The Taxation Paid

The taxation paid by businesses is usually derived from an adjusted profit value derived from the profit and loss account (P&L). The depreciation charge applied in the accounts using IAS GAAP is disallowed as a deduction. The business then is allowed a deduction related to capital expenditure according to the local corporate taxation rules. In the UK these tax deductions are known as capital allowances and for the purposes of this book I will refer to this as government depreciation. The depreciation shown in the annual report I will call manager's depreciation.

Where a business invests in growth Capex it will be able to claim government depreciation on the relevant expenditure. This means that a business investing in growing its capacity or output enjoys a lower charge for taxation than a business that is merely maintaining its fixed assets. Growth companies pay less tax per dollar of profit than mature companies because they can deduct more government depreciation from their taxable profit.

We should now understand what the effects of growth are on the first four values in the cash flow template. We can now consider restating them.

If you are comfortable with manipulating numbers and using spreadsheets, it is not particularly difficult to adjust all the four numbers individually. The analyst can identify appropriate drivers for change and use them to restate each of the figures to arrive at an adjusted total for the no-growth cash flow available to satisfy finance providers. Here are some examples of the data that might be used to adjust the actual cash flow values to no-growth estimates:

- Operating cash margin – percentage growth in sales, percentage increase in outlets, percentage increase in floor space, percentage increase in volume output, percentage increase in production units, percentage change in tonnage extracted.
- Movement in net working assets – retail, consumer or producer inflation indexes, to take out the increase due to inflation, the remainder being due to growth or other factors. The amount of increase due to growth can be derived from the analysis of historic debtor, inventory and creditor days.

- Net Capex – the maintenance Capex value if disclosed, IAS depreciation as an estimate of maintenance Capex or some percentage of cost if depreciation data is local or heavily accelerated and not representative of maintenance capital expenditures.
- Taxation – using the assumptions made in the net Capex section adjust the taxation for the capital allowances related to growth expenditure at a notional marginal percentage derived from local government depreciation rates.

There may be situations where the time and effort involved in performing this sort of scenario analysis is justified. However, in many situations there is no need to examine the no-growth scenario in so much detail in order to gain benefit from it.

A more straightforward starting point is to make one simple adjustment to the actual cash flows: replace the actual Capex with an estimate of the no-growth or maintenance Capex and see what effect this has on the values disclosed. Why are we doing this?

Firstly, of all the values in the template, Capex is the one that typically shows the most variation between growth and mature businesses.

Secondly, there is a certain degree of offset between the change net working assets value and the taxation paid. When adjusting these values to examine the no-growth scenario, the net working asset value is likely to go down and the taxation paid value will typically rise due to their being less government depreciation available as a deduction.

Thirdly, this single adjustment is usually sufficient to reveal if the business is stressed in cash flow terms or not.

PHIBRO ANIMAL HEALTH CORPORATION

Phibro is a global leader in animal health and performance products based in the US. It was recently listed on the Alternative Investments Market in the UK. Over the three years shown the business has been developing rapidly. The turnover values for the group are shown in Table 8.4.

Table 8.4   Three years of sales data for Phibro

PHIBRO ANIMAL HEALTH SUMMARY OF TURNOVER YEARS ENDED 30th JUNE	20X8 $'000	20X7 $'000	20X6 $'000
TURNOVER	511 437	453 045	398 402
% INCREASE IN TURNOVER NOMINAL	13%	14%	

It should be clear from this that Phibro is a growth company. Examination of the financial information disclosed by Phibro reveals that this growth was achieved historically, mainly through organic growth. In the future, further expansion is expected to come from both organic growth and by acquiring businesses in their field of operations.

In Chapter 7 on analysing growth cash flows I characterised this sort of business as an investor/acquirer. It is making the necessary investments to grow its output as well as acquiring other companies when appropriate. As I mentioned then, this type of entity constitutes a very high risk combination because of the high rate of change being faced by the group. The need to manage the new investment as well as assimilate third party businesses into the group at the same time is extremely challenging for management.

Phibro's cash flows for the last three years summarised in Jury's Cash Flow Template format (Table 8.5).

Table 8.5   Three years of cash flows for Phibro

PHIBRO ANIMAL HEALTH CONSOLIDATED STATEMENT OF CASH FLOWS YEARS ENDED 30th JUNE	20X8 $'000	20X7 $'000	20X6 $'000
OPERATING CASH MARGIN	36 778	24 441	22 455
(INVESTED)/GENERATED FROM NET WORKING ASSETS	−24 212	−3260	5616
NET CAPITAL EXPENDITURE	−19 589	−10 120	−5097
TAXATION	−4640	−5596	−5084
CASH FLOW AVAILABLE TO SATISFY FINANCE PROVIDERS	**−11 663**	**5465**	**17 890**
NET INTEREST	−28 275	−29 171	−22 178
NET DIVIDENDS	0	0	0
OTHER NON-OPERATING INCOME/(EXPENDITURE)	717	−1809	−205
NET CASH GENERATED/(ABSORBED) BEFORE FINANCING	**−39 221**	**−25 515**	**−4493**
Financed by:			
INCREASE/(DECREASE) IN EQUITY	41 046	−577	0
INCREASE/(DECREASE) IN DEBT	−6829	29 286	−542
(INCREASE)/DECREASE IN CASH	5004	−3194	5035
TOTAL CHANGE IN FINANCING	**39 221**	**25 515**	**4493**

Let us review this information. The most striking item here is the interest payments. Examination of the balance sheet, which is reproduced later in this chapter (Table 8.6), reveals that the group at the 20X8 year end carries $249 million

Table 8.6   Three years balance sheets for Phibro

Consolidated balance sheets As of June 30	2008	2007	2006
		(in thousands)	
ASSETS			
Cash and cash equivalents	$ 6994	$ 11994	$ 8688
Accounts receivable, net	90 869	76 112	58 990
Inventories	110 437	89 394	96 803
Prepaid expenses and other current assets	17 304	14 003	12 165
Total current assets	225 604	191 503	176 646
Property, plant and equipment, net	75 188	53 592	51 326
Intangibles, net	5996	7382	8784
Other assets	18 287	19 373	11 520
	$325 075	$271 850	$248 276
LIABILITIES AND SHAREHOLDERS' DEFICIT			
Loans payable to banks	$ —	$ —	$ 8500
Current portion of long-term debt	435	546	1317
Accounts payable	54 064	45 998	41 639
Accrued expenses and other current liabilities	40 515	42 761	49 499
Total current liabilities	95 014	89 305	100 955
Domestic senior credit facility	5850	8485	—
Long-term debt	241 418	240 080	209 810
Other liabilities	21 185	22 019	21 264
Total liabilities	363 467	359 889	332 029
Commitments and contingencies			
Preferred shares	—	—	521
Common shares	7	6	6
Paid-in capital	40 622	800	856
Accumulated deficit	(93 143)	(96 646)	(89 932)
Accumulated other comprehensive income	14 122	7801	4796
Total shareholders' deficit	(38 392)	(88 039)	(83 753)
	$325 075	$271 850	$248 276

of debt, with negative equity of $38 million. Phibro is a highly leveraged entity. It is, what we call technically bankrupt, its liabilities exceed its assets on the balance sheet.

It appears that, sometime in the past, Jack Bendheim, the owner of the business, rather than selling the group, chose to realise much of the value built up in the business by leveraging it and extracting the resulting cash flow as some sort of dividend or share buy-back, I have inferred this from the information disclosed as the available annual reports do not go back far enough to confirm this explicitly. In 20X8, 3i (a UK-based private equity house) acquired 29.9% of the business from BFI Co LLC, the family investment vehicle controlled by the family of Jack Bendheim. This was achieved by buying 19.5% from BFI for $57.2 million, and by buying the remaining 10.4% following the admission of Phibro to AIM in April 20X8 for a consideration of $44.6 million. After expenses this is what constitutes the $41 million new equity in the Cash Flow Template.

Reviewing the cash flow template in the previous two years we can see why this additional fundraising became necessary. The business has not been generating sufficient cash available to satisfy finance providers to cover the groups interest burden. In 20X7 the shortfall was in excess of $25 million. In analysing this performance we have one further problem, the shortfall in cash generation might be due to the growth investments needs of the business. Phibro's no-growth cash flows for the last three years are summarised in the template below. The only adjustment that has been made is to substitute the amortisation value for net Capex in the template. As expected, this means the template no longer balances (Table 8.7).

Table 8.7   Three years of no-growth restated cash flows for Phibro

PHIBRO ANIMAL HEALTH NO-GROWTH RESTATEMENT OF CASH FLOWS YEARS ENDED 30th JUNE	20X8 $'000	20X7 $'000	20X6 $'000
OPERATING CASH MARGIN	36778	24441	22455
(INVESTED)/GENERATED FROM NET WORKING ASSETS	−24212	−3260	5616
NO-GROWTH MAINTAINANCE CAPEX ESTIMATE	−10007	−10717	−13991
TAXATION	−4640	−5596	−5084
CASH FLOW AVAILABLE TO SATISFY FINANCE PROVIDERS	**−2081**	**4868**	**8996**
NET INTEREST	−28275	−29171	−22178
NET DIVIDENDS	0	0	0
OTHER NON-OPERATING INCOME/(EXPENDITURE)	717	−1809	−205
NET CASH GENERATED/(ABSORBED) BEFORE FINANCING	**−29639**	**−26112**	**−13387**
Financed by:			
INCREASE/(DECREASE) IN EQUITY	41046	−577	0
INCREASE/(DECREASE) IN DEBT	−6829	29286	−542
(INCREASE)/DECREASE IN CASH	5004	−3194	5035
TOTAL CHANGE IN FINANCING	**39221**	**25515**	**4493**

Remember that this adjustment gives us a crude representation of what the cash flow of the business might look like if Phibro had not invested in growth in each of the three years. Comparing this with the previous version is illuminating. In 20X6 the actual Capex was just 36% of the amortisation charge for that year. Clearly this is not a sustainable reduction as it implies the group was failing to invest enough to maintain its existing fixed assets in this particular year, perhaps because of the need to prioritise interest payments. The values for 20X7 were similar in both summaries because Capex in 20X7 was almost the same as amortisation. Since we are looking at a proxy for the cash flows of the business when mature this implies a shortfall in the generation of operating cash margin in 20X7 of some $26 million. This is a significant deficit. This deficit was covered by an increase in debt.

In 20X8 the CATS Finance Providers deficit has reduced significantly in the no-growth example, as there was significant growth Capex in this year, which the restatement removes. However, CATS Finance Providers is still negative before finance costs, perhaps because of the exceptional level of net working asset investment in this year. Bear in mind the increase in net working assets is probably a one-off and is unlikely to keep repeating at this level in future years, unless the business continues to increase output dramatically.

The analysis reveals that there is a gap of about $30 million between the actual cash-flow generation performance of Phibro and its cash-flow obligations on a no-growth basis. Given the nature of the business and the sector it operates in it is difficult to see how this shortfall could be met from improvements in operating performance alone. This implies, in the absence of significant restructuring, that the business may collapse into official bankruptcy at some point in the future. (In this case the senior lenders are likely to end up owning the business.)

We have been able to develop much of this hypothesis from Jury's Cash Flow Template alone. This implies this an efficient way of gaining such insights. Bear in mind that a good analyst should analyse all of the information available before coming to any conclusions about the business. The fact that the Phibro balance sheet is significantly negative is also a big clue about its financial condition.

9

Analysing the Cash Flows of
Start-up Businesses

In Chapter 3 I introduced the concept of start-up, growth, mature, decline as a way of comprehending the significance of cash flow information. One of the problems with the English language is that terminology expressed in English is often imprecise, meaning different things in different contexts. Terms in English are vulnerable to misunderstanding if the context in which the term is used is not defined.

The term 'start-up' can mean too many different things. We need to explore this difficulty further.

Early in the entrepreneurial process it means the intention to turn an idea into a business. Three years later the business may still be called a start-up because it has not yet begun to sell product. Indeed the term start-up may be used until the business turns a profit. From an analytical point of view this is a problem because the entrepreneurial entity is changing fundamentally throughout this process.

So, how do we analyse start-ups from a cash flow point of view?

In the early stages there is no cash flow from the business because trading with customers has not yet commenced. Earlier in the book I used the term 'charity' in a derogatory fashion for such situations because at this point owners and investors are essentially giving money to the entrepreneurial entity who, in turn, gives it to other stakeholders (employees, suppliers) with no immediate cash inflows arising.

Let us call the business a 'start-up project' for this period, reserving the term 'start-up' for the point in time when the business achieves regular (recurring) operating cash flow from customers. So, the test I am using for a start-up project to become a business is as follows:

> The business has reached a point where it has demonstrated it can successfully produce a product or service and sell it to customers, who then continue to consume it.

There are still many uncertainties about the future viability of the business at this point. The price charged for the product needs to generate sufficient returns to satisfy finance providers. If the owners of the business are selling goods or services below this price as a penetration strategy the viability of the business is not proven until it charges an economic price for its output which may be sometime later. There may also be volume targets that need to be achieved before economies of scale come into play. The management challenge is still immense. The business has not demonstrated viability until it achieves cash break-even on a regular period-by-period basis.

Other uncertainties such as competitor response, technology change, shifts in fashion change, new regulations or recession may also affect the business to some degree. However, these are issues faced by all businesses. They are a consequence of being part of a sector or market. In other words, they are a consequence of being in trade (we also label these types of risk as 'business risk').

ANALYSING THE CASH FLOWS OF A START-UP PROJECT

As everyone who has invested in such situations knows, the only real cash flow indicator that can be examined in this phase is the 'cash burn' rate. What is this?

We can identify the liquidity available to the project, in the form of cash already raised together with any other irrevocably committed financing and compare this with the monthly cash flow cost of continuing to pursue the idea on which the start-up project is founded. If we divide the amount of liquidity available by the expected average monthly cash burn we get a period of time expressed in months to the point at which liquidity is completely consumed. This is the cash burn rate. Here is an example.

Burning Limited	
Cash and facilities available	£1.5 million
Monthly cash consumption	£0.15 million
CASH BURN RATE 10 months	(£1.5 million divided by £0.15 million)

It implies the window of opportunity available to the start-up project sponsors to make sufficient progress with their project to either be cash positive, or to be in a position to raise further investment from finance providers. If no action to refinance is taken and no progress is made to improve the cash flow position, the business will collapse at about this point.

The progress benchmarks are generally non-financial at this point. To illustrate this, Table 9.1 shows the typical steps required to get a new product to market.

Investors will generally continue to invest in a project if they can observe what they consider to be reasonable progress (top to bottom in Table 9.1). In many business segments this can take years. Jury's Template cash flows in this period are substantially negative with a negative operating cash margin, investment in net

Table 9.1   The entrepreneurs route to success

SUMMARY OF THE ENTREPRENEURIAL PROCESS

Come up with an idea for a new product!
Research the viability of the idea
Can it be manufactured?
Can it be manufactured at an acceptable price?
Who are the customers?
Why will they adopt the product?
In what volumes will they want it?
Who will invest in the start-up project?
Create business plan and financing proposal

Identify potential investors
Get investment

SIGNIFICANT CASH OUTFLOWS USUALLY START HERE
Design the product
Prototype the product
Prove the product viability
Establish financial control function
Establish production function

Design manufacture of the product
Who? How? Where?
Build pilot plant
Commence pilot production, prove process
Establish marketing, selling
Build production plant
Commence mass production

Design marketing of the product
Literature
Web site
Advertising and promotion
Sales organisation

Sell the product

OPERATING CASH INFLOWS USUALLY START HERE
Evidence of true customer adoption and market acceptance
Evidence of medium term business viability

DEFINITION POINT FOR 'START-UP' IS HERE
Grow sales
Grow production
Control the business

**CASH BREAK-EVEN OCCURS SOME PERIODS LATER HERE – THE
BUSINESS GRADUATES TO 'GROWTH' TYPE SOMETIME IN THIS
PERIOD**

---

working assets and net Capex. All cash inflows are coming from finance providers. The junior stock market in the UK (known as AIM – the Alternative Investments Market), has many businesses of this type.

NXT plc was established to exploit flat panel loudspeaker technology, which the group had developed and protected with a number of patents. The initial business model was to licence the technology to manufacturers for various uses such as in-car entertainment, domestic and commercial sound systems, flat panel TV, and so on. This business model had worked successfully for ARM, the UK-based low power semiconductor designer. ARM does not make any chips; it simply designs them and then licences the design to chip foundries, who then produce the chips. Over time it became clear that although this model worked for ARM it could not generate adequate added value for NXT plc as manufacturers were not willing to pay a royalty large enough to provide a reasonable operating cash margin to NXT. This may be because NXT competes with an existing mature technology which essentially puts a ceiling on the maximum price the market is willing to pay for their product (there is a close substitute for their product).

As a result of this NXT plc has steadily downsized its activities to move closer to break even and has extended the business model into providing greater services to their target markets. In Hong Kong they have established a facility that will design and implement products for their customers. In essence they have moved closer to producing the product themselves without actually doing so. They have also continued to develop the technology behind the product becoming experts in resonance and flat panels in general. The cash flows of NXT summarised into Jury's Cash Flow Template format are shown in Table 9.2.

As we can see, the business has never produced a positive operating cash margin. Whilst it continues to creep closer and closer to cash break-even at the CATS Finance Providers line it is still some £2.5 million away at the end of 20X8. In order to break even it need revenues some two to three times larger than it currently enjoys. Turnover growth over the last 12 months was 5% nominal. It may be that there simply is not sufficient margin in the product to support a business operating on any other model than primary manufacture. This business is still a start-up as it has not yet demonstrated that there is a viable business model, its present level of activity is significantly below that required to do so.

So, if we are analysing start-up projects, the two issues we are concerned with is the cash burn rate compared to the progress made towards true viability and the possibility of raising further finance or achieving cash break-even.

Table 9.3 shows the balance sheet of NXT at the 30 June 20X8. Let us use this to consider the cash burn rate.

We can see from the cash flow NXT is burning about £2.5 million a year. The balance sheet shows no debt and about £1 million of surplus cash. This means, if we assume no change, the business has to raise further finance within the next six months, or restructure to get its business costs in line with its revenues.

Table 9.2 Six years cash flows for NXT

NXT plc SUMMARY CASH FLOW	20X8 £'000	20X7 £'000	20X6 £'000	20X5 £'000	20X4 £'000	20X3 £'000
At 30th June						
OPERATING CASH MARGIN	−2775	−4228	−3853	−5754	−7998	−9070
(INV)/GEN FROM NET WORKING ASSETS	−212	757	151	529	−430	465
NET CAPITAL EXPENDITURE	−13	−58	2	−58	−40	−139
TAXATION	346	382	378	389	538	1780
CASH FLOW AVAILABLE TO SATISFY FINANCE PROVIDERS	**−2654**	**−3147**	**−3322**	**−4894**	**−7930**	**−6964**
NET INTEREST	21	74	211	297	401	322
NET DIVIDENDS	0	0	0	0	0	0
OTHER NON-OPERATING INC/(EXP)	0	0	0	118	0	0
NET CASH IN/(OUT) BEFORE FINANCING	**−2633**	**−3073**	**−3111**	**−4479**	**−7529**	**−6642**
Financed by:						
CHANGE IN EQUITY INCREASE/(DECREASE)	3033	6	138	2544	9388	0
CHANGE IN DEBT INCREASE/(DECREASE)	0	0	0	−66	764	412
CHANGE IN CASH (INCREASE)/DECREASE	−400	3067	2973	2001	−2623	6230
TOTAL CHANGE IN FINANCING	**2633**	**3073**	**3111**	**4479**	**7529**	**6642**

Table 9.3   NXT consolidated balance sheet

NXT plc **Consolidated Balance Sheet** **At 30th June 20X8**	**20X8** **£'000**
Assets	
Non-current asets	
Property, Plant and Equipment	43
Intangible assets	301
Long-term debtors	50
	394
Current assets	
Trade and other receivables	1079
Current tax recoverable	175
Cash and cash equivalents	945
	2199
Total assets	**2593**
Equity and liabilities	
Share capital	1436
Deferred share capital	22 682
Share premium account	86 595
Other reserve	282
Stock option reserve	571
Retained earnings	−109 825
	1741
Non-current liabilities	
Long-term provisions	0
	0
Current liabilities	
Trade and other payables	431
Short-term provisions	421
	852
Total liabilities	852
Total equity and liabilities	**2593**

AFTER THE POINT DEFINED ABOVE AS 'START-UP' EARLIER IN THIS CHAPTER

The key value that measures success from a cash flow point of view is the operating cash margin, until this is consistently positive the business has not yet demonstrated its viability. So, we are most interested in the operating cash margin value or, more importantly, its trend. Is this improving over time? Until this goes positive the business has not generated enough cash flow from customers to cover its regular operating cash overheads. Once this has become consistently positive we will normally start thinking of the business as a 'growth' business. See Chapter 7 on analysing growth cash flows to analyse the performance from this point.

In most cases the overall cash flow will still be negative for some time. This is due to the investment needs of the business to grow production constantly in order to match customer demand.

The analytical emphasis changes from ensuring sufficient cash is available to fund the burn rate to monitoring the trends in each of the values in the template. The ideal scenario is to monitor what is happening on a monthly basis. The key question is: are the monthly cash flows improving over time?

If you are analysing listed businesses you may only have access to quarterly, half yearly or annual data, nevertheless the same logic applies: are we seeing incremental increases in the operating cash margin and general improvement towards cash break-even?

Table 9.4 shows the summary cash flows of NXT for the six months to 31 December 20X8, the period immediately following the cash flow summary shown earlier.

Table 9.4   NXT cash flow update

NXT plc SUMMARY CASH FLOW	20X8 £'000 6 months
OPERATING CASH MARGIN	299
INV/(GEN)FROM NET WORKING ASSETS	−1226
NET CAPITAL EXPENDITURE	−36
TAXATION	188
CASH FLOW AVAILABLE TO SATISFY FINANCE PROVIDERS	**−775**
NET INTEREST	3
NET DIVIDENDS	
OTHER NON-OPERATING INC/(EXP)	0
NET CASH IN/(OUT) BEFORE FINANCING	**−772**
Financed by:	
CHANGE IN EQUITY INCREASE/(DECREASE)	0
CHANGE IN DEBT INCREASE/(DECREASE)	0
CHANGE IN CASH (INCREASE)/DECREASE	772
TOTAL CHANGE IN FINANCING	**772**

For the first time NXT has achieved break-even at the operating cash margin. The cash outflow seen above is associated mainly with a big increase in trade and other receivables due to a significant increase in royalty and licensing income. There was adequate cash to finance this in the business. Working asset investment like this is unlikely to recur at this level unless turnover continues to increase dramatically. It may be that we can now start to think of NXT as a growth business!

10

Analysing the Cash Flows of Decline Businesses

In Chapter 3 I introduced the concept of assessing business cash flows by relating them to the pattern we expect to see for a business in the life cycle of the markets in which it operates. The final part of the business life cycle we need to examine is decline.

I define this as a business operating in a market where demand is falling. It is a consequence of change, which may be technological, environmental, demographic or be related to consumer tastes or fashion, and it occurs at some point in all industries and markets.

I do not mean a business that is being badly managed, although the label decline is also used in general English for this, a business can be badly managed in any of the four phases of its potential life.

Over the past 20 years there have been huge global changes in places where goods are manufactured. I have first hand experience of the effects of globalisation on the footwear and clothing industries in particular, as I have lived in an area seriously affected by these changes for much of my life. In both industries the majority of volume production of product for the mass market in the UK now takes place in other countries.

Many other industries, such as shipbuilding, car manufacturing, electronics and engineering have also faced similar pressures. These changes have come about due to a number of factors which have reduced the economic cost of operating at a distance from consumers. It is a combination of containerisation, cheap air travel, global courier services, computerisation, the fax machine and subsequently the internet, and a relatively benign regulatory environment, that has made it cost effective for large producers to supply global markets from a handful of factories situated in economies with a low cost of labour.

Any business in a high labour cost economy where the production process is necessarily labour intensive has been vulnerable to being undercut (that is, competitors selling what you produce at a price you cannot match without losing money) and eventually being pushed out of their traditional markets by similar businesses operating in lower cost economies.

What choices do businesses have when faced by such a situation? Remember that the goal of wealth maximising businesses is to seek to optimise cash flows at all times, even in decline.

There are both offensive and defensive strategies available for businesses. Offensive strategies are as follows:

- Relocate production to a low cost location.
- Use technology to gain an offsetting cost advantage for higher labour costs.
- If economies of scale are available at a larger size, acquire other similar businesses to gain sufficient volume to take advantage of them.
- Use the cash flow from declining markets to diversify the business into new markets that require similar core competences to those exploited in the markets being abandoned.
- Use the cash flow from declining markets to diversify the business into completely new markets for the business.

Defensive strategies are as follows:

- Exit now or later by selling the business.
- Exit now or later by winding the business down in a orderly way and realising the assets.
- If the decline is in its early stages recognise the volume decline as inevitable and manage the business to maintain cash flow whilst reducing operating capacity until it is no longer economic to continue.

Generally, owners and managers seek continuity. Indeed, the nature of capital investment (spend now, get benefits later) means that it is necessary to think and plan in terms of years in order to get a return from the initial investment. So it is unusual to see owners and managers who are content to manage a business in a decline market by accepting the turnover fall until exit is inevitable.

Generally they seek instead to diversify the business away from the decline market into new markets (for the business). They use the cash flows from the existing mature and decline business areas to make their entry into the new market, which may be start-up, growth or mature. Nokia is a good example of this, originally commencing its existence as a paper works in 1865. Nokia Corporation as we know it today was formed from the merger of Nokia Ab, the Finnish Rubber Works and the Finnish Cable works which formally merged in 1967.

HOW DOES DECLINE AFFECT CASH FLOWS?

One of the consequences of decline is that price competition between the remaining competitors in a market is likely to be intense. This is because each individual business is still trying to maintain or grow its volume output, even though the overall volume consumed by the market is dropping. Due to overcapacity amongst producers the market is oversupplied with product so allowing customers to seek lower and lower prices by threatening to transfer to other suppliers.

So, we expect to see a steady erosion of the operating cash margin over time, indeed this is a late signal that the business is facing permanent rather than temporary problems in the choice of markets in which it chooses to compete.

Dawson International is a leading supplier of cashmere to the textile industry. Based in Scotland, it operates in three divisions spinning, knitwear and home furnishings. It has been in steady decline for the last decade (Table 10.1).

Table 10.1   Eight years sales and profit data for Dawson International

**DAWSON INTERNATIONAL
TURNOVER AND OPERATING RESULT**

	20X7	20X6	20X5	20X4	20X3	20X2	20X1	20X0
Ongoing operations	47.7	53.5	63.9	70.2	68.3	61.2	75.5	90.7
Acquisitions – Dorma bed linen	44.9	48.5	47.7					
Discontinued operations								10.3
TURNOVER	**92.6**	**102**	**111.6**	**70.2**	**68.3**	**61.2**	**75.5**	**101**
Operating profit/(loss)	**−1.1**	**−3.1**	**3.9**	**2.6**	**−18.1**	**−8.3**	**−4.3**	**−1.7**

In 20X5 Dawson acquired the bed linen business of Dorma. I have continued to show the split of turnover after this date so the decline in the underlying Dawson business is clear (Table 10.1). The turnover of the cashmere business has almost halved in eight years. This is likely to be due to competition from suppliers of the same products who are situated in countries with lower costs, particularly with lower labour costs.

The cash flows of Dawson International for the same eight years are summarised in Table 10.2. The operating cash margin is generally negative. This item contains both the positive or negative cash margin from trading in the year and the one-off costs associated with reducing the size of the business year on year. One of the features of the legal and regulatory environment of developed nations is that there are barriers to exit (the opposite of barriers to entry) in the form of redundancy costs (payments required by law in the UK to employees to compensate them for the loss of their employment) when labour numbers are reduced, together with other one-off costs associated with the reduction in size or cessation of business.

In some years working asset investment is contributing to cash flow, as the value invested in inventory and debtors less creditors reduces. Capex is low and in some years the proceeds of disposal of Capex is also contributing to cash flows. One of the difficulties of being in decline is that if you sell off your fixed assets cheaply to someone else you may create a competitor with lower costs than your own until those fixed assets wear out. The solution to this problem used to be to sell the assets into a territory where you do not compete. However, this does not

Table 10.2 Eight years cash flows of Dawson International

DAWSON INTERNATIONAL
SUMMARY TEMPLATE CASH FLOWS

Amounts in £ millions	20X7	20X6	20X5	20X4	20X3	20X2	20X1	20X0
Operating cash margin	-4.3	-2.5	1.3	0.2	-9.6	-7.4	-2.1	0.8
Change in net working assets	0.2	-5.7	5.3	0.2	5.1	-4.8	11.8	-13.4
Net Capex	2.6	-1.4	-2.3	0.3	-0.9	0.2	-2	0.2
Cash taxes	-0.3	-0.4	-0.5	0.3	0.1	0	-0.2	-0.2
CASH FLOW AVAILABLE TO	**-1.8**	**-10.0**	**3.8**	**1**	**-5.3**	**-12**	**7.5**	**-12.6**
SATISFY CAPITAL PROVIDERS								
Net interest	-0.9	-0.7	-0.7	-1.2	-1.1	-0.2	0.1	0.1
Net dividends	0.0	0.0	0	0	0	0	0	-25
Other	0.0	-1.1	-6.9	16.5	1.3	-1.1	1.1	8.8
NET CASH INFLOW/(OUTFLOW)	**-2.7**	**-11.8**	**-3.8**	**16.3**	**-5.1**	**-13.3**	**8.7**	**-28.7**
Increase/(Decrease) in equity	0.0	0.0	1.4	0	0	0	0	0
Increase/(Decrease) in debt	6.0	1.9	-0.7	1.8	3.5	-0.7	0.3	-0.6
(Increase)/Decrease in cash	-3.3	9.9	3.1	-18.1	1.6	14	-9	29.3
FINANCING CASH FLOW	**2.7**	**11.8**	**3.8**	**-16.3**	**5.1**	**13.3**	**-8.7**	**28.7**

work any more as the goods produced using the discounted assets can still end up competing in your market due to the ease with which goods move internationally.

With the exception of the Dorma acquisition the Dawson group has been steadily selling off businesses and assets. The most recent transaction being the sale and leaseback in 20X7 of the manufacturing site at Kinross generating £3.5 million cash. The business carried net debt of £5.7 million at the end of 2007. The cash flows of Dawson International represent a good example of decline-phase cash flows.

In a true decline scenario the first management challenge is to recognise that the situation is almost certainly irreversible and inevitable. I have observed many instances where owners and managers appear unable to accept that this is the situation they are now in. They continue to run their business as if it were mature, despite falling turnover, cash flow and profits and, if they remain in denial, collapse into bankruptcy or are taken over by others who are more realistic about the real future prospects of the business. Those managers who do recognise their business is now operating in decline markets can then act to optimise the impact of the subsequent decline for all the stakeholders in the business, sometimes for many years. Finally, at some point in the future, they can make a planned and orderly exit from the markets affected.

CONCLUSIONS ABOUT DECLINING MARKETS

Any adverse trend in the performance of a business is a warning sign. The difficulty faced by managers in declining markets is recognising that what is happening to their business is more than the effect of short-term competitive changes, and that their situation is unlikely to improve unless they recognise that in the long term their existing market position is no longer viable.

The most important management action is to recognise the inevitability of decline once it is established and that in the long term there are no positive outcomes for the business without a dramatic change in the business model.

After that the choices available are as shown in the section on strategies at the beginning of the chapter. Managers who fail to recognise this and act will almost certainly end up with a failed business at some point in the future.

11

What to do about Bad
Cash Flows

In this chapter we are going to consider how to approach the situation where we discover 'bad' cash flows in a business we are analysing. I am using the term 'bad' as shorthand for any situation where we identify a set of cash flows that is not in accordance with our understanding of what constitutes a satisfactory cash flow performance. When we are examining 'bad' cash flows, the context needs to be considered before we discuss what actions can be taken.

If you are approaching this situation as an analyst, you are almost certainly examining the cash flows in the context of either a credit decision or an investment decision. The questions you are seeking to answer are likely to be as follows:

• What is the cause of the cash flow shortfall?
• Is the cause of the cash flow shortfall temporary or permanent?
• How long will it be before the business recovers its performance?
• Will the business default on its loans, debt or trade creditors?
• Will the business survive?

If you are approaching this situation as a manager, director or entrepreneur running the business entity you will also be keen to know the answers to the questions above. However, in these circumstances, we can ask two more questions in addition to those above:

• Were the causes of the shortfall inside or outside our control?
• What actions can we take to remedy the situation?

So, we will approach this subject initially from the viewpoint of the analyst, after which we will consider the problems faced by the manager.

THE ANALYST'S VIEWPOINT

Let's start by attempting to identify some analytical logic to help us with this problem. A neutral cash flow is one where the value of the cash inflows is sufficient to cover the cash outflows. This is not working very well as a maxim because all cash flow statements balance! The inflows must match the outflows.

So, what then do we need to focus on? Lets start with the statement from Chapter 6:

> In the long run the Cash Available to Satisfy Finance Providers must be sufficient to cover interest, dividends and scheduled debt repayment.

There are two key totals in Jury's Cash Flow Template, these are:

- The Cash Available to Satisfy Finance Providers.
- The Net Cash Generated/(Absorbed) before financing.

The Cash Available to Satisfy Finance Providers Total

This total is important because it is what it says it is! This is the cash *available* to satisfy finance providers. For cash flow to be 'satisfactory' we need sufficient cash here to cover interest, dividends and scheduled debt repayment in any particular period. However, we know already from the earlier sections on start-up and growth that there will be situations where we *expect* the cash flows to be negative at this total.

So the first point is that the state of development of the business is highly relevant. Is it start-up/growth or is it mature/decline?

If it is start-up/growth the question is whether the cash flow shortfall exceeds our expectation of what is reasonable. Again, this will be a subjective judgment based on business plans, trends and sector knowledge.

If the business with the shortfall is a mature/decline business we know there is definitely a problem because the cash flow at this total should always be sufficient to cover interest, dividends and scheduled debt repayment at this total. If the business is failing to achieve this we need to seek to understand why.

The Net Cash Generated/(Absorbed) before Financing Total

If a business is positive at this total it is generating cash from that period's activity.

If a business is negative at this total it is expending more cash than it has generated from the period's activity. This then has to be financed; the cash can come from exiting cash reserves held over from previous trading periods, or from new debt or equity.

Let us consider each of the questions posed earlier.

What is the Cause of the Cash Flow Shortfall?

Initially we should consider the other information revealed by Jury's Cash Flow Template. Examining each of the first four values disclosed and comparing it with previous periods should provide insights as to which value or values are deficient.

The operating cash flow may have dropped; a good way to check this is to look at the operating cash flow to sales ratio. If this is trending down it implies there is a problem with margins.

The net working asset investment may have risen significantly. Chapter 8 discusses the possible causes of such an event in some detail. It may be necessary to disaggregate the various components of the net working asset change value to ascertain which item is the culprit.

The Capex may be high relative to the historic trend. This can be assessed by comparing the Capex value to sales and to depreciation as a percentage. If the value is high the next question to answer is: will future improvements in cash returns offset this?

The taxation value may have risen. Why has this occurred? If the taxation paid value relates to the previous period. The answer is probably to be found in the previous year's accounts.

The goal should be to understand the cause of the cash flow shortfall.

Is the Cause of the Cash Flow Shortfall Temporary or Permanent?

The challenge here is to come to some view as to whether the negative trend observed is a one-off, an effect associated with the economic or sector cycle, or a more permanent change in the market caused by technological obsolescence, fashion or overall market decline.

Is the cause only going to affect this periods values or will it affect future periods?

How Long will it be before the Business Recovers its Performance?

Will the Business Default on its Loans, Debt or Trade Creditors?

Will the Business Survive?

In seeking to answer these questions we are moving towards an attempt to predict the future. We are moving from analysing known historic performance, to considering the extent of a range of possible future outcomes.

In order to arrive at any conclusions about these three questions the goal should be to understand the probable duration of any shortfall (if temporary) and then assess whether the business has the cash or financing resources to survive the interim period until cash flow recovers.

This is inevitably an imperfect process because of the dynamic nature of business. The most important variable is probably the quality of management. Good managers will react early to any negative trend in the business with a range of initiatives designed to recover cash flow performance. Less good managers will under react, being both slow to respond and limited in the scope of the initiatives they choose to take.

Other key issues to consider are (amongst other things) the effect of changes in the economy, the sector fundamentals, technology change, fashion change, regulatory change, market effects such as competitor changes, commodity price change and currency effects.

CONCLUSIONS FROM THE ANALYST'S VIEWPOINT

'Bad' cash flows can occur at any time in the life cycle of a business. It can occur in the start-up phase, or any of the other three phases already discussed, these being growth, mature and decline. Until this chapter I have concentrated on explaining what 'good' cash flows should look like in each of the four phases, the negative inference being that anything that is not 'good' is 'bad'.

Once we have identified that the cash flow performance of an entity is somehow inadequate, the key question then becomes; how inadequate (or how 'bad')?

There are literally hundreds of possible negative scenarios, which might explain an observed cash flow shortfall. Rather than attempt to list them, which would inevitably result in omissions, it is more elegant to use the logic just described.

THE MANAGER'S, DIRECTOR'S OR ENTREPRENEUR'S VIEWPOINT

If you are responsible for the management of a business entity you will almost certainly have a good deal more information available to you than anyone else to assist in ascertaining the cause of any negative trends in cash flow. In addition to the above questions it may be helpful to consider the further questions noted below.

Were the Causes of the Shortfall Inside or Outside our Control?

A well-run business should have a range of management information – about sales, costs, asset performance and efficiency – that is not available to external analysts and others interested in the business. This should provide managers with a major advantage in understanding the causes of any cash flow shortfall they experience.

Internal issues that may give rise to cash flow shortfalls are (amongst other things), lack of volume, changes in the mix of products produced, shortfalls in resources such as skilled labour, errors and mistakes, system and machinery failures, inventory build up and losses and poor financial control including credit control.

External issues that may give rise to cash flow shortfalls are (amongst other things), raw material and labour shortages, environmental risks such as adverse weather events and volcanic activity, political and risk events such as riot, revolution, legal and regulatory changes, theft and fraud, changes in the nature and structure of the competition, fashion change, technology change and social change.

What Actions can We Take to Remedy the Situation?

There are literally hundreds of possible actions managers can take when faced with adverse cash flow trends.

If the operating cash margin is in decline the logic is well understood, we can lower costs and/or increase revenue and margins. There are many other sources of information in books and on the web on cost control, manufacturing efficiency and selling and marketing. None of these things are easy to achieve in competitive markets, due to the existing intensity of competition.

If the net working asset investment is increasing we can consider reducing inventory relative to sales. Concepts originating in Japan such as just-in-time manufacture and business process engineering are relevant here. Improving financial control systems and monitoring and controlling inventory properly may help. We can also improve credit control and consider changing our trading model to generate cash faster from sales. Finally we can look at ways of taking more credit from suppliers.

If the net Capex is increasing, we can look at ways of getting more from our existing assets, do we work our machines 24 hours a day, seven days a week? Can we increase output by achieving better machine efficiencies?

If taxation is increasing, are there routes available to reduce the liability?

CONCLUSION FROM A MANAGER'S VIEWPOINT

Whatever actions are chosen the most important thing is probably to act early and act with sufficient initial vigour to have a materially positive impact on the cause of the cash flow shortfall. When examining the history of failed business all too often we can observe that managers failed to recognise that the problem they were facing was as severe as it turned out to be and that the actions they took to remedy this were too little and too late.

One of the biggest problems in making significant changes to any established business is that when changes are made there is usually a lead-time of some months before any positive effects can be observed. This is why early detection and response to any adverse trends is so important.

It is far better to overreact to a perceived threat and then scale back the actions taken later, than under react and find you are in even more trouble as time passes.

Forecasting cash flows can be a powerful technique to assist managers and analysts in understanding the likely future performance of the entity. This is covered in section two of the book.

12

Cash Versus Profit as a Measure of Performance

In order to put in context the quality of cash flow information compared to the P&L it is first necessary to understand something of the history of the P&L, the assumptions that underpin its use and the areas in accounts that are vulnerable to manipulation by those seeking to bias their reporting of performance. Finally, this is contrasted with the information about performance disclosed in the cash flows.

HISTORY OF THE P&L

For centuries, profit has been the accepted measure of success in business, a good business being one that is consistently and highly profitable. The concept of profit (as opposed to loss) being that the business received more in *income* than it spent on *costs* in a particular measurement period.

In a cash business (a business where all the income is received as cash and all the costs are paid for in cash at the time of purchase) the cash surplus and the profit is the same amount. In the sixteenth and seventeenth centuries this simple approach to performance measurement was probably adequate for most businesses. In the eighteenth century the industrial revolution bought new problems and opportunities, one major innovation was the pooling of capital by investors to undertake larger and larger projects. First the canals and then the railways were constructed, to facilitate the movement of both raw materials and finished goods. At the same time factories came into being to exploit the economies of scale created by mechanisation: originally water powered, subsequently steam powered. As energy markets developed in sophistication diesel fuel, gas and electricity subsequently took over as the energy source to power the plant and machinery in the factory.

These innovations, which resulted in the development of the accounting concept of depreciating assets, bought further complexity to the measurement of profit. In the last century other innovations such as pension funds, deferred taxes, ever more complex opportunities for provisioning and the accounting for financial instruments such as swaps, options and futures have made the identification of profit ever more technical and demanding.

In many ways the profit and loss account has been overwhelmed by the desire of regulators and rule setters to fairly state profit after allowing for all these additional complexities, in a particular period. It has moved the profit and loss account from being a straightforward two column summation of income and cost to being a dense multi column (sometimes as many as eight columns for two years numbers) table of figures disclosing values relating to continuing and discontinued operations, associates and joint ventures, reorganisation and restructuring and other matters outside the identification of profit from trading activities, such as the gain or loss on hedging activities.

SO, WHAT CAUSES THE DIVERGENCE BETWEEN PROFIT AND CASH FLOW?

There are a number of different factors at work. A good place to start is to understand the effect of the fundamental accounting concepts on the recognition of profit. The IASB summarises these in a document that is not a standard, it is entitled 'Framework for the Preparation and Presentation of Financial Statements'.

WHAT ARE FUNDAMENTAL ACCOUNTING CONCEPTS?

In order to reduce and summarise the operations of a business down to a few pieces of paper (the accounts) we need to make some rules and assumptions about how we proceed. These are known as fundamental accounting concepts.

Essentially we are seeking to summarise the transactions of the entity (there may be millions of these) down to something users can comprehend.

The fundamental accounting concepts can be summarised in the order they appear in the Framework as follows:

- Accrual basis
- Going concern
- Prudence
- Comparability

Other important ideas that affect profit recognition are:

- Materiality
- Substance over form
- Neutrality
- Completeness

The Framework also mentions other qualitative characteristics of financial statements:

- Understandability
- Relevance
- Reliability
- Faithful representation

Let us examine each one in turn and understand its effect on profit and cash flow recognition.

Accrual Basis

Financial statements disclose the actual sales achieved and costs incurred in a period rather than the cash paid or received in respect of the input or output. What this means, for a manufacturer for example, is we recognise the sales value of the goods despatched and the costs of the raw materials consumed and overheads incurred in achieving those sales in a particular measurement period. The cash received from customers or paid to employees and suppliers may occur some time before or after the income or cost is recognised. The idea is to report in monetary values what is actually physically occurring in a particular period. So, sales or turnover typically represents the physical goods despatched in a particular period.

In order to do this we need to adjust the transaction records at a particular period end to take account of accruals (and prepayments). We accrue for costs for which we have not yet recorded as a transaction. Examples are: goods received not yet invoiced by the supplier and expenses which are billed periodically such as telephone and energy bills. We also accrue for labour costs where we have not yet paid for the labour.

Certain expenses are paid for in advance; insurance is one example of this type of cost. Here the opposite happens to an accrual. We remove from the profit and loss account that part of the cost that is paid for in advance (which is the prepayment). Similarly, if customers have paid in advance for goods not yet delivered we don't show this as sales until the goods are despatched in a later period (this is known in accounts as deferred income).

As a consequence of this it should be clear that the value of cash received from customers in a particular period is not the same as the sales or turnover recognised in the same period. The same can be said for all cost and expense items.

Going Concern

This is the term used to identify the assumption made when we prepare financial statements that the business will continue to trade into the future indefinitely. This assumption allows us to avoid showing our assets and liabilities in the balance sheet at their realisable value at the date of the balance sheet (because we have no intention of selling them at this time).

Inventories are valued at the lower of cost or net realisable value, the assumption being that unless the inventory is impaired it will be sold for more than its original cost value later, however, we only show that profit when it is actually sold in a future period.

Likewise, fixed assets are carried in the balance sheet at their original cost less accumulated depreciation, this being a fair estimate of their value to the business given the assumption that we continue to use them in the future and as long as they remain productive.

Depreciation is another idea related to the going-concern concept. Depreciation is a concept introduced to spread the cost of fixed assets over their useful life evenly in the profit and loss account. This is achieved by transferring a proportion of the historic cost of an asset from fixed assets to the profit and loss account each period. The key point to grasp about depreciation is that it is non-cash. You do not write a cheque or make a payment to anybody in respect of depreciation. It is an internal accounting adjustment. The result is that the reported profit and loss does not leap about as it would if we showed fixed asset purchase as an overhead. The idea behind depreciation is that we should spread the cost of the asset in the P&L account over the number of years we expect to have the benefit of that asset. Depreciation is an invention designed to make the accounts more useful, it is inherently artificial.

Prudence (or Conservatism)

Financial statements do not deal with profit and loss in the same way. The prudence concept dictates that we should treat profit and loss differently. We should only recognise a profit when we have earned it; however, we recognise a loss as soon as we are aware of it, which may be years before the loss actually results in cash outflows. The treatment of profit and loss is thus asymmetric.

The recognition of profit or loss is largely driven by the accounting policies governing recognition of sale. IAS 18, which deals with this issue, says that we should recognise a sale when the business selling has transferred to the customer the significant risks and rewards of ownership of the goods. For example, this wording allows a retailer to recognise a sale when the goods are initially sold despite the possibility that the customer may have the option to return the goods within a given period for a full refund.

When we recognise a loss we normally make a provision for the expected future costs associated with the event causing the loss in the next arising financial statements. Inevitably, this is an estimate and is therefore vulnerable to manipulation by the preparers of accounts.

Comparability (or Consistency)

This is the assumption that the same accounting policies are used and applied consistently each period. In the 1960s, companies would change accounting policies each year so making the values disclosed not comparable with the previous period. This practice was controlled by allowing companies to change policies only if they improved the quality of financial reporting and by making companies restate all previous period data as if the new policy had applied throughout, so preserving consistency within one set of published accounts.

Materiality

Financial statements are only materially correct. The Framework defines information as material if its omission or misstatement would influence the economic decisions of users taken on the basis of the financial statements. This means if some element of the accounts is wrong but the error or difference is small it may not be adjusted for in the final financial statements.

Substance over Form

Financial statements should disclose the economic reality of the business rather than the strict legal form. A good example of this is the accounting treatment of financial leases. When a business buys an asset in a financial lease arrangement it is required to show the asset as if it were purchased at the start of the lease and show the amount outstanding as a debt item in the liabilities, even though in law the asset is still owned by the lessor.

This is because the business has the future economic benefits of the asset, indeed it may have to insure it, maintain it and protect it as well! Economically this arrangement is almost identical to ownership in terms of responsibilities and rewards.

The concept of substance over form allows the preparer of accounts to ignore the strict legal nature of a transaction where it may mislead the user regarding the true economic reality.

Neutrality

The Framework states that accounts should be free from bias. The reality is they are not. The main reason for bias is taxation. Generally businesses will seek to disclose a little profit as possible in order to minimise taxation liabilities, auditors are generally comfortable with this because they don't normally get sued when companies disclose less profit than they have actually made.

Where a business is listed on a stock exchange the opposite bias applies, the directors will be under considerable pressure to deliver constant improvements in sales and profits. If performance is inadequate it will be tempting to use whatever leeway is available within GAAP to improve the numbers.

So, in performing any analysis, it is prudent to assume there may be a bias until there is sufficient evidence to the contrary.

Completeness

The Framework explains that, to be reliable, accounts must be complete within the bounds of materiality and cost. An omission can cause information to be false or misleading and thus unreliable.

For this reason, rather than reading a set of financial statements from the beginning, I always turn initially to the section containing the audited accounts, which usually starts at somewhere in the middle of the report. Auditors make considerable efforts to ensure there is no material omission in the audited accounts. So, in this section I will find disclosure, usually in the notes, of all the bad news. The chairman's report and the operating and financial review at the beginning of the accounts do not form part of the audited accounts, so the usual way of dealing with bad news in this part of the accounts is to omit it! Generally these parts of the accounts are a bit like an advertisement; highlighting the things the business wants you to know about with glossy pictures and elegant graphs of the good news. Bad news is simply omitted, or, if already in the public domain as news, dealt with as a positive experience.

When the part of the accounts containing the real information is encountered, (the audited accounts) the information may be printed in a small font in grey ink on a light grey background, (I have observed this a number of times). Notes are laid out in a way that makes them as confusing as possible to decipher. Key subtotals may be omitted in the financial statements and the notes to avoid any negative values and make data appear superficially better than it is. In other words presentational tricks are used to make information difficult to decipher unless you are an expert.

Analysts and others who are seeking to understand the real performance of a business should initially concentrate their attention on the audited part of the annual report and accounts, this is where the most useful and significant disclosures are likely to be found.

CONCLUSIONS – FUNDAMENTAL ACCOUNTING CONCEPTS

The reason for explaining the fundamental accounting concepts is twofold, firstly it is surprising how many users of accounts, are unaware of some or all of these concepts, despite the fact that they are assumed by preparers and auditors of accounts to by fully familiar with both the ideas themselves and the implications of these ideas when it comes to misstatements in accounts. In other words, if we view the accounts as an artificial representation or model of the business, (which they are), these fundamental accounting concepts are the underlying assumptions which underpin the model.

Secondly, most forms of accounting abuse arise from either failing to report data in accordance with the spirit of the relevant concept, or by exploiting conflicts between the different concepts.

Accounting Abuse

Before continuing we need to understand what accounting abuse means. This is the term generally used to describe a practice of disclosure in accounts that is within GAAP, the law and any other regulations dealing with financial reporting, but results in disclosures in the accounts that are misleading for the user.

This is to distinguish accounting abuse from fraud and misrepresentation, which is lying in accounts or inventing the information or other data that is relied upon by others. In most legal jurisdictions this is a criminal (as opposed to civil) offence. Most major corporate collapses involve an element of fraud.

Table 12.1 shows many of the typical accounting abuses and techniques used to misrepresent data in the profit and loss account.

Table 12.2 shows many of the typical accounting abuses and techniques used to misrepresent data in the balance sheet.

Provisioning

It should now be evident that the main conduit for the manipulation of accounts is provisioning. The practice of provisioning comes about to recognise in one period the effects of actions or omissions in that period that will give rise to losses in future periods, provisions are necessary due to the impact on the accounts of the accruals and the prudence concept.

The problem for analysts and other users of accounts is that provisions are inherently subjective. The directors estimate what they believe the future cost might be, typically by reference to past experience, and estimate the provision required. Businesses that do not seek to manipulate their accounts usually apply some sort of guideline to this process, and, if in doubt will over-provide.

Businesses that seek to manipulate their accounts usually do so because the directors believe that external stakeholders, equity or debt providers will seek change in order to protect their exposure to the business. They use provisions to smooth their profit reporting, seeking to disclose profit when the underlying business is in fact loss making or insufficiently profitable.

Depreciation is also vulnerable to director subjectivity, because the amount charged for depreciation in respect of each asset is determined by estimating the useful life of the asset and its residual value and then writing off the difference using either the reducing balance or the straight-line method. No one actually knows the useful life of the asset or its residual value at that point in the future, so these values can also be biased should the directors wish to make them so.

Table 12.1   Abuses relevant to the Profit and Loss Account

Heading	Abuse	Concept incorrectly applied
Sales or turnover	Acceleration of recognition ahead of reality. Cut off manipulation, taking sales from one period into another Increase/decrease of bad debt reserve for reasons other than bad/doubtful debts	Prudence, consistency if there has been a change in recognition of sale
Cost of sales/other overheads	Inappropriate deferral of cost into later periods Cut off manipulation Inappropriate capitalisation of cost	Prudence, consistency if there has been a change in recognition of cost
Inventory	Increasing/decreasing provisions for, slow moving, obsolete and damaged inventory	Prudence, consistency
Operating provisions, such as warranty provisions, returns, guarantees	Increasing/decreasing provisions for profit/loss effect rather than because of commercial need	Prudence, consistency, accruals
Reorganisation and restructuring	Excessive provision taken, treated as exceptional, material and shown separately Provisions then used to move cost from profit and loss account in subsequent years so increasing reported profit	Consistency, accruals
Asset write down	Excessive write down used to reduce need for depreciation in future years	Consistency, accruals
Ownership level change of subsidiaries, associates, joint ventures, investments	Used to reduce eliminate need to consolidate losses, may not be an arms length arrangement	Substance over form

Table 12.2   Abuses relevant to the Balance Sheet

Heading	Abuse	Concept incorrectly applied
Fixed assets	Excessive write down to reduce depreciation in future years	Prudence, consistency
	Excessive revaluation upwards to improve leverage ratio	
	Overstated carrying values in recession conditions not subjected to impairment adjustment	
Depreciation	Under-depreciating	Prudence, consistency
Connected party debtors, related company trade or financing	Shown as asset when worthless	Prudence
Inventory	Overstated to create profit. Understated to reduce taxes	Prudence, consistency
Debtors	Recognised as a debtor despite being uncollectable	Prudence
Operating liabilities	Understatement/omission of known liabilities	Prudence
Provisions	Understated to preserve profits	Consistency
	Overstated to hide profits, defer profit to future period or reduce taxes	
Rents, operating leases, preference shares, pension deficits, off balance sheet debt	All these items are quasi-debt (like debt or interest on debt)	Substance over form

Cash Flow Versus Profit

The foregoing extended explanation of fundamental accounting concepts and accounting abuse was necessary in order to justify my next assertion.

> Cash flows are a more reliable indicator of performance than profits.

Why is this?

We have seen above that many of the problems with profit recognition stem from the complexity of the modern profit and loss account and the need for subjective estimates in order to satisfy the fundamental accounting concepts underlying the model of the business the financial statements represent. In contrast the cash flow statement seeks to represent the cash flowing through the business and no more, it shows where the cash was generated and where the cash was spent.

In doing so we remove or eliminate most of the accounting issues that cause the profit value to be vulnerable to accounting abuse. How does this happen?

In reporting the operating cash margin, we are seeking to report the cash received from customers for goods or services less the cash paid to suppliers, employees and others for inputs. Depreciation is added back (essentially eliminated). The profit or loss on disposal of fixed assets (essentially a depreciation adjustment on disposal) is added back. Provisions are added back (also eliminated). The only abuse that may continue to affect the operating cash margin is manipulation of the inventory value. However, this potential distortion is cancelled out by the change in inventory in line two of the template.

Rather than dealing with the value of fixed assets the cash flow statement only shows the money spent on new fixed assets (Capex) and the money received on selling old fixed assets (the proceeds of sale). The cash flow statement only shows the realised gains or losses on the disposal of investments in other businesses (investment, joint venture, associate or subsidiary) and financial instruments, it does not attempt to deal with unrealised gains and losses.

In other words, most of the abuses that are possible in the profit and loss account and balance sheet are not possible in the cash flow statement.

Statisticians talk in terms of data quality. What they are discussing is whether the data they are using to come up with a hypothesis about the data is good enough. There are many errors that can arise in data sets, measurement errors, variation in the frequency and range of the data measured, transposition errors, errors of omission, (counting what you see as opposed to what is actually there), loss of data, falsification of data, and so on. So, in terms of data quality:

The cash flow statement represents better data quality, because it is less vulnerable to bias due to estimation error.

In this case 'estimation error' means errors in the estimates underpinning the accounts, such as depreciation and provisioning.

CONCLUSION

When seeking to assess the performance of a business entity a summary of a businesses cash flows in Jury's Cash Flow Template format is probably a better place to start than the P&L. This is because reported cash flows are significantly less vulnerable to manipulation by those responsible for the preparation of accounts than reported profits or losses.

13

Cash Flow Analysis and Credit Risk

This chapter is focused on the needs of bankers, credit analysts and others involved in business or corporate lending and the management of credit exposures and credit risk.

Before reading this chapter it is assumed that the reader has read and digested the earlier chapters on summarising and evaluating cash flows in Jury's Cash Flow Template format.

WHAT IS CREDIT RISK?

Credit risk is usually defined as the probability of default. Default is the failure by one party to pay cash due to another party at the time specified by some contract between them.

The contract may be related to financing activities such as lending, leasing, factoring or invoice discounting. Lending encompasses the provision of short-, medium- and long-term loans, such as overdrafts, syndicated loans and mortgages, the issuance of bonds, debentures, commercial paper, medium-term loans, convertible bonds and all other forms of debt.

Alternatively, the contract may be related to some form of trade activity such as the supply of goods or services (trade credit) or the supply of higher value capital goods with some sort of deferred payment arrangement (vendor financing, leasing, hire purchase, project financings).

Thirdly the contract may relate to some form of investing activity, such as investments in derivative financial instruments such as swaps, options or any other asset where a counterparty pays (or receives) periodic variable payments to (from) the seller of the derivative.

For those readers less familiar with the workings of capital markets it should be clear from the wide variety of credit related activities summarised above that credit risk is a major issue for virtually every participant in financial markets. Credit risk is everywhere in business and in capital markets. It needs to be managed carefully to avoid losses due to non-payment of interest and or principle due from counterparties.

CASH VERSUS PROFITS

From a cash flow perspective a simple bank loan consists of:

1. A cash outflow to the customer at the commencement (the advance).
2. A series of variable or fixed, cash interest payments over the duration of the loan.
3. Repayment of the loan in cash instalments during the loan period or as a lump sum of cash at the end.

The first observation is that it is cash that repays outstanding interest and debt due, not profits. It would appear logical then to centre the credit risk analysis process on cash flows rather than the condition of the profit and loss account and balance sheet. Chapter 12 – Cash Flow Versus Profit deals in some detail with the issues affecting profit as a measure of performance.

Put simply, if the business runs out of cash it will be unable to honour its contracts to deliver cash to third parties as agreed. It is the cash flow that is primary rather than profits or the state of the balance sheet.

Having said this, should cash flow generation turn negative, the state of the balance sheet becomes highly relevant as it determines the window of opportunity available to restore the cash flow generation.

WHICH CASH FLOWS SHOULD WE BE INTERESTED IN?

The cash flow available to satisfy finance providers is *exactly* what it says it is. It represents the cash generated by the business that is *available* to satisfy lenders and other investors' needs. It does *not* mean that this money automatically gets paid to them.

Why is this a key value? Table 13.1 shows the cash flows of Dairy Crest plc, a milk processor and dairy product producer, which we looked at in the Chapter 6 covering the analysis of mature business cash flows.

In examining the template we notice that the first four values represent the following. The operating cash margin represents the cash generated from trading by the business. The amount invested or generated from net working assets represents the need of the business to invest each period in its net working assets, the net Capex represents the need of the business to invest each period in its fixed assets. Finally the business is obliged by law to pay the taxes due to the government on a regular periodic basis.

In the long run, all these payments are essential if the business is going to sustain itself into the future. The business can always defer some or all of these expenditures temporarily, however, this does not eliminate the need to make the expenditure later. So, in the long run, the cash available to satisfy finance providers is essentially the cash available for debt service.

Table 13.1   Six years cash flows of Dairy Crest

DAIRY CREST PLC
TEMPLATE SUMMARY CASH FLOWS
Six years to 31ˢᵗ March 20X7

	20X7 £m	20X6 £m	20X5 £m	20X4 £m	20X3 £m	20X2 £m
Operating cash margin	97.0	89.7	122.4	126.4	111.0	100.6
Change in NWA	−2.8	−16.3	20.6	10.2	−6.1	−52.1
Net Capex	−26.6	−34.6	−29.5	−29.7	−27.0	−52.3
Cash taxes	−6.1	−15.5	−12.6	−8.7	−4.1	−5.3
CASH FLOW AVAILABLE TO SATISFY CAPITAL PROVIDERS	**61.5**	**23.3**	**100.9**	**98.2**	**73.8**	**−9.1**
Net interest	−15.3	−16.4	−17.7	−20.6	−22.0	−18.7
Net dividends	−18.8	−16.6	−23.9	−19.9	−17.4	−15.9
Other	−235.0	−43.7	−9.7	6.6	−93.4	1.1
NET CASH INFLOW/(OUTFLOW)	**−207.6**	**−53.4**	**49.6**	**64.3**	**−59.0**	**−42.6**
Inc/(Dec) in equity	39.7	0.7	3.6	0.2	1.0	4.4
Inc/(Dec) in debt	178.4	39.9	−42.6	−57.7	65.2	35.9
(Inc)/Dec in cash	−10.5	12.8	−10.6	−6.8	−7.2	2.3
FINANCING CASH FLOW	**207.6**	**53.4**	**−49.6**	**−64.3**	**59.0**	**42.6**

Why do I say this when dividends are also shown after interest in the template? When a business is operating normally both interest service and dividend payment takes place because the business has generated sufficient cash for it to do so. Should there be problems with cash generation debt normally has priority over equity in any situation where there is a conflict. If a business defaults on any payment due to the lender the provisions of a typical contract between the lender and the customer usually give the lender some control over the business, directly or indirectly. In other words, in most situations where there is a conflict over which finance provider gets cash, lenders have priority over equity providers. To put this another way, the equity providers are usually last in the queue. They can take cash out of the business (as dividends or equity redemption) only after all the other stakeholders are satisfied.

So, to evaluate the historic performance of a business in generating sufficient cash to satisfy its debt obligations we can restate the cash flows as shown in Table 13.2.

In the lines below the *cash available to satisfy finance providers* total we see the interest and dividends deducted to arrive at a new total, which represents the cash flow available for debt repayment.

Table 13.2   Six years restated cash flows of Dairy Crest

DAIRY CREST PLC
TEMPLATE SUMMARY CASH FLOWS – DEBT SERVICE AVAILABILITY
Six years to 31st March 20X7

	20X7 £m	20X6 £m	20X5 £m	20X4 £m	20X3 £m	20X2 £m
Operating cash margin	97.0	89.7	122.4	126.4	111.0	100.6
Change in NWA	−2.8	−16.3	20.6	10.2	−6.1	−52.1
Net Capex	−26.6	−34.6	−29.5	−29.7	−27.0	−52.3
Cash taxes	−6.1	−15.5	−12.6	−8.7	−4.1	−5.3
CASH FLOW AVAILABLE TO SATISFY CAPITAL PROVIDERS	**61.5**	**23.3**	**100.9**	**98.2**	**73.8**	**−9.1**
Net interest	−15.3	−16.4	−17.7	−20.6	−22.0	−18.7
Net dividends	−18.8	−16.6	−23.9	−19.9	−17.4	−15.9
CASH FLOW AVAILABLE FOR DEBT REPAYMENT	**27.4**	**−9.7**	**59.3**	**57.7**	**34.4**	**−43.7**

WHY INCLUDE THE DIVIDEND?

For most public companies servicing the dividend is as important to the directors as paying interest. This is because any reduction or elimination of dividend payments will result in a substantial fall in the quoted price of the company's equity. This of course is only the case for public companies. Dairy Crest falls into this category, therefore we leave the dividends in the revised template.

Private businesses can do as they wish with the dividend. Indeed, to understand how to treat different types of business, we need to segment our types of business some more before we properly understand the implications of both size and public versus private company status. We will do this later in this chapter. However, for the moment, let us carry on examining Table 13.2. Let us just say at this point that it is up to the user whether to include dividends or not when making the analysis of debt service capability.

The final step in the exercise is to compare the amount of cash available for debt repayment with the total amount of net debt in the business. It is convenient to express the resulting values as a ratio as follows.

$$\frac{\text{Total Net debt}}{\text{Cash available for debt repayment}} = \begin{array}{l}\text{The number of years to repay debt} \\ \text{assuming no change in the business}\end{array}$$

This value is useful because it can be compared across a sample of both healthy and failed companies to come up with some typical values. The values noted below can be used as a starting point for consideration.

No of years to repay	What it means
0–6	Typical range for healthy mature companies
6–10	Leverage high, cash flow fully utilised
10+	Too much debt, business disposals and/or restructuring may be required to reduce debt in the near future.

Table 13.3 shows the Dairy Crest example with the above calculation completed.

In 20X2 and 20X6 the cost of interest and dividend service exceeds the cash flow available to satisfy finance providers. In these years Dairy Crest is either borrowing or spending surplus cash or both to finance the difference. In 20X2 the problem was caused by the increase in the investment in net working assets. In 20X6 the problem was a significant reduction in the operating cash margin compared to the previous year and the effect of some acquisition activity.

Table 13.3   Six years further restated cash flows of Dairy Crest

DAIRY CREST PLC
TEMPLATE SUMMARY NO GROWTH CASH FLOWS – DEBT SERVICE
YEARS TO REPAY
Six years to 31ˢᵗ March 20X7

	20X7 £m	20X6 £m	20X5 £m	20X4 £m	20X3 £m	20X2 £m
Operating cash margin	97.0	89.7	122.4	126.4	111.0	100.6
Change in NWA	−2.8	−16.3	20.6	10.2	−6.1	−52.1
Net Capex	−26.6	−34.6	−29.5	−29.7	−27.0	−52.3
Cash taxes	−6.1	−15.5	−12.6	−8.7	−4.1	−5.3
CASH FLOW AVAILABLE TO SATISFY CAPITAL PROVIDERS	**61.5**	**23.3**	**100.9**	**98.2**	**73.8**	**−9.1**
Net interest	−15.3	−16.4	−17.7	−20.6	−22.0	−18.7
Net dividends	−18.8	−16.6	−23.9	−19.9	−17.4	−15.9
CASH FLOW AVAILABLE FOR DEBT REPAYMENT	**27.4**	**−9.7**	**59.3**	**57.7**	**34.4**	**−43.7**
TOTAL NET(DEBT)/CASH	**−444.9**	**−280.5**	**−227.5**	**−279.7**	**−345.2**	**−284.9**
NUMBER OF YEARS TO REPAY	**16.2**	**never**	**3.8**	**4.8**	**10.0**	**never**

In 20X3 and 20X7 the measure, *number of years to repay* is 10 years or above. The reason for the increase in both years is that the group has made significant acquisitions using debt to finance them. When this situation is observed the area of doubt is whether the operating cash margin will rise sufficiently as a result of the acquisition to offset the negative effect of the extra debt taken on to finance the acquisition. After the acquisition in 20X3 the operating cash margin did increase, leverage appeared sensible in 20X4 and 20X5 as a result. Whether the same behaviour will be seen in 20X8 depends on the nature of the business acquired and management's ability to successfully integrate it into the group.

The final check we can make is to do the same analysis as above but restating the cash flows on a no-growth basis. This concept has already been explained more fully in Chapter 8, Growth and Mature – Further Analysis Issues. The reason we are doing this is to remove any distortions caused by the fixed asset investment pattern. The idea is that we substitute the value charged as depreciation this value being a proxy (or estimate) for the replacement (or maintenance) Capex requirement of the business for the actual Capex.

This restatement of the cash flows (Table 13.4) reveals that the actual Capex of Dairy Crest has been below depreciation for the last five years. In some industries this could imply underinvestment in fixed assets, a strategy which eventually

Table 13.4   Six years restated no-growth cash flows of Dairy Crest

DAIRY CREST PLC
TEMPLATE SUMMARY NO GROWTH CASH FLOWS – DEBT SERVICE
YEARS TO REPAY
Six years to 31st March 20X7

	20X7 £m	20X6 £m	20X5 £m	20X4 £m	20X3 £m	20X2 £m
Operating cash margin	97.0	89.7	122.4	126.4	111.0	100.6
Change in NWA	−2.8	−16.3	20.6	10.2	−6.1	−52.1
No-growth maintenance capex	−40.6	−38.3	−34.4	−36	−35.8	−37
Cash taxes	−6.1	−15.5	−12.6	−8.7	−4.1	−5.3
CASH FLOW AVAILABLE TO SATISFY CAPITAL PROVIDERS	**47.5**	**19.6**	**96.0**	**91.9**	**65.0**	**6.2**
Net interest	−15.3	−16.4	−17.7	−20.6	−22.0	−18.7
Net dividends	−18.8	−16.6	−23.9	−19.9	−17.4	−15.9
CASH FLOW AVAILABLE FOR DEBT REPAYMENT	**13.4**	**−13.4**	**54.4**	**51.4**	**25.6**	**−28.4**
TOTAL NET(DEBT)/CASH	**−444.9**	**−280.5**	**−227.5**	**−279.7**	**−345.2**	**−284.9**
NUMBER OF YEARS TO REPAY	**33.2**	**never**	**4.2**	**5.4**	**13.5**	**never**

results in a loss of cost effectiveness relative to more technologically advanced and capital intensive competitors. However, in the food processing industries this is quite common to observe, it is probably due to the very homogeneous nature of the products produced and the maturity of the technology in the plant and machinery used in processing. There are also cash inflows from the disposal of fixed assets as the processing and distribution of the product becomes more centralised and streamlined. Put simply, capital investment needs appear to be lower than in markets where there is more product and technology change. So, in reality, the leverage issues identified in the first actual cash flow debt service years to repay example (Table 13.3), could be worse as the underinvestment in fixed assets cannot continue indefinitely.

Dairy Crest is a good example of the effectiveness of this technique for examining the ability of a business to support its leverage. Using the template the analyst is able to avoid being bogged down in the overwhelming amount of data disclosed in a typical annual report and concentrate on exactly the cash flow values that matter. To further demonstrate the power of this technique let us look at some other examples.

BRITISH TELECOM AND 3G LICENCES

Table 13.5 shows the cash flows of BT plc, the UK's largest telecom business from 1999 to 2001. In the year 2000, BT acquired UK licence number three in the 3G auctions, bidding £4003 million for it. BT also went on to acquire control of Viag Intercom who had bid £5164 million for a licence in Germany. BT also spent about £13 billion on other acquisitions designed to position the group as a major contender in the 3G mobile market.

The restated no-growth cash flows in the table show what the cash flows of BT would look like in 2001 if it had not bid for the 3G licences, (some of the price paid being part of Capex). In other words, we are looking at what BT would look like, with no new growth investment in Capex in the three years. This reveals that, by the end of 2001, it would take 1164 years to repay debt from the cash flow of the existing business! The only way this debt could be reduced on a sensible timescale was by breaking up the group. Over the next few years BT sold its Yellow Pages business (now called Yell) and its mobile phone business (now known as mmO$_2$) to reduce the debt back to manageable levels.

Table 13.5   Three years cash flow data for BT Group

BT Group
TEMPLATE SUMMARY ACTUAL CASH FLOWS

	2001 £m	2000 £m	1999 £m
Cash generated from operations	6193	6095	6067
(Invested in)/Generated from Net Working Assets	−296	−241	−30
Net Capital expenditure	−8524	−3425	−3077
Taxation paid in period	−669	−1311	−630
Cash available to satisfy capital providers (CATS Fin Pro)	**−3296**	**1118**	**2330**
Net Interest	−727	−163	−328
Net Dividends	−1432	−1364	−1186
Other non-operating income/(expenditure)	−13 672	−6732	2156
Net cash generated/(absorbed) before financing	**−19 127**	**−7141**	**2972**
Financing:			
Increase/(Decrease) in equity	185	559	174
Increase/(Decrease) in debt	19 550	5400	−632
(Increase)/Decrease in cash	−608	1182	−2514
Total change in financing	**19 127**	**7141**	**−2972**

BT Group
TEMPLATE SUMMARY NO-GROWTH CASH FLOWS – DEBT SERVICE YEARS TO REPAY

	2001 £m	2000 £m	1999 £m
Cash generated from operations	6193	6095	6067
(Invested in)/Generated from Net Working Assets	−296	−241	−30
Depreciation (maintenance capex proxy)	−3045	−2752	−2581
Taxation paid in period	−669	−1311	−630
Cash available to satisfy capital providers on a no growth basis (CATS Fin Pro on a no-growth)	**2183**	**1791**	**2826**
Net Interest	−727	−163	−328
Net Dividends	−1432	−1364	−1186
Cash available for debt service	**24**	**264**	**1312**
Total net debt of BT	**−27 942**	**−8700**	**−953**
YEARS TO REPAY	**1164.3**	**33.0**	**0.7**

CONCLUSIONS ABOUT THIS STYLE OF ANALYSIS

Using Jury's Template as a primary tool for credit risk evaluation offers a number of advantages to the credit analyst.

1. It shows the actual cash available for interest service and debt repayment, a value that does not appear anywhere in a published cash flow statement.
2. It points to the reasons for any shortfall, for example it could be reduction in the operating cash margin, or a significant increase in the amount invested in net working assets. This can then be researched further if necessary, in order to properly understand what has occurred.
3. If the cash flows are summarised into the template on a multi year basis, as shown in many of the examples in this book, it conveys an impression of the historic effects of both economic and sector cycles on the business, and the degree of variability in the cash flows of the business itself.

INTEREST, DIVIDENDS AND DEBT REPAYMENT – THE IMPLICATIONS OF SIZE

It is common to see the credit functions within large lending institutions segment the corporate market into three categories, these are:

1. Large/major corporates.
2. Medium-sized/mid corporates.
3. Other smaller businesses.

This segmentation is also of assistance in understanding how to use the debt service, years to repay restatement of the template.

Large Corporates

Large corporates can be defined as businesses that don't need banks for borrowing purposes! If they wish, they can raise debt directly from investors, by issuing commercial paper, medium-term notes or corporate bonds. This doesn't mean they don't borrow from banks, indeed, they are often huge borrowers from banks, it means that, unlike smaller businesses, they are not restricted to banks alone as the source of debt finance. This means that businesses of this size are largely insulated from issues to do with the availability (or lack of) bank lending.

Typically they are very large businesses such as oil and mineral extraction companies, consumer goods producers, and large industrial groups. Essentially, many of these businesses carry *permanent* debt. Depending on the groups' view as to what leverage is appropriate, they will finance a certain percentage of their

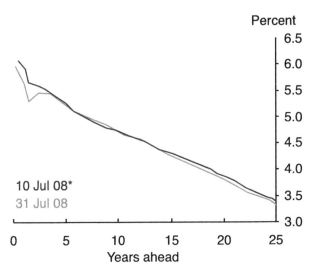

Figure 13.1   UK instantaneous commercial bank liability forward curve

balance sheet with debt permanently. The debt itself may short-, medium- or long-term debt. Whether they borrow short or long depends on the state of the interest rate yield curve. Generally they will seek to source debt as cheaply as possible, changing the structure of their debt portfolio as the yield curve changes. Whether the debt is short or long when it is due for repayment it is simply replaced with new debt. Figure 13.1 shows an example of a yield curve published by the Bank of England whose components consist of commercial debt priced mainly off LIBOR.

It should be clear from Figure 13.1 that, in July 2008, it was a lot cheaper to borrow money at a 15 to 20 year duration than it was to borrow short-term.

So, to summarise, large corporates generally have permanent debt. They do not repay as such, rather rolling over debt that is due into some new form of debt.

This means they generally only need to have sufficient cash available to satisfy finance providers to service interest and dividends. Remember for large corporates the dividend is as important to the directors as interest, any reduction or failure to pay dividends would have an immediate adverse effect on the share price of the quoted equity. As we saw when discussing what happens to large, mature businesses when they fail to generates sufficient cash, if businesses of this size run into cash flow problems they will usually borrow in the early stages rather than cut or eliminate the dividend.

Unless their leverage has increased beyond what could be considered normal they don't actually make repayment as such, when debt is due for repayment they simply roll it over into a new debt instrument. The exception to this is when they make a large acquisition or other investment which takes their debt above what would be considered normal leverage for a business of this type, then the business will need sufficient cash flows to reduce the debt, in addition to achieving interest and dividend service.

Smaller Businesses

These businesses are usually private companies, they may also be public companies listed on junior stock markets around the world. Unless they are very large, most private companies seeking debt finance must obtain it from commercial banks in the form of overdraft facilities, factoring, leasing, loans, mortgages, and so on. From a credit risk analysis perspective, the key difference between small and large corporates is that they may not be able to roll over debt whenever they wish if the supply of credit is restricted or liquidity has disappeared from the lending market, a scenario that arises quite regularly, usually due to economic recession. This means they must be able to make both interest and repayment of principal as required, even when the cash flows are stressed. For smaller businesses repayment of principle is compulsory, rather than optional, even in a recession, if they wish to avoid bankruptcy. Conversely, smaller companies rarely need to pay dividends if they do not wish to do so. For them, the dividend is optional. This means they only need to have sufficient cash available to satisfy finance providers to service interest and debt principal repayment due.

Medium-Sized Corporates

Mid corporates are larger private companies and smaller public companies. Mid corporates are in the worst situation, they are also obliged to raise most if not all of their finance from commercial banks. This means they are in the same position as smaller private companies when it comes to debt repayment. If they are listed they may also need to regard their dividend payments as obligatory, or risk a substantial fall in stock price. This means they need to have sufficient cash available to satisfy finance providers to service interest, dividends and debt principal repayment.

COVENANTING AND CASH FLOWS

For centuries it has been usual practice for lenders to restrict the use to which money lent to borrowers is put using a variety of methods. This represents a form of risk reduction for the lender. A good example of this is acquiring property using a mortgage. The borrower of a mortgage typically never actually has possession of the money they have borrowed. The advance typically going, via a lawyer or notary, directly to the seller of the property concerned at the time the borrower acquires it. This practice occurs because the provider of funds does not wish to allow the borrower the opportunity to use the funds for any other purpose. It is a restriction on the use of the funds, designed to avoid the risk of misappropriation.

Covenants are another form of restriction negotiated between the lender and the borrower. They are legally binding undertakings to do, or not do certain things whilst the loan remains outstanding. Amongst other things, they usually restrict the rights of the managers of the business to do things that reduce the resources available to service and repay the loan. Restrictions on things such as dividends, employee loans, Capex, asset disposals, acquisitions, share repurchase, bonuses and new debt are typical.

When a borrower breaches a covenant this typically gives the lender the right to demand immediate repayment of all outstanding debt. Usually the borrower will not be able to do this (as they cannot easily replace the debt when their business is deteriorating), and they cannot immediately repay it from cash flow. So the economic effect of such a covenant is to transfer control of the business to the borrower who can then demand whatever outcome they prefer (change of management, restructuring, disposal of the business or bankruptcy).

Financial covenants are one type of covenant. They typically place a limit on the relationship between two values taken from the published financial information of the borrower. Typically, financial covenants seek to define that the borrower maintains, throughout the period of the loan:

1. A certain minimum net worth in the business.
2. A minimum working capital in the business.
3. A limit on the total leverage of the business.
4. A minimum interest cover.
5. A minimum debt service cover.

Research into the precise covenants adopted by individual lenders reveals a wide variation in the minutiae of defining the covenant. They are often described in loan documentation in terms of balance sheet and profit and loss account values. The first two financial covenants above are typically defined by reference to values taken from the balance sheets. As this book is about cash flow, I only wish to examine and comment on those matters within covenanting that are related to cash flows. Generally, this is the last three items above.

Leverage Covenants

Generally, leverage covenants are also couched in terms of balance sheet values such as debt to net worth or tangible net worth. Sometimes leverage covenants are related to cash flow proxies such as debt to EBITDA. The use of EBITDA in this way requires significant further examination and explanation.

Traditionally, EBITDA had no profile as a measure of anything until the 1980s. Two things brought EBITDA to prominence, the emergence of the leveraged buyout and the dot-com boom.

EBITDA and the Leveraged Buyout

Due to the massive leverage typically mobilised in a leveraged buyout the business may have little or no positive equity and no profits after interest service, accordingly leverage ratios based on traditional approaches are of little use. Lenders, looking for an alternative, which would be meaningful when lending 100% debt to a business entity, identified EBITDA as a value against which they thought they could meaningfully covenant.

EBITDA and the dot-com Boom

The dot.com boom spawned many new technology businesses, typically focused around the emergence of the internet, who had no meaningful earnings in their formative phase. In the terms I offered earlier in Chapter 9 they represented 'Start-up Projects'. Net income, earnings after tax, earnings before tax and earning before interest and tax and EBITDA were all negative. EBITDA was seen as the first earnings value that went positive when a business approached cash break-even. EBITDA was then seized upon as a proxy for value creation by those venture capitalists who were buying and selling these businesses, who then used EBITDA multiples as a way of expressing their view of the value of an entity. This method of deriving a value becoming common despite the fact these business were typically still loss making start-up projects who had not yet established they had a viable business to exploit. When the dot-com bubble collapsed it became clear that most would never achieve viability.

Thirdly, lenders, and to a certain extent their lawyers, are traditionally conservative. They have traditionally expressed covenants in terms of balance sheet and profit and loss account values, even when they are seeking to apply a covenant in terms of cash flow. As I said earlier, EBITDA is seen as a cash flow proxy. It is seen as a substitute, derived from the P&L, for the OPERATING CASH MARGIN value from Jury's Template. In a published cash flow statement the equivalent value is assumed to be the cash from operations value (excluding interest and taxes) before working asset investment. Typically the value of EBITDA will be similar to the OPERATING CASH MARGIN, however, *they are not the same*! A review of a published cash flow statement reveals many other items that are added back to EBIT in addition to depreciation and amortisation in order to arrive at the OPERATING CASH MARGIN. These items have been covered in detail in the earlier chapters of this book.

I have explained earlier that debt is serviced and repaid from cash flows, not profit. It follows that covenants should ideally follow this logic, and be defined in cash flow terms. By defining covenants in EBITDA terms the covenant may fail to achieve the intended outcome.

By covenanting the relationship between total debt and the OPERATING CASH MARGIN, we are essentially creating another form of debt service covenant; it is labelled as a leverage covenant because one of the elements is total debt or net debt. However, it triggers more like a debt service covenant.

Interest Service Covenants

Before we had cash flow statements in accounts, the traditional way of covenanting interest service was the interest cover ratio. This was the relationship between operating profit (EBIT) and the interest payable, expressed as a multiple of the interest payable. For example the interest cover ratio might be set at 3.5 times. This means that the EBIT should never be less than 3.5 times the interest payable in a particular period.

Following the development of cash flow statements it was common to see two kinds of interest cover ratios in loan documents. The first one is to covenant OPERATING CASH MARGIN to interest paid as a multiple. This is the cash flow equivalent of the P&L derived interest cover ratio.

The second is to covenant the CASH AVAILABLE TO SATISFY FINANCE PROVIDERS value from the template as a multiple of interest paid/(due) in a period. As should be clear from previous chapters this value does represent the cash available for debt service, so this is probably the most meaningful value against which to covenant.

Debt Service Covenants

Debt service covenants are similar to interest service covenants; the only difference is that, instead of covenanting a multiple of interest service, we also bring in any principal repayment due. So, the relationship covenanted as a multiple is the relationship between OPERATING CASH MARGIN or the CASH AVAILABLE TO SATISFY FINANCE PROVIDERS and the sum of interest service and principal debt repayment due in the period.

CONCLUSION

Debt is serviced and repaid from cash flow, not profit. It follows that lenders and credit functions should be cash flow centric rather than P&L centric in performing analysis of the creditworthiness of existing and potential borrowers, and other counterparties.

14

Cash Flow Analysis and Performance Measurement

This part of the book is intended for entrepreneurs, managers, investors and others who are interested in using cash flow information to assess or monitor the viability, health or performance of a business.

Before reading this chapter it is assumed that the reader has read and digested most of the earlier chapters on summarising and evaluating cash flows in Jury's Cash Flow Template format.

HOW CAN WE USE CASH FLOW INFORMATION?

Those who are interested in analysing business performance can use the data contained within Jury's Cash Flow Template in a variety of ways.

When buying or valuing a business we can think of the valuation as being in two parts.

1. The value of the present (largely derived from the existing surplus cash flow generated).
2. The value of the future, which can be considered as the present value of the potential growth of the future surplus cash flows of the business.

The template provides an elegant way of summarising the existing performance of the business. A review of the historic cash flow patterns in the template will reveal the extent and cyclicality of the ability of a business to generate cash surpluses for investors. I recommend that analysts prepare a spreadsheet with sufficient history in it to see the business through a full economic cycle. Given the recent pattern of global economic behavior it may be appropriate to go back up to twelve years in order to achieve this.

Analysis of the historic cash flow performance will also reveal the past relationships between growth and investment in working assets and fixed assets, so acting as a reasonableness check on any assumptions made about future performance.

The second issue all business controllers face is the need to monitor and control the businesses in which they are interested. Again, the cash flow template can be used as a primary indicator of performance. As a controller I should be able to target a particular level of operating cash margin, usually from some sort of budgetary, planning or forecasting process. This in turn will imply a given level of working asset investment, and capital investment. All these values can then be forecasted and targeted.

This target can then be used to compare with weekly, monthly or quarterly performance. Each major component of the template can be broken down as required to reveal more information about performance as required.

The other benefit of using the template as a primary reporting tool is that managers become more aware of the cash flow implications of changes in the way the business operates. For example, step changes in volume output of the business will have working asset and possibly capex effects, which are, to a certain extent, predictable.

WHAT IS SUCCESS IN BUSINESS?

In order to identify what cash flow measures we are going to seek to focus on we need to discuss what constitutes success in business. We are seeking to identify concise, elegant measures that can be used for performance assessment.

In the earlier chapters I briefly discussed what success is – firstly discounting profits or growth as measures on their own because they fail to take account of the amount of capital expended to get the particular level of profits or growth achieved.

I also indicated that the current thinking was that the best measure of success is to look at the increase in the value of a business period on period. Unfortunately, the value of a business is not only influenced by its ability to generate cash surpluses both now and in the future, but also by external factors such as economic conditions, the availability of finance, fashion trends in investment and technological and social change.

So, we need to try to identify a measure that we can use which is generated from the internal data available in a business. Of all the possible ratios to consider, the most appropriate is probably return on investment. What do we mean by this?

Investment is the cash invested in the business; return is the excess cash generated over the economic cost of the cash invested in the business. Applying even this apparently simple measure is not straightforward because the cost of equity is difficult to estimate with any reliability. It is generally assumed to be higher than the cost of debt, because the future expected returns from the equity are assumed to be more risky than the returns to debt.

Technically we should be using both the opportunity cost of debt and the opportunity cost of equity in arriving at the cost of capital. The concept is as follows: as an investor in, or owner of, a business I expect to receive on my investment a return at least as good as I could get investing in other investments of similar risk. Analysts generally use historic returns data from stock markets to estimate what these values might be for debt and for equity and combine them into a single percentage expected return estimate which is typically known as the *weighted average cost of capital.*

This value is specific to the business to which it relates because it contains various assumptions unique to that business. These are: an assumption about the long term leverage of the business; an assumption of the extra return required on all equity relative to debt; and an adjustment for the relative riskiness of the particular sector in which the business operates relative to the overall market. Once we have identified this value we can apply it to the amount invested in the business to come up with the expected periodic cash generation required to compensate investors. This can then be compared with the actual Cash Available to Satisfy Finance Providers total as a value and a percentage.

CASH FLOWS AND INVESTMENT

Investors are another class of stakeholder who may see benefits from understanding the cash flows of businesses they invest in. Investors in quoted equity face many problems. The easiest way to comprehend this is to use the concept of the perfect investment.

What is the Perfect Investment?

A little thought should yield the following insights. The perfect investment would yield massive returns, be growing strongly and have negligible business risk! This is essentially the holy grail of investing.

Whilst, occasionally, companies appear that fit this profile for a period, they are the rare exception rather than the norm. Generally companies cannot be all three things at the same time. If a company is growing strongly and yielding good returns it is probably in a growth market where there are significant business risks to do with technology, adoption and competitor behaviour. Companies facing negligible business risk are usually in mature, low margin sectors such as utilities and food retail.

Going back to our perfect investment we could also add that the investor ideally wants to identify such an investment in five minutes! Investors have further problems to do with the overwhelming amount of information they have to interface with in order to pick a share, in the form of regulatory announcements and filings, annual and periodic reports, prospectuses, news, databases, analysts recommendations, comparative analysis and so on.

As a consequence they seek shortcuts. They seek to identify measures of performance that appear simple and are convenient to use. Examples of this are measures such as Earnings per Share and Dividend Yield, both of these being derived from the profit and loss account.

They also need to consider the affordability of a share or stock. Is too expensive or cheap, given the existing and future prospects of the business? Investors use measures such as the Price Earnings ratio (PE ratio) and Tobin's Q ratio (which seeks to capture the relationship between the market value of a business and the replacement value of the same business, which is assumed to be similar to the book value).

All of these measures are vulnerable to manipulation or abuse. This was explained in detail in Chapter 12 – Cash versus Profit. Cash flow data compared to the number of shares and share price may represent better, less biased, indicators of current performance and the relative affordability of a share.

For example, from an investor viewpoint, the two most important values from the template are probably the OPERATING CASH MARGIN and the CASH AVAILABLE TO SATISFY FINANCE PROVIDERS values. Why is this?

The OPERATING CASH MARGIN is the cash generated from going round the working asset cycle. It represents the difference between the cash costs of producing the product or service and the resulting cash revenue when it is sold. It is the reason the business exists. In a successful mature business it pays for all the necessary cash outflows below it in the template. Loosely it can be considered to be the cash flow equivalent of operating profit (EBIT). It is the most important number in the template because, in the long run, it pays for everything else. In other words, the perfect business (or investment) is one that generates massive (and ideally, growing) OPERATING CASH MARGIN.

The CASH AVAILABLE TO SATISFY FINANCE PROVIDERS is also important because it represents the residual cash flow available to reward investors. As I mentioned earlier this doesn't mean that investors actually receive any or all of it.

As a measure it is similar to Earnings per share in nature, which identifies the value of the earnings after tax, minority share interests and preference share dividends attributable to each ordinary share in the business. This doesn't signify that the shareholder receives their earnings per share as, for example, a dividend. Earnings per share represents how much of the earnings of the business each share notionally 'owns'.

The CASH AVAILABLE TO SATISFY FINANCE PROVIDERS is similar in concept to another term used by analysts, the enterprise cash flow. This means the cash flow generated by the enterprise, before we consider how this is split between the debt and equity investors. Bear in mind that the enterprise cash flow is the cash flow of the entity when debt free. This is important because, as interest is tax deductible, the taxation actually paid by the business varies depending on the amount of debt carried by the entity. So, the CASH AVAILABLE TO SATISFY FINANCE PROVIDERS is not the same as the enterprise cash flow.

Both of these values can be compared with the capital invested in the business, the market capitalisation of the equity and the total debt outstanding, or be

Table 14.1 Six years of cash flow based returns data for Nokia

Nokia TEMPLATE SUMMARY CASH FLOWS Years to 31st December	20X8 €m	20X7 €m	20X6 €m	20X5 €m	20X4 €m	20X3 €m
Operating cash margin	7457	8474	6163	5390	5193	6545
Change in NWA	−2546	605	−793	−366	299	−194
Net Capex	−966	−800	−748	−593	−643	−631
Cash taxes	−1780	−1457	−1163	−1254	−1368	−1440
CASH FLOW AVAILABLE TO SATISFY CAPITAL PROVIDERS	**2165**	**6822**	**3459**	**3177**	**3481**	**4280**
Net interest	66	260	271	374	219	341
Net dividends	−2042	−1748	−1553	−1530	−1391	−1354
CASH FLOW AVAILABLE AFTER INTEREST AND DIVIDENDS	**189**	**5334**	**2177**	**2021**	**2309**	**3267**
Debt	none	none	none	none	none	none
Equity invested (Share cap & share premium)	3994	4189	2953	2724	2552	2560
Number of shares at the year-end millions	3697	3846	3966	4172	4593	4761
Share price on or near 31st Dec in euros	11.5	26.42	15.51	15.45	11.4	13.75
Market capitalisation (millions)	42 516	101 611	61 513	64 457	52 360	65 464
Cash flow return on capital invested (CATS Fin Pro/Equity Invested %)	54%	163%	117%	117%	136%	167%
Cash flow return on market capital invested (CATS Fin Pro/Mkt Cap %)	5%	7%	6%	5%	7%	7%

Table 14.2 Six years of cash flow based returns data for Dairy Crest

DAIRY CREST PLC TEMPLATE SUMMARY CASH FLOWS	20X8 £m	20X7 £m	20X6 £m	20X5 £m	20X4 £m	20X3 £m
Operating cash margin	115.8	97	89.7	122.4	126.4	111
Change in NWA	−7.4	−2.8	−16.3	20.6	10.2	−6.1
Net Capex	−20.8	−26.6	−34.6	−29.5	−29.7	−27
Cash taxes	−6.7	−6.1	−15.5	−12.6	−8.7	−4.1
CASH FLOW AVAILABLE TO SATISFY CAPITAL PROVIDERS (CATS Fin Pro)	**80.9**	**61.5**	**23.3**	**100.9**	**98.2**	**73.8**
Net interest	−30.7	−15.3	−16.4	−17.7	−20.6	−22
Net dividends	−23.5	−18.8	−16.6	−23.9	−19.9	−17.4
CASH FLOW AVAILABLE AFTER INTEREST AND DIVIDENDS	**26.7**	**27.4**	**−9.7**	**59.3**	**57.7**	**34.4**
Net debt	**474.8**	**444.9**	**280.5**	**227.5**	**279.7**	**345.2**
Equity invested (Share capital & share premium)	**103.5**	**99.8**	**60.1**	**59.4**	**55.8**	**55.2**
Number of shares at the year-end millions	132.3	127.2	124.8	123.4	122.6	120.7
Share price on or near 31st March in pence	478.75	666.5	477	485	394.5	330.83
Market capitalisation (millions)	**633.39**	**847.79**	**595.3**	**598.49**	**483.66**	**399.31**
Cash flow return on capital invested (CATS Fin Pro/Equity Invested + Net Debt %)	14%	11%	7%	35%	29%	18%
Cash flow return on market capital invested (CATS Fin Pro/Mkt Cap + Net Debt %)	7%	5%	3%	12%	13%	10%
Cash flow return on equity invested (CATS Fin Pro- Net Interest/Equity invested %)	49%	46%	11%	140%	139%	94%
Cash flow return on market capitalisation (CATS Fin Pro- Net Interest/Mkt Cap %)	8%	5%	1%	14%	16%	13%

considered before or after debt service as a per share value by dividing the totals by the number of shares in issue.

Bear in mind that whether a business is growth or mature has a huge impact on what we expect to see. For the reasons explained earlier in the chapters on growth and mature, due to the fast pace of change, and volume increase, growth businesses may have little OPERATING CASH MARGIN and negative CASH AVAILABLE TO SATISFY FINANCE PROVIDERS. Restating their cash flows on a no-growth basis may be necessary to get a better picture of their underlying performance.

Table 14.1 shows the cash flows of Nokia with some cash flow to equity ratios appended. As Nokia has no debt (it runs a huge surplus cash position) I have only calculated the cash flow return on equity values.

Mature companies are likely to be more amenable to performance measurement in this way as we expect them to have low investment needs and be cash positive at both the OPERATING CASH MARGIN value and the CASH AVAILABLE TO SATISFY FINANCE PROVIDERS value. M&A activity may distort the picture and need to be adjusted for. The cash flows of Dairy Crest together with a variety of cash flow based returns ratios are summarised in Table 14.2.

This analysis makes it clear that Dairy Crest has struggled to generate an adequate performance since making major acquisitions in 2006 and 2007. Further comparison with a sector peer group would reveal more about whether the current performance is typical or not.

CONCLUSION

Entrepreneurs, managers and investors will typically have grasped the utility and value of looking at a business through the application of Jury's Cash Flow Template as they have proceeded through the earlier parts of this book. The concepts introduced above are merely suggestions as to how this knowledge might be utilised. Users can and should tailor the concepts offered to their particular needs.

15

Analysing Direct Cash
Flow Statements

This chapter explains the nature of direct cash flows, the difference between indirect and direct cash flows and how to analyse them into Jury's Cash Flow Template.

IAS 7 – Cash Flow Statements – gives preparers the option of reporting cash flows using the direct method, whereby major classes of gross cash receipts and gross cash payments are disclosed, or the indirect method.

The standard goes on to say, 'Entities are encouraged to report cash flows from operating activities using the direct method. The indirect method provides information which may be useful in estimating future cash flows and which is not available under the indirect method.' Later on in the chapter we will see whether this advice is acted upon.

Direct cash flows are rare, I have never yet seen an example from the UK, US, Germany or France and indeed many other countries, all of which seem to prefer to use the indirect method for preparing cash flow statements.

When they do appear in the published accounts of large businesses it is usually because the local GAAP used to prefer it or required it, and this habit has been continued when IAS GAAP was adopted. So the same information forms the published cash flow statement for the annual report and any filings required for US listings such as the form 20-F for overseas filers.

Both of the examples used in this chapter are Portuguese listed companies, as Portuguese companies generally continue to offer direct cash flow statements in their annual reports.

Unicer – Bebidas de Portugal, SGPS, S.A. is Portugal's largest beverages company. Its core business is beers and bottled spring waters. Unicer trades in segments that also include juice and soft drinks, wines, coffee, production and sale of malt and hotel management. The Unicer cash flow statement is reproduced in Table 15.1.

Table 15.1 Unicer direct cash flow statement

CONSOLIDATED FINANCIAL STATEMENTS
ANNUAL REPORT AND ACCOUNTS 2006
UNICER – Bebidas de Portugal, SGPS, S.A.

	Notes	20X6	20X5
CASH FLOW FROM OPERATING ACTIVITIES			
Receipts from customers		465.732.523	445.548.238
Payments to suppliers & employees		(344.379.427)	(310.043.874)
NET CASH FROM OPERATING ACTIVITIES		**121.353.096**	**135.504.364**
Interest paid			
Income tax paid		4.229.044	(3.501.577)
Other receipts/payments from operating activity		(44.278.973)	(62.233.978)
Net cash from operating activities		**81.303.167**	**69.768.809**
CASH FLOWS FROM INVESTING ACTIVITIES			
Purchase of tangible fixed assets		(32.794.582)	(33.806.897)
Tangible fixed assets		759.626	1.510.380
Purchase of intangible assets		(4.093.855)	(2.516.414)
Financial Investments			(114.412)
Subsidies received		522.773	700.627
Interest received			4.297
Net cash used in investing activities		**(35.606.038)**	**(34.222.419)**
CASH FLOWS FROM FINANCING ACTIVITIES			
Bank loans payments		(4.489.304)	
Interest and similar costs paid		(9.207.578)	(8.010.690)
Proceeds from bank loans		1.063.843	2.230.761
Dividends paid – Equity holders		(31.500.000)	(31.500.000)
Dividends paid – Minority interest		(270.651)	
Net cash from financing activities		**(44.403.690)**	**(37.279.929)**
(Decrease)/increase in cash and cash equivalents		1.293.439	(1.733.539)
Cash and cash equivalents, beginning of year		1.865.362	3.598.901
Effects of exchange rate changes			
Cash and cash equivalents, end of year	28	**3.158.801**	**1.865.3**

Table 15.2   Comparison of cash from customers to turnover for Unicer

UNICER Amounts expressed in €	20X6	20X5
Receipts from customers	465 732 523	445 548 238
Sales and services rendered	479 758 364	442 960 881
Difference	**−14 025 841**	**2 587 357**

WHAT IS DIFFERENT ABOUT A DIRECT CASH FLOW STATEMENT?

A careful examination of the cash flow statement (Table 15.1) will reveal that it is the section *cash flow from operating activities* that is different to a cash flow prepared using the indirect method. The other sections are typically the same as would be disclosed in an indirect cash flow statement.

Instead of starting with a profit value the direct cash flow statement starts with receipts from customers and payments to suppliers and employees. This represents exactly what it says it does. However, the receipts from customers is not the same as turnover. Why is this? Let us compare the two values (Table 15.2).

The receipts from customers represents the cash received from customers during the financial year. It does not represent the amounts billed to customers. In other words it encompasses both the turnover billed and the change in the outstanding receivables. In 2006 the group received €14 025 841 less in cash than it billed. This implies that trade debtors should have increased by the same amount. Ideally we would like to reconcile this to the movement in trade receivables in the balance sheet. Let us look at this in Table 15.3.

Whilst receivables have increased the value is approximately half of the number we are looking for. Where then is the rest of the difference? Unfortunately, this is not clear from the accounts, and, indeed, may never be explained from the other information available in the annual report. I can seek other values in the balance

Table 15.3   Identifying the change in trade receivables for Unicer

UNICER Amounts expressed in €	
Receivables from customers 20X6	81 809 764
Receivables from customers 20X5	74 194 153
Difference	**7 615 611**

sheet that might represent part of the difference such as 'other receivables'. It is also possible that movements on liabilities such as 'deposits received on returnable packaging in transit' might constitute part of the movement. Finally the accounts reveal that loans are made to customers, which are paid off via discounts granted on sales volumes. This type of arrangement is a common practice amongst brewers, who will often assist a customer with loans and supply the equipment needed by the retailer to serve the product in exchange for an exclusive supply arrangement. This means movements on customer loans may also be involved.

So, it seems we don't necessarily get more information in a direct cash flow after all. Indeed in this case we get less information than we would have obtained from an indirect cash flow statement from the same business. How does this affect the template?

When the available values are summarised into the template (Table 15.4) we lose the split between the operating cash margin and the changes in the amounts invested in the net working assets of the business. In Chapter 8, *Growth and Mature – Further Analysis*, I noted that there was much useful information about management quality that can be implied from the changes in the net working

Table 15.4 Two years summary cash flows for Unicer

UNICER – Bebidas de Portugal, SGPS, S.A. SUMMARY CASH FLOWS Amounts expressed in €	20X6	20X5
OPERATING CASH MARGIN (INVESTED)/GENERATED FROM NET WORKING ASSETS	77 074 123	73 270 386
NET CAPITAL EXPENDITURE	−36 128 811	−34 812 931
TAXATION	4 229 044	−3 501 577
CASH FLOW AVAILABLE TO SATISFY FINANCE PROVIDERS	**45 174 356**	**34 955 878**
NET INTEREST	−9 207 578	−8 006 393
NET DIVIDENDS	−31 770 651	−31 500 000
OTHER NON-OPERATING INCOME/(EXPENDITURE)	522 773	586 215
NET CASH INFLOW/(OUTFLOW)	**4 718 900**	**−3 964 300**
Financed by:		
INCREASE/(DECREASE) IN EQUITY		
INCREASE/(DECREASE) IN DEBT	−3 425 461	2 230 761
(INCREASE)/DECREASE IN CASH	−1 293 439	1 733 539
TOTAL CHANGE IN FINANCING	**−4 718 900**	**3 964 300**

assets. This information is essential to the analyst and should not be omitted before attempting to assess the information contained within the template.

One way of dealing with this problem is to extract from the balance sheet what appear to be the relevant values and 'reverse engineer' the change in net working asset data from this. In order to achieve this I have gone through the notes to the accounts selecting the values which appear to represent the net working assets of Unicer. Notice I have excluded all assets and liabilities relating to the fixed assets, corporate taxation and debt of Unicer as these are not part of the net working assets. I have also excluded non-cash items such as movements in provisions, accruals and prepayments. Table 15.5 shows the required data from the balance sheet of Unicer.

There is much useful information about changes in the business here for the analyst. Inventories have not moved much at all. Receivables from customers has increased by about €8 million. This has been offset by a reduction in the amount due from government of about €10 million, leaving a net change of €2 million reduction in total receivables. Trade payables have increased by about €9 million this is offset by modest reductions in other liabilities taking the final increase in creditors to about €6.5 million. The overall net effects on net working assets is a reduction of about €8 million. In the cash flow template this represents a cash inflow to the business. We can reverse engineer this information into the template as shown in Table 15.6.

Table 15.5   Identifying the net working asset change values for Unicer

UNICER **Amounts expressed in €** **SUMMARY OF CHANGE IN** **NET WORKING ASSETS**	**20X6**	**20X5**	**Change**
Inventories	**26 921 820**	**26 647 525**	**−274 295**
Receivables from customers	81 809 764	74 194 153	−7 615 611
Other receivables	25 498 523	24 896 153	−602 370
Other assets – government receivables	8 852 406	19 201 043	10 348 637
TOTAL ASSUMED RECEIVABLES	**116 160 693**	**118 291 349**	**2 130 656**
Deposits received on packaging in transit	16 755 114	18 127 286	−1 372 172
Other non-current creditors	1 833 032	2 373 262	−540 230
Trade payables	39 822 122	31 034 865	8 787 257
Other payables	13 796 725	13 675 230	121 495
Other liabilities – government payables	4 590 088	5 060 630	−470 542
TOTAL ASSUMED PAYABLES	**76 797 081**	**70 271 273**	**6 525 808**
TOTAL NET WORKING ASSETS	**66 285 432**	**74 667 601**	**8 382 169**

Table 15.6   Restated 20X6 cash flows for Unicer

UNICER – Bebidas de Portugal, SGPS, S.A. SUMMARY CASH FLOWS Amounts expressed in €	Original 20X6	Restated 20X6
OPERATING CASH MARGIN	77 074 123	68 691 954
(INVESTED)/GENERATED FROM NET WORKING ASSETS		8 382 169
NET CAPITAL EXPENDITURE	−36 128 811	−36 128 811
TAXATION	4 229 044	4 229 044
CASH FLOW AVAILABLE TO SATISFY FINANCE PROVIDERS	**45 174 356**	**45 174 356**
NET INTEREST	−9 207 578	−9 207 578
NET DIVIDENDS	−31 770 651	−31 770 651
OTHER NON-OPERATING INCOME/(EXPENDITURE)	522 773	522 773
NET CASH INFLOW/(OUTFLOW)	**4 718 900**	**4 718 900**
Financed by:		
INCREASE/(DECREASE) IN EQUITY		
INCREASE/(DECREASE) IN DEBT	−3 425 461	−3 425 461
(INCREASE)/DECREASE IN CASH	−1 293 439	−1 293 439
TOTAL CHANGE IN FINANCING	**−4 718 900**	**−4 718 900**

At this point we have the same level of information in the right hand column as we would have obtained from an indirect cash flow. However, remember this is our estimate of the change in net working assets, derived from selected balance sheet data. It should be viewed as approximate rather than exact.

Table 15.7 shows another example of the operating cash flow section of a direct cash flow taken from the form 20-F of Portugal Telecom.

Again, with the direct cash flow of Portugal Telecom we have the same problem, whilst there is a little more analysis of the various elements of the operating cash flows, we still do not get any disclosure of the movements in the net working assets.

CONCLUSIONS ABOUT DIRECT CASH FLOWS

The direct cash flow discloses more information about the cash inflows and outflows that generate the operating cash flow of the business than an indirect cash flow. However, in doing so, the disclosures found in an indirect cash flow relating

Table 15.7 Three years cash flow data for Portugal Telecom

PORTUGAL TELECOM, SGPS, SA
CONSOLIDATED STATEMENT OF CASH FLOWS
FOR THE YEARS ENDED 31 DECEMBER 20X7 AND 20X6
(Amounts stated in Euro)

	Notes	20X7	20X6	20X5
OPERATING ACTIVITIES				
Collections from clients		7 070 397 265	6 763 769 410	6 503 131 136
Payments to suppliers		(3 653 519 418)	(3 277 388 237)	(3 411 857 036)
Payments to employees		(654 757 374)	(653 682 324)	(625 591 295)
Payments relating to income taxes	44.a	(206 528 920)	(51 626 295)	(67 361 504)
Payments relating to post retirement benefits	9.4	(284 159 570)	(580 789 898)	(699 806 967)
Payments relating to indirect taxes and other	44.b	(610 407 039)	(572 755 719)	(534 931 734)
Cash flow from operating activities from continued operations		1 661 024 944	1 627 526 937	1 163 582 600
Cash flow from operating activities from discontinued operations	20	198 182 708	194 134 513	228 717 368
Cash flow from operating activities(1)		1 859 207 652	1 821 661 450	1 392 299 968

to changes in the amounts invested in net working assets are lost. This data can be estimated by extracting the changes in the various net working asset values from the balance sheet and adjusting the operating cash flow value accordingly.

Other than this the content of the rest of a direct cash flow is essentially the same as an indirect cash flow. The restatement and analysis of these values into the template being the same process as for an indirect cash flow statement.

16

Generating a Cash Flow Summary from Profit and Loss Account and Balance Sheet Data

This chapter deals with the process of estimating cash flow information from profit and loss account (P&L) and balance sheet data.

Before reading this chapter it is essential that the reader has read and digested the earlier chapters on summarising and evaluating cash flows in Jury's Cash Flow Template format. Virtually all of the terminology used in this chapter has been introduced and explained earlier in the book.

THE NATURE OF THE PROBLEM

There are a variety of risk management scenarios where there may be a desire on the part of the analyst or a counterparty to identify and assess the cash flow performance of a business that does not publish a cash flow statement. Those involved in credit-based transactions and those who are considering the purchase of a business are two examples.

Small- and medium-sized businesses in the UK are not required to publish cash flow statements when they file accounts. This concession to smaller businesses is common in other parts of the world. Business performance information is typically presented to an analyst or other interested parties in the form of a profit and loss account (P&L) and balance sheet. Secondly, much management information, particularly in product-based companies is focused around P&L and balance sheet information.

So, if we wish to examine an entities cash flow performance, what can we do about this problem?

Earlier in the book we found out that cash flow statements can be prepared using two possible methods, the direct method and the indirect method. The indirect method derives the cash flow statement from P&L and balance sheet data. It follows that it should be possible for an analyst to do the same in the absence of a published cash flow statement and, indeed, it is!

Before we examine the process, it is important to understand the limitations of assembling the estimated cash flow information in this way. What we will end up with is typically not identical to the equivalent published cash flow statement. It will be an approximation of the true cash flow performance. Typically, the numbers we end up with are likely to be within, say, 10% of the actual cash flow values, indeed, they may be considerably more accurate than this.

Why do these differences arise?

Accruals and Prepayments

The values disclosed in the P&L and balance sheet are adjusted for items that have been used or consumed but not invoiced or paid for (accruals) and items that have been paid for in advance but not fully consumed (prepayments). These adjustments do not represent cash flows and should be reversed. This concept has already been explained in detail in Chapter 12 – *Cash Versus Profit as a Measure of Performance.*

It is not usually possible to adjust for these individually because there is typically no disclosure of them individually. However, in situations where the business is operating normally this should not distort the resulting cash flow estimation too much because the same process of identifying and adjusting for accruals and prepayments occurred at the beginning of the financial period. In other words when we use an income or expense value from the P&L for cash flow estimation purposes, we are not using the actual cash flow received or paid in the period (of say 12 months), we are using a value that represents the 12 months actual physical sales or cost consumed. Both relate to 12 months of income or expense, however, the cash received or paid typically lags the values reported in the P&L by the credit period granted or received from customers and suppliers.

Lack of Disclosure

When we studied the detailed restatement of the operating cash flow of a business in Chapter 4 we discovered a whole variety of adjustments that might be required to restate the operating profit (EBIT) value (or other profit value starting point), to reflect the corresponding OPERATING CASH MARGIN. Typically, some of these adjustments will not be disclosed when working from P&L and balance sheet data. Therefore, we won't be aware of them and, as a result, they will be absent from our final estimates.

The most significant adjustment to profit is typically depreciation/amortisation; this is usually disclosed in the P&L and or balance sheet. We may also have disclosure of the profit/loss on disposal of fixed assets in the notes to the P&L. We are unlikely to have detailed information disclosed about movements in provisions and other non-cash items. Ideally, we should have all these in order to correctly arrive at the OPERATING CASH MARGIN.

Changes in the Composition of a Group

If we are seeking to identify the cash flows of a group, and the group has acquired or disposed of subsidiaries during the year, the changes identified from the balance sheet for both working assets and fixed assets are unlikely to match the values that would be revealed were there a cash flow statement available. To illustrate why this might be the case consider inventory. If I acquire a business during the year with holdings of inventory this will be measured and consolidated at the period end, however the opening inventory of the acquisition will not be in the opening balance sheet inventory value. If we are aware of this problem we can attempt to adjust for it if there is sufficient disclosure. Usually this is not the case.

SO, IS AN ESTIMATED CASH FLOW SUMMARY USEFUL?

Does this mean there is no value in trying to create a summary of cash flows from P&L and balance sheet data? I believe the process is still meaningful, because of the concept of materiality. If we identify the significant values approximating to the actual cash flow values we will still obtain a useful impression of the overall cash flow performance of the entity under examination. It is not necessary for our cash flow values to absolutely correct for us to gain beneficial insights about the cash flow performance of the entities.

So, what is the process?

Rather than attempting to reconstruct a complete cash flow statement in accordance with IAS GAAP the recommended approach is to come up with a best estimate of the cash flow values that appear in each line of Jury's Cash Flow Template. This requires far less knowledge of double entry bookkeeping and the preparation of statutory accounts than would be required to attempt to complete a statutory cash flow statement. Let us now examine each line of the template and discuss how best to identify the appropriate values for each line (Table 16.1).

The contents of each line of the template have already been explained in detail in Chapters 1, 2 and 4. I do not intend to repeat that material here. It is assumed that readers have already familiarised themselves with this material. I will simply summarise what each line of the template represents before explaining the various methods for developing a best estimate from the P&L and balance sheet data. Readers should revisit the earlier chapters if they are unfamiliar with any of the terms or methods mentioned.

1. OPERATING CASH MARGIN

The operating cash margin in the template represents the cash received from selling goods and services less the cash costs of producing them. In a cash flow statement prepared using the indirect method this value is derived by taking a profit value

Table 16.1   Labelling the content of the template

DATA LINE NUMBER	JURY'S CASH FLOW TEMPLATE SUMMARY CASH FLOW HEADINGS
1	OPERATING CASH MARGIN
2	(INVESTED)/GENERATED FROM NET WORKING ASSETS
3	NET CAPITAL EXPENDITURE
4	TAXATION
Sub-total	**CASH FLOW AVAILABLE TO SATISFY FINANCE PROVIDERS**
5	NET INTEREST
6	NET DIVIDENDS
7	OTHER NON-OPERATING INCOME/(EXPENDITURE)
Balancing total	**NET CASH IN/(OUT) BEFORE FINANCING** Financed by:
8	CHANGE IN EQUITY INCREASE/(DECREASE)
9	CHANGE IN DEBT INCREASE/(DECREASE)
10	CHANGE IN CASH (INCREASE)/DECREASE
Balancing total	**TOTAL CHANGE IN FINANCING**

from the P&L, adjusting it for non-cash income or expense items and removing any other income or expense recognised as profit or loss which does not relate to operations.

The first quick crude estimate of the OPERATING CASH MARGIN is *EBITDA (earnings before interest, tax, depreciation and amortisation)*. In the simplest situation, where there are no other adjustments for non-cash items, *EBITDA* is the OPERATING CASH MARGIN. When there are a number of adjustments disclosed, the add-back of depreciation and amortisation is usually by far the largest item adjusted for.

Typically there will also be a value disclosed in the notes to the P&L for the *profit and loss on the disposal of fixed assets*. This also represents a non-cash adjustment to depreciation and should also be used to adjust the starting EBIT value. Be careful to get the signage right when adding back or deducting the value.

In some situations there may also be some disclosure of *movements in provisions* in the notes to the accounts (this may be also deduced indirectly by looking at the changes in any operating provisions disclosed separately in the opening and closing balance sheet). If there is adequate disclosure of *movements in operating provisions* the EBIT value can also be adjusted for these items.

These are typically the main items. If there is any other disclosure of items relevant to the estimation of the OPERATING CASH MARGIN then they can also be adjusted for to further improve the quality of the resulting estimate.

2. (INVESTED)/GENERATED FROM NET WORKING ASSETS

The amount invested or generated from net working assets in the template represents the sum of the change during the reporting period in the amounts invested in inventory, debtors (receivables) and creditors (payables).

The usual way of determining this value is to take the opening and closing values for the three items from the opening and closing balance sheet and identify the differences. An illustration of this is shown in Table 16.2.

Table 16.2   Identification of the change in net working assets for Tesco

TESCO PLC SUMMARY OF NET WORKING ASSET CHANGE	20X8 £m	20X7 £m	Change £m
Increase in inventories	2430	1931	−499
Increase in trade and other receivables	1311	1079	−232
Increase in trade payables & other payables	−7177	−6046	1131
Totals	**−3436**	**−3036**	**400**

When working out the change value be careful to get the signage right. For example, an increase in inventories is a cash outflow (we have to expend cash in order to increase the number of boxes in our warehouse). An increase in debtors is also a cash outflow (we are lending more money to our customers). Conversely an increase in creditors is a cash inflow (our suppliers are lending more money to us).

There is sometimes difficulty in deciding which elements of current assets, current liabilities and non-current liabilities represent working asset values. Let us consider each in turn.

Current Assets

- Inventories. This value may be disclosed as one number; alternatively it may be shown as raw materials, work-in-progress and finished goods.
- Debtors and prepayments. This is the value we would typically take for working assets, this may be disclosed separately as trade debtors, other debtors and prepayments. Other debtors relating to asset or business disposal should be excluded from the working asset calculation.
- Other current assets such as cash and cash equivalents, pension fund surpluses, and items relating to investments (equity and debt) and financial instruments should also be excluded.

Current Liabilities

- Exclude current liabilities relating to dividends, interest and taxation, they are dealt with elsewhere in the template.
- Exclude current liabilities relating to pension fund deficits and asset or business acquisition or disposal. What should be left is the operating liabilities such as trade creditors, accruals and other creditors, we require the sum of these values.

Non-current Liabilities

- As with current liabilities you will find two kinds of item, non-current liabilities relating to debt and other non-current liabilities. Exclude all non-current liabilities relating to debt and financial instruments.

Typically what is left is any creditors due after more than one year and the provision for deferred tax. All we require for the working assets value is any operating creditor due after more than one year. Deferred tax should be excluded.

3. NET CAPITAL EXPENDITURE

The net capital expenditure in the template is the amount spent on new fixed assets in the period, less any proceeds of sale of any old fixed assets disposed of in the period.

If there is a note in the accounts in respect of fixed assets it should be possible to identify the value of the additions to fixed assets in the period from the note. This represents the value of the fixed assets purchased and delivered in the period. Note that there may be outstanding creditors in respect of fixed assets at the end of the year, in other words this value does not necessarily represent the cash spent on new fixed assets. However, typically, it will not be materially different to the cash flow value, and where there is little purchase of fixed assets near the end of the year, may be the same value.

In the simplest and fastest cash flow estimation exercise, this may be the only value you need for the template. This is because there is typically little value in the disposal of old fixed assets. If there are any proceeds of disposal the value is usually immaterial when compared with the expenditure on new fixed assets. There are of course exceptions to this, if the business has disposed of entire factories, or moved from one factory to another or made other substantial disposals there may be significant values involved in the disposal of fixed assets. Such events would normally be considered sufficiently material for there to be specific disclosure in the accounts of the sums involved.

A second method involves the use of some simple accounting tricks to obtain an estimate. The following logic gives a materially correct answer if there are no material disposals in the period.

Opening fixed assets + additions − depreciation = Closing fixed assets

This means if you have a value for the opening and closing net book value of fixed assets from the two balance sheets and a value for depreciation from the P&L or notes you can develop an estimate for the value of fixed asset additions. The above statement can be rearranged so that:

Additions = Closing fixed assets − opening fixed assets + depreciation

This may be more than adequate when dealing with the accounts of smaller businesses. Where there is a fixed asset note in the accounts the other information in the note together with the profit/(loss) on disposal from the notes to the P&L can be used to identify the proceeds of disposal as follows:

Original cost of assets disposed of − accumulated depreciation of assets

disposed of − loss/(profit) on sale of fixed assets

= Proceeds of sale of assets disposed of

If a loss on disposal of fixed assets is disclosed − deduct it.
If a profit on disposal of fixed assets is disclosed − add it.

---

4. TAXATION

The item taxation in the template represents the cash paid in taxes on corporate profits in the financial period.

Initially it would appear logical to use the corresponding P&L charge for taxation. However, this could lead to error for a variety of reasons.

- The P&L charge to taxation consists of two things:
  1. The taxation charge on profits for the year.
  2. The movement in the deferred tax provision.
     We need to exclude the movement in the provision for deferred taxes as it is a non-cash item.
- The taxation recognised in this period is not necessarily paid in the same period. We have a lag between recognition in the P&L and payment.

  In the UK if the business is small or medium sized it pays taxes nine months after the year-end. This means this year's tax charge in the P&L is paid in the following year. If the business is large, tax is paid quarterly on account with a final payment in the first quarter of the following year. Internationally there is no consistent rule; taxation is paid over to the respective government in accordance with the tax legislation for the country concerned. It may be necessary to find out what the rules are before developing an estimate for the tax paid in the period.

There are other ways of estimating the tax paid value. Once again we can use some simple accounting tricks to identify the value if we have sufficient detail in the notes on creditors. Here is another chunk of accounting logic:

Opening tax creditor + tax payable on profits for the year − tax payment
    for the year
= Closing tax creditor

It is usual to show the tax creditor separately in the notes relating to current liabilities. This means we can identify the opening and closing tax creditor, the tax charge for the year should be in the taxation note relating to the P&L. This means we can identify the tax paid during the period. The above statement can be rearranged so that:

Tax payment for the year
= Opening tax creditor + tax payable on profits for the year
    − closing tax creditor

CASH AVAILABLE TO SATISFY FINANCE PROVIDERS

Summing the four values arrived at above gives us our first sub-total from the template, the cash available to satisfy finance providers. This may be sufficient information if all the user of this method is seeking to do is see whether a business is cash generative or not. However, it is better to try to complete the whole template because the resulting difference that is likely to arise in the two balancing values (due to the problems noted at the beginning of the chapter) should give the analyst an idea of the scope of any error in the estimation process (i.e. is the difference large or small?).

5. NET INTEREST

The net interest value in the template is the cash interest received less the cash interest paid. If the net debt in the business is relatively constant throughout the period the P&L charge is typically a reasonable estimate of the cash interest paid or received. Once again, the P&L interest charge will have any accrued interest added, however, this will also have been adjusted for at the beginning of the year. So the P&L charge should be close in value to the cash interest paid.

The only exceptions to this would be situations where interest has been recognised in the P&L but has not actually been paid. The use of deep discount bonds or payment in kind notes would achieve this result. Private equity debt structures often have features like this.

A useful check is to try to reconcile the average net debt for the year to the interest paid. It is now common for the liabilities notes to detail both the individual debt items and the associated interest rate being paid on them, which facilitates this process.

6. NET DIVIDEND

The net dividend in the template is the value of dividends received less the value of any dividends paid in the period.

It is common practice for businesses to pay a dividend twice a year. The first dividend paid in an accounting period is known as the interim dividend payment (being an interim partial payment of the dividend which will be paid on the profits for the relevant accounting period). The second payment is known as the final dividend and is typically paid out sometime in the following accounting period, however, this dividend is recognised as a cost in the current financial period. This means the value of dividends shown in the P&L is not a good measure of the cash dividends paid. Typically the cash dividends paid in a given period will be the final dividend for the previous accounting period and the interim dividend for the current accounting period. It may be possible to estimate this value from the notes to the accounts.

There is another way to estimate this value, we can use the same accounting trick we have used for taxation. Here is another chunk of accounting logic:

Opening dividend creditor + dividends declared for the period
− dividend payments for the period = Closing dividend creditor

It is usual to show the dividend creditor separately in the notes relating to current liabilities. This means we can identify the opening and closing dividend creditor, the dividends declared for the year should be in the dividend recognised in the P&L. This means we can identify the dividend paid during the period. The above statement can be rearranged so that

Dividend payments for the period
= Opening dividend creditor + dividends declared for the period
− closing dividend creditor

The value of dividends received is usually the cash value. This is because we don't usually recognise a dividend as income, until we have received it. Note that if a business due to receive a dividend knows its payer has declared (but not paid) a dividend it is possible the business receiving such a dividend could show this as income with a corresponding debtor for the dividend due. It should be evident from the notes to the accounts if this is the case.

7. OTHER NON-OPERATING INCOME/(EXPENDITURE)

The value of other non-operating income/(expenditure) in the template picks up the remaining cash flows that are not part of the Categories 1 to 6 and are not financing cash flows. Typically these are cash flows relating to the following:

- The purchase or sale of interests in subsidiaries.
- The purchase or sale of interests in associates or joint ventures.
- The purchase or sale of other equity or debt interests in other businesses (this includes investment activities and long-term customer finance where not dealt with by adding a line for vendor finance to the template. It does not include financial instruments unless bought as investments).
- The receipt of grant or other assistance from governments and others.

Many smaller businesses will go for years without having any of these items in their cash flows. In larger businesses the buying and selling of interests in other businesses is more common. Again the notes to the P&L and balance sheet should tell us something about these types of activities if they are relevant to cash flow analysis.

NET CASH IN/(OUT) BEFORE FINANCING

This is the second key total from the template. This represents the net cash inflow/(outflow) for the period before financing. This value should balance with the value of the financing cash flows and cash movement when adjusted for signage issues.

8. CHANGE IN EQUITY

The change in equity from the template represents the cash change in equity during the accounting period. Remember that the movement in retained profits, which is a change to equity in the balance sheet, is not a cash flow. What we are seeking to identify is the cash received in respect of new equity issued and/or the cash spent on buying back equity or treasury shares.

A review of the notes to the balance sheet, if they are available, should reveal this information. If there are no notes the movement on share capital and any share premium account should correspond to the cash received from the sale of new equity assuming the equity was, in fact, exchanged for cash. Bear in mind that if a business, or an interest in a business, was acquired the equity may have been exchanged for shares or net assets instead.

9. CHANGE IN DEBT

The change in debt from the template represents the movement in the capital value of interest bearing liabilities for the period. If the balance sheet or notes contain a split of the *creditors due within one year* and the *creditors due after one year* it should be straightforward to extract the various debt items, summarise them and identify the change to debt during the year.

Remember that debt for the purposes of this analysis is defined as any liability that is interest bearing. This includes, for example, loans, overdrafts, mortgages, debentures, bonds, finance leases, commercial paper, items recognised as finance leases and factoring advances.

Once all the debt items have been identified it should be straightforward to calculate the movement between opening and closing values. An increase in debt is a cash inflow (positive) a decrease in debt is a cash outflow (negative).

10. CHANGE IN CASH

The change in cash and cash equivalents from the template represents the movement in cash and cash equivalents during the period. Cash equivalents is the term used in the IAS standard on cash flows for cash surpluses held in a business as short-term bank deposits or invested in short-term debt securities.

Identify the values of cash and any cash equivalents from the balance sheet and notes. Calculate the movement for the period. Once this is done introduce the movement to the template values with the signage reversed.

TOTAL CHANGE IN FINANCING

The final total from the template is the total change in financing. This is the sum of the change in equity, debt and cash. Take care to get the signage of all three values correct. When summarising a published cash flow statement this template value should be the same as the net cash in/(out) before financing value from the template, but with the signage reversed. In a template developed from the opening and closing balance sheets and associated P&L data it is unlikely these values will be the same. This is due to the problems identified at the beginning of the chapter. Generally we would expect the two values to be similar. If the two totals are materially different this suggests an error has been made during the development of the estimated cash flows in the template. If so, consider the following;

- Have you used all the values disclosed in the balance sheet or deliberately omitted them if not relevant?
- Have you checked all the signage is correct?
- Have you checked all calculations are correct?
- If the difference remains does the data (or lack of it) suggest a plausible reason why it might occur? If so, can we validate this?

Table 16.3   Profit and loss account for Pizza Express

Pizza Express plc
Abridged Profit & Loss Account
Year to 30th June 2XXX

	2XXX £m
Group Turnover	126.6
Cost of Sales	−88.4
Gross Profit	**38.2**
Sales, general & administrative costs	−3.1
Depreciation	−5.4
Operating profit	**29.7**
Net interest payable	−0.3
Profit on ordinary activites before tax	**29.4**
Taxation	−5.9
Profit on Ordinary activites after taxation	**23.5**
Dividends on equity shares	−2.7
Retained profit for the finncial year	**20.8**

Tables 16.3 and 16.4 shows an example of the process of assembling the cash flow template data based on historic data taken from the published accounts of Pizza Express plc. Certain values have been amended to ensure the resulting template balances precisely.

Have a go!

Should you wish you can attempt to summarise the above data (Tables 16.3 and 16.4) into the template format before looking at the information in Table 16.5 which summarises how it is done. This is the best way of learning even if you don't finish the task as it gets you to internalise the information presented in your own mind.

Alternatively you can reverse engineer the information provided in the answer to understand its derivation (Table 16.5).

Table 16.4   Balance sheets for Pizza Express

Pizza Express plc
Abridged Balance Sheets
For the year ended 30th June 2XXX

	Current Year 2XXX £m	Previous Year 2XXW £m
Fixed Assets		
Tangible Assets	84.6	65.7
Current Assets		
Stocks	5.1	4.1
Debtors	4.7	5
Cash at bank and in hand	6.2	5.4
	16	**14.5**
Total Assets	**100.6**	**80.2**
Creditors		
Within one year		
Overdraft	0.6	11
Other loans	3.9	5.6
Dividends	2.8	2.1
Other creditors	26.2	21.2
Total short creditors	**33.5**	**39.9**
After one year		
Loans	0	0
Other creditors	0.1	3.1
Total long creditors	**0.1**	**3.1**
Provisions for liabilities & charges	0	0.4
Capital & Reserves		
Called up share capital	7.1	6.9
Share premium account	45.1	35.9
Profit & Loss Account	14.8	−6
	67	**36.8**
Total Liaibilities	**100.6**	**80.2**

Table 16.5 Jury's cash flow template data

Pizza Express plc
Cash Flow Statement derived from the P&L and Balance Sheet
For the year ended 30th June 2XXX

	2XXX £m
Cash from operations	
Operating profit	29.7
Add back depreciation	5.4
Change in Provisions	−0.4
CASH FROM OPERATIONS	**34.7**
Change in Net Working Assets	
Change in Stocks	−1
Change in Debtors	0.3
Change in short other creditors	5
Change in Long other creditors	−3
TOTAL CHANGE IN NWA	**1.3**
Net Capex	−24.3
Taxation	−5.9
CASH FLOW AVAILABLE TO SATISFY CAPITAL PROVIDERS	**5.8**
Net Interest	−0.3
Net Dividends	−2
NET CASH INFLOW/(OUTFLOW)	**3.5**
Change in Equity Inc/(Dec)	9.4
Change in Debt Inc/(Dec)	−12.1
Change in Cash (Inc)/Dec	−0.8
Total funding cash flows	**−3.5**

Notes to the Case Explaining the Derivation of Each of the Values in the Answer

Cash from Operations

The operating profit and depreciation values come direct from the profit and loss account.

The change in provisions is derived from the difference between the balance sheet values headed Provision for Liabilities and Charges. Note that the provision has reduced in the balance sheet signifying a reversal, this will increase profit by the same amount. As this is not a cash flow we reduce the Cash from Operations accordingly.

Change in Net Working Assets

These values are the differences between the previous and current balance sheet values for the items listed. Take care to get the signage right.

Net Capex

Uses the formula shown earlier:

Additions = Closing fixed assets − opening fixed assets + depreciation
So, additions = 84.6 − 65.7 + 5.4 = 24.3

This means the value of additions is 24.3. This goes into the template as −24.3 as it represents a cash outflow.

Taxation

As we have no information about the opening and closing tax creditor we cannot use the formula approach, we only have the P&L data so we will use this value, as it is the only data we have.

There may be a significant error in the use of this estimate. We should bear this in mind if there is a significant difference when we try to balance the template at the end of the process.

The value used is therefore −5.9

Net Interest

The value used is the value disclosed in the P&L, namely −0.3

Net Dividends

Uses the formula shown earlier:

Dividend payments for the period
  = Opening dividend creditor + dividends declared for the period
    − closing dividend creditor
Dividend payments for the period = 2.1 + 2.7 − 2.8 = 2.0

This means the value of the dividends paid is 2.0. This goes into the template as −2.0 because it represents a cash outflow.

Change in Equity Inc/(Dec)

This represents the sum of the change in the Called up Share Capital and the Share premium account.

Change in Debt inc/(Dec)

This represents the sum of the change in the Overdraft and Other Loans in Creditors within one year and the change in Loans in the creditors after one year.

Change in Cash (Inc)/Dec

This represents the change in Cash at bank and in hand.

   If all the amounts have been correctly extracted from the source data and entered into the template with the correct signage this particular template will balance as I have engineered the values to ensure it does so. In a real example do not expect to get a precise balance, if this example were based on the real values the error caused by not having the true taxation paid value available would almost certainly throw out the balancing totals.

CONCLUSION

This method of estimating the template values from the published profit and loss and balance sheet data will in most cases result in a summary of the cash flows in template format that is within a few percent of reality. This method will typically provide sufficient information to assess the state of the cash flow performance of an entity in the absence of a published cash flow statement.

Summarising Historic Free Cash Flow

This chapter deals with the identification and analysis of the historic free cash flows of a business. Before we commence the actual process of analysis it is probably useful to offer some brief contextual remarks to those readers who are less familiar with the fundamentals of corporate finance theory.

THE ORIGIN OF FREE CASH FLOW

In the last 50 years we have seen the development of a new methodology for assessing the value of a project, based on the idea of forecasting and then discounting the future cash flows relating to the project to arrive at the present value of the project. Sometime later it was recognised that this method could also be used to arrive at the valuation of a business (this in turn coming from the insight that a business can be viewed as a bunch of projects in various stages of their life cycles).

In order to complete the process of valuing a business in this way it is typical to forecast the future free cash flows of the business a number of years into the future and then discount them using an estimate of the businesses cost of capital; the resulting annual free cash flow values then being summed.

The estimated cash flows after the forecast period are dealt with by assuming they represent a perpetuity of some kind, the value which is, in turn, also discounted to find its present value. The resulting value is known as the residual value.

As this is a forecasting exercise the process of completing this is dealt with in Section 2 Chapter 20. Before attempting to develop a forecast of the future cash flows of the business for the purposes of valuation it is always wise to first identify and assess the historic performance of the business in some detail.

If performing such an exercise for real I would recommend taking the most recent 10 years' accounts from the entity concerned (if the business has been in existence for more than this period) and summarising each of the three primary accounting statements into a spreadsheet programme in columnar format. It may surprise you that I consider there is any value in looking at accounting information from anything up to a decade into the past. However, the benefit of this exercise is that we should be able to see how the business performed throughout the duration of at least one economic cycle.

Businesses vary dramatically in the extent to which they are affected by economic cycles, it is important to understand the degree to which the cash flows of a business entities are likely to be affected should a recession arise at some point in the future. The best starting point for this is to examine the historic performance through at least one economic cycle. It may be necessary to go back further if there has been an extended period without severe recession as we have recently experienced.

Having summarised the accounting information in this way we should be able to assess the variability of sales, profits and cash flows throughout the cycle. Once the relevant figures have been identified it may make everything clearer if we then graph the data. We can then take this further and compare the graphed data with other similar businesses, economic and sector indices and other relevant sector indicators to assess the relative overperformance or underperformance of the business through the economic cycle.

Having prepared a summary of the last 10 years' cash flow statements we are now in a position to take things to the next step. Using the techniques outlined in Chapters 2, 3 and 4 we can then summarise this data into the template format. This gives us an overview of the cash flow performance of the business for the previous 10 years.

WHAT THEN, ARE THE FREE CASH FLOWS OF A BUSINESS?

Let us start with a definition and then examine what this actually means.

The free cash flow of an entity is the cash flow the business would generate, before finance costs, assuming the business has no debt.

The free cash flow of an entity for a given period is the sum of the four values shown in Table 17.1.

The observant amongst you will notice that the above summation is very similar to Jury's cash flow template! This is not an accident – the first three values are the same. However, there is one key difference: Jury's cash flow template shows

Table 17.1   Template illustrating the elements of free cash flow

Example Limited Summary of the historic free cash flows	2XX0	2XX1	2XX2	2XX3	2XX4
Operating cash flow					
(Invested)/Generated from Net Working Assets					
Net capital expenditure					
Unlevered taxes					
FREE CASH FLOW (The sum of the four items above)					

the actual taxes paid rather than the unlevered taxes as shown in Table 17.1. The cash flow template was originally designed to facilitate and simplify the process of analysing historic cash flow statements. As such it deals with cash flows *as they are*. There are no adjustments made to the published values, they are simply summarised into the template.

In order to arrive at a summary of the historic free cash flows from a set of template cash flows it is necessary to adjust the last of the four values. We need to adjust the actual tax paid to show the taxes the business would have paid as if it had no leverage. This exercise is often referred to as 'unlevering the actual tax charge'.

Why do we need to perform this adjustment?

In summarising the free cash flows we are seeking to identify the cash flows available to investors from the business before we have any knowledge as to how the business is financed. The description usually used for this process is 'identifying the *enterprise* free cash flows'. The cash flows of the enterprise being the residual cash generated from the operating assets of the business before we consider the effects of financing.

At this point we do not know whether there is any debt finance used in the business or not. Another way of looking at this is that we are seeking to identify what the cash flows of the business would look like if the business was financed entirely by equity. Why is this important?

THE CASH FLOW EFFECTS OF DEBT FINANCING

When debt is used to finance a business, the interest paid on the debt is normally allowable as a tax deduction before the calculation of the amount of corporate taxes due in a period. For example, if we assume a tax rate of 30% for a business, when we pay €1000 of interest to a bank this is going to save us €1000 × 30% = €300 when we pay our taxes. In other words the actual net interest cost of debt for the corporate is €700 rather than the €1000 paid to the bank because we are able to reduce our taxes by €300 as a consequence of paying interest of €1000. So, the actual cost of debt for a business is the after-tax cost of debt.

Thus, when we observe the actual tax charge of a business we are looking at the taxes due after this deduction in respect of the interest paid in a particular period.

In order to arrive at the unlevered tax charge we adjust the actual tax charge as follows. Identify the net interest paid in the period, multiply this value by the applicable tax rate and add the resulting total to the actual taxes. The resulting value, known as the unlevered tax charge, represents the amount of tax the business would have paid if the business had been financed entirely by equity. Table 17.2 shows an example.

The typical way to effect this adjustment to the template cash flows would be to create the appropriate functionality within a spreadsheet and then develop a summary of the free cash flows. These values can then be examined and

Table 17.2 Identifying the unlevered tax value

Example limited	
Actual corporation tax payable for the period	$500 000
Net interest payable in the period	$1 500 000
Tax rate applicable to interest 30%	
Tax value of the deduction for interest	$450 000
Unlevered taxes for the period	$950 000
(this being $500 000 + $450 000)	

subjected to analysis by looking at trend data and by comparing with other similar businesses. It can also be compared with data such as stock price, market capitalisation, dividends, stock indexes and other economic data to gain insights about the behaviour and variability of the free cash flows. This kind of analysis is invaluable should it be necessary to attempt the exercise of predicting the future free cash flows of the business.

Table 17.3 shows the identification of the historic free cash flows of Dairy Crest the milk processing business examined earlier in the book.

The second example of the identification of the historic free cash flows (Table 17.4) is a restatement of Vestas, the wind turbine business. I have assumed a tax rate for the first two years of the sample as the accounts are no longer on the company web site.

It should be clear from a comparison of the two examples shown that the free cash flows of Vestas are significantly more volatile than the cash flows of Dairy Crest. There are two years where the free cash flows are significantly negative, this being due to investment in fixed and working assets.

Dairy Crest is an example of a typical mature company, Vestas is an example of a typical growth company.

Table 17.3   Derivation of the free cash flow of Dairy Crest

DAIRY CREST PLC
TEMPLATE SUMMARY CASH FLOWS
Six years to 31ˢᵗ March 20X7

	20X7 £m	20X6 £m	20X5 £m	20X4 £m	20X3 £m	20X2 £m
Operating cash margin	97.0	89.7	122.4	126.4	111.0	100.6
Change in NWA	−2.8	−16.3	20.6	10.2	−6.1	−52.1
Net Capex	−26.6	−34.6	−29.5	−29.7	−27.0	−52.3
Cash taxes	−6.1	−15.5	−12.6	−8.7	−4.1	−5.3
CASH FLOW AVAILABLE TO SATISFY CAPITAL PROVIDERS	**61.5**	**23.3**	**100.9**	**98.2**	**73.8**	**−9.1**
Net interest	−15.3	−16.4	−17.7	−20.6	−22.0	−18.7
Effective Tax rate	30%	30%	30%	30%	30%	30%
Tax shelter value of interest	−4.6	−4.9	−5.3	−6.2	−6.6	−5.6

DAIRY CREST PLC
HISTORIC FREE CASH FLOWS
Six years to 31ˢᵗ March 20X7

	20X7 £m	20X6 £m	20X5 £m	20X4 £m	20X3 £m	20X2 £m
Operating cash margin	97	89.7	122.4	126.4	111	100.6
Change in NWA	−2.8	−16.3	20.6	10.2	−6.1	−52.1
Net Capex	−26.6	−34.6	−29.5	−29.7	−27	−52.3
Ungeared taxes	−10.7	−20.4	−17.9	−14.9	−10.7	−10.9
HISTORIC FREE CASH FLOW	**56.9**	**18.4**	**95.6**	**92.0**	**67.2**	**−14.7**

Table 17.4   Derivation of the free cash flow of Vestas

VESTAS Summary group cash flow statement Year ended 31st December	20X7 €m	20X6 €m	20X5 €m	20X4 €m	20X3 €m	20X2 €m
OPERATING CASH MARGIN	639.0	353.0	44.1	36.5	171.9	145.6
(INV)/GEN FROM NET WORKING ASSETS	190.0	376.0	186.8	−15.5	11.2	−244.4
NET CAPITAL EXPENDITURE	−317.0	−168.0	−126.6	−118.4	−111.1	−136.0
TAXATION	−128.0	−91.0	−40.6	−10.3	−8.6	−13.3
CASH FLOW AVAILABLE TO SATISFY FINANCE PROVIDERS	**384.0**	**470.0**	**63.7**	**−107.7**	**63.4**	**−248.1**
NET INTEREST	0	−40	−42.4	−40.5	−21.4	−13.9
Effective tax rate	34%	31%	21%	32%	30%	30%
Tax shelter value of interest	0.0	−12.4	−8.9	−13.0	−6.4	−4.2

VESTAS HISTORIC FREE CASH FLOW Six years to 31st December 20X7	20X7 €m	20X6 €m	20X5 €m	20X4 €m	20X3 €m	20X2 €m
OPERATING CASH MARGIN	639.0	353.0	44.1	36.5	171.9	145.6
(INV)/GEN FROM NET WORKING ASSETS	190.0	376.0	186.8	−15.5	11.2	−244.4
NET CAPITAL EXPENDITURE	−317.0	−168.0	−126.6	−118.4	−111.1	−136.0
UNGEARED TAXATION	−128.0	−103.4	−49.5	−23.3	−15.0	−17.5
HISTORIC FREE CASH FLOW	**384.0**	**457.6**	**54.8**	**−120.7**	**57.0**	**−252.3**

CONCLUSION

The term 'free cash flow' is used to describe the amount of cash generated by a business that is available to satisfy the finance providers to the business, before we have any knowledge of how the business is actually financed. It shows us the cash flow the business would generate if it were completely financed by equity.

When debt is used to finance a business this has a beneficial effect on the actual cash flows before interest service. In most jurisdictions interest is allowed as a tax deduction in arriving at the taxable profit. This means as the interest paid increases the tax charge reduces, so increasing the available free cash flow. This is one of the reasons the leveraged buy-out market and the private equity market have been able to establish themselves as a permanent part of the financial landscape.

Section Two
Forecasting Cash Flows

18

Introduction

I have chosen to deal with forecasting cash flows as a separate section because it represents a different universe of risk for those engaged in the process, when compared to the task of analysing historic cash flows. What follows is a discussion of the major points of difference between the analysis of historic cash flows (and data in general) and the process of forecasting cash flows (and forecasting in general).

FORECASTING VERSUS ANALYSING HISTORIC DATA

In examining historic cash flows we are essentially conducting our analysis exercise after the fact. We are seeking to make published and other historic data more useful and accessible by manipulating and simplifying it. This is similar to the process carried out by a detective in seeking to solve a crime. The facts (clues) are there, it is a matter of identifying them and piecing them together to tell the full story of what actually happened.

In most situations we will make an assumption that the published cash flow data that represents the starting point for our analysis is fact. Occasionally, due to accounting manipulation and abuse, fraud or misrepresentation, this assumption will turn out to be wrong, so invalidating our analysis of what actually happened. From this initial insight we can immediately attempt a maxim.

All assumptions are dangerous.

For example, if you have developed a comprehensive historical cash flow analysis of a business from published audited accounts, perhaps because your organisation or client intends to purchase the entity owning the business and then presented your report and witnessed the subsequent acquisition of the business, only to find much later that all the cash flow data on which your analysis was based was fictional, you could find yourself in trouble, simply because you made this perfectly reasonable assumption.

Why is the assumption reasonable? Normally, we would assume that the financial information used for the analysis was produced by a competent individual (who was probably qualified to do so by some accounting organisation). Secondly, it was then audited by another organisation (the auditors) who were specifically tasked with checking the data and who have a general duty to identify fraud if it is evident from their enquiries. Typically they would also certify in the audit or other report that they consider the published data that results from the whole exercise to be materially accurate.

Observation of the real world suggests that in, say, ninety-nine cases out of a hundred the assumption that the accounting data we are using fairly reflects the activities of the underlying entity would turn out to be reasonable. The problem posed by my example scenario is you would have been caught out by the one case in a hundred.

This issue of how we deal with risks that are remote, occur infrequently and have possibly severe consequences, has become more topical of late. This is largely due to the monumental errors of assumption made by hundreds of intelligent, extremely well paid investment bankers. If you wish to consider the whole subject of infrequent event risk in more detail I would recommend a book called *The Black Swan* by Nicholas Taleb. His insights about infrequent event risk are invaluable to anyone involved in forecasting.

So, the purpose of this largely philosophical discussion about risk is to prepare you for my first key observation about forecasting.

All forecasts are fantasies.

At first sight this may appear an extreme position to take. After all, I can forecast that the sun will rise tomorrow and, as long as I am situated somewhere on the planet's surface, there is a very high probability it will do so. However, there will eventually come a day, hopefully many millions of years into the future, when something else happens. In other words, there are many future expected events that we assume to be certain, when in fact they are not *absolutely* certain. It is the gap between assumed to be certain and absolutely certain which causes problems.

It's not what you do know (and should have analysed thoroughly) which surprises you, it's the unknown or unexpected risk event that catches you unawares and unprepared.

If you don't wish to be caught out by infrequent event risk it is always important to be aware of, and consider the possible consequences of what you don't know as well as what you do know when taking business decisions. This is one of the most important observations about risk I can offer the reader.

FORECASTS AND PREDICTION

So, when we developing a forecast, are we attempting to predict the future?

In the context of preparing a cash flow forecast the answer must be no. Again, there is extensive literature on the subject of attempting to predict the future.

Essentially, this is what a gambler seeks to do. Those readers who have studied the subject will know that the laws of probability have a significant influence on the *process* of gambling (not the outcome of a specific bet, which is fundamentally uncertain). What mathematical analysis reveals is that we may appear to predict the future successfully a number of times. However, our outcomes are in fact simply luck and we are still bound by the rules of probability, eventually we will make a prediction that will fail, and suffer a negative outcome. Unfortunately the laws of probability don't tell us exactly *when* this will happen.

A Forecast is a Plausible Future Scenario

What then are we attempting to do when we prepare a forecast? I would put to you that we are seeking to develop what I call *plausible future scenarios*. What do I mean by this?

Let us start with the word *plausible*. Forecasts are not right or wrong as such, because they are not based on scientific fact, they are simply plausible. In other words, they represent what we think is more or most likely to happen in the future, rather than some other less likely scenario. A single forecast is subject to the laws of probability, it represents one probable future. There are always other parallel probable futures.

So, taken even more literally, *plausible* means we like this forecast more than any other forecast. This, then, is a subjective judgment; it is more plausible to us. In other words prejudice and opinion are also a factor to consider in the process of preparing and using forecasts.

The term *future scenarios* is more self-explanatory. Let me repeat this because it is so important: forecasts are not right or wrong as such. In order to create a forecast it is necessary to make certain assumptions about the future. The forecast itself, which consists of apparently factual numbers with the same authority as any other accounting information, is actually nothing more than a scenario based on the particular set of assumptions used to make it. It is neither right nor wrong. It follows from this that much of the difficulty in forecasting arises from the assumptions we make and the way we use them in our forecast model. A forecast does not represent fact (what will happen), it represents what might happen, given a particular set of circumstances (the assumptions).

REASONS FOR PREPARING CASH FLOW FORECASTS

Why do we prepare cash flow forecasts? The usual reason for doing this is to assist with some sort of decision making in the present.

The preparation of a cash flow forecast starts with its purpose. What is the forecast for?

Typical reasons for preparing forecasts of a businesses cash flow are:

- Do we have enough cash to run our business next month, quarter, year?
- Do we have enough cash to buy, invest in X?
- When do we think we will we get paid by our customers?
- Can we afford to pay for asset X?
- How do we pay for asset X?
- How much should we invest in project X?
- How much do we think business X is worth?

In order to assist us in making these decisions it may be helpful to create one or more forecasts of the expected cash inflows and outflows relevant to the decision. In other words, the purpose of the forecast should dictate the *scope* of the forecast.

There are a number of issues that necessarily need to be considered in defining the scope of the exercise before commencing the preparation of the forecast.

One of the early architectural decisions required in the process is dealing with the time base. Is it a daily, weekly, monthly, quarterly or annual forecast, or a combination of various different timescales? This is a decision that needs careful consideration because it is usually not practical to change the timescale of a forecast model after it has been created.

Secondly, the level of detail is important. Too much detail will make preparation more expensive and time consuming, too little detail will mean important cause and effect relationships within the forecast may be overlooked. This is why the preparation of a good forecast is an art rather than a science. A good forecast is elegant in the way it captures the input data, uses it and displays the required information without unnecessary complexity.

FORECASTS AND THE COST OF NEGATIVE EVENTS

Returning to the subject of the benefits of forecasting, I would put it to you that the major pay-off from a good forecast is that it improves your understanding of what *might* happen in the future. This is because it provides information about cause and effect and other limitations in the execution of the project. This is particularly apparent when you manipulate the variables in the completed model to simulate different outcomes or scenarios. I will illustrate this with an example.

In the world of project finance it is normal to have to deal with vast forecasts extending for 50 years or more into the future. I have seen such documents associated with the financing of infrastructure such as major toll bridges (e.g. the second suspension bridge crossing the Bristol Channel in the UK), the construction of mobile telephone networks and oil and gas projects such as LPG plants and their associated transport infrastructure.

The reason for the extreme length of these forecasts is that it is necessary to forecast the construction costs, and the revenues and costs of the subsequent operation of the asset until the point when the asset has paid back the capital invested to construct it in the first place. This may be 35 years or more for a toll bridge for example.

Once a forecast model for such a project has been constructed, it can then be manipulated in order to assess the consequences of events not occurring as predicted.

One common risk in the construction phase of any project is the consequences of delay. Delay can occur for many reasons, some of which are under the control of the project managers. Examples are, shortage of labour and raw materials, delay in the construction of critical sub-components by suppliers, disputes with suppliers, regulatory delays and strikes. Another group of events, which are not completely under the control of management, may also cause delays. Examples are catastrophic failure of major items of plant such as cranes critical to the construction process, a collision with the structure whilst under construction and extreme weather events such as extremely high or low temperatures, wind, hurricane and so on, which give rise to damage and/or delay.

When the effects of this sort of event are modeled in a forecast, usually by extending the construction phase by three to six months in the model, it is normal to discover the project is no longer viable! Delay turns out to be extremely expensive. Why is this?

If we consider the cash flows of the project, the construction phase is when all the cash required to construct the asset is being spent, and the end of construction is the point at which the cash outflows are at their highest point in the whole life of the project. The monthly interest accruing at this point is so high that a delay of as little as three months may make the project non-viable in terms of delivering a positive return to its sponsors.

The sponsor will only be aware of this if a comprehensive financial model of the project has been constructed and then been manipulated to assess the impact of such possible events. This high cost of delay turns out to be typical in all 'lumpy' projects.

Lumpy Projects

What do I mean by a lumpy project? A lumpy project is one where you have to spend all the money required at the beginning in order to get the benefit of the asset required. Bridges and tunnels are good examples; a half built bridge or tunnel is of no economic benefit to any one other than base jumpers and mushroom farmers! Contrast this with building or extending a factory. As the need for space grows additional space can be constructed, there is no need to build a huge factory at the inception of the project. This ability to chop up the project turns out to be very valuable to the sponsor, not only because it reduces the financial outlay in the early years of the project, but also because it introduces a valuable option not available to the sponsors of bridge or tunnel projects, the option to abandon further investment if not viable or not required. The option to abandon can save you money many years in the future if events turn out to vary significantly from those predicted at the inception of the project.

Anyone working in project finance is already likely to be aware of these insights about project risk. However, for those of us who have not previously been involved in significant capital expenditure decisions this information may be invaluable. Once we are aware of this risk (of delay) we can plan and manage accordingly to mitigate it. (In the context of risk management 'to mitigate' means to minimise the effect of, or remove, the risk completely.)

Forecasting and the Economic and Financial Consequences of Negative Risk Events

Once the economic and financial consequences of possible negative risk events are properly understood, this is likely to change the amount of time and effort allocated to dealing with them before they occur. If we have the appropriate analytical skills to build these risk analysis models, knowledge of the effects of risks can come directly from our examination and manipulation of the financial model constructed to examine the risks of the project and their financial consequences.

All this work can be performed before any capital is committed to the project itself. For the manager or entrepreneur this is invaluable as it involves only a minimal financial outlay in preparing these models, which then provide a powerful risk management tool. Indeed the analysis may reveal that the project, although superficially attractive, is actually unviable.

By modelling any project properly there is the possibility of developing a sort of beneficial feedback loop. By manipulating the model we gain insights into the costs and consequences of variations in our assumptions, which changes our priorities about mitigating those risks, which reduces their possible impact on the project. Corporate finance theory tells us that if we reduce the risk of a project whilst keeping the financial outcome constant we have increased the value of the project. This implies risk reduction is valuable in its own right. We know this to be true because there are whole industries in the market place whose sole function is to reduce risk – hedging currency risk is an example. Futures markets exist because they provide an economically useful service; they offer producers and users of commodities the ability to fix their prices many months into the future.

The example we have discussed above deals with the management of one particular risk, the risk of delay. Typically, there are many more risks that should also be examined and assessed for their probability and effect before committing to a project.

Examples are: variation in the rate of adoption of the product or service; changes in the volume and price of our output; the effects of difficulties with sourcing key raw materials; disruption to output due to labour shortages or strikes; temporary loss of capital assets for various reasons; and changes in inflation rates, interest rates and taxes.

A good cash flow model provides an elegant tool to achieve this because, if constructed well, it should mimic the financial behavior of the actual project, or indeed any other set of cash flows given the circumstances input as assumptions.

So, forecasts are invaluable for the management of future risk, not because they predict the future (they don't), but because they enable us to consider the financial and other effects of the future changes we have chosen to model *before they occur*. Put simply, the intelligent use of forecast models can improve our ability to successfully manage the future into the present. They are proactive rather than retrospective.

This is important because I believe the primary goal of management *is* to successfully manage the future into the present.

OTHER BENEFITS OF FORECASTING MODELS

When someone new to forecasting initially produces a model for the first time they are obliged to make a number of assumptions. Let us assume they use their best endeavours to develop a model of the monthly cash flows of a business for the next 12 months.

As soon as one month has passed they will be able to compare their model of the cash flows of the business with what actually happened. Learning from the differences between the model and reality they will be able to reiterate the model with improvements and modifications to the structure and the assumptions.

At the end of the second month they will be able to do this again, and so on, in the third and subsequent months. This iterative process delivers a number of benefits; it obliges the person responsible for the model to confront the differences between the forecast and what actually happened each month, so improving their understanding of the behaviour of the assumptions used to generate the model. In other words it makes the users understand the risks affecting the cash flows of the business better. When this information is shared with the management team responsible for the business it should result in a better understanding of the risks affecting the whole business and, if appropriate actions are taken, improve the overall performance of the business.

If no initial forecast is made there is no template in place to compare with reality. This typically results in the management viewing unexpected change rather like the weather (sometimes bad things happen and there is nothing we can do about it), rather than being considered as a foreseeable risk and managed accordingly.

The use of forecasts is, of course, similar to the use of budgets. However, a budget is usually present to serve a number of other objectives such as cost allocation, manufacturing performance measurement and management accountability.

It is better to use a rolling cash flow forecast for the purpose of evaluating and understanding the future risks faced by the business.

Forecasting is best carried out as an ongoing, iterative process: as reality diverges from the forecast this becomes part of the forecasting process itself.

Enough has now been said in the abstract about cash flow forecasting; let us now start to consider a number of issues relevant to the forecasting models we can use to help us manage risk. However, before we do this we need to consider other risks that are inherent in the forecast modelling process itself.

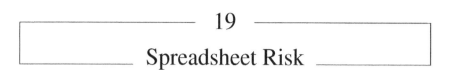

19

Spreadsheet Risk

INTRODUCTION

We could of course start developing our cash flow model by summarising the required cash flow information on paper, perhaps using some sort of multi column pad. Indeed for some very simple tasks this may be more than adequate. However, whilst this may be satisfactory for capturing the source data, its shortcomings would soon become evident as soon as we start to try to manipulate the data.

In order to present the financial information required, in a way that is both organised and capable of easy manipulation, we need a software tool. The main tool of choice for most analysts is spreadsheet software. The first ever spreadsheet software, called Visicalc, was invented in 1979 and was initially released on the Apple platform. As this occurred before software patents were invented it was never patented. This allowed many others to develop their version of the spreadsheet, the most famous of these being Microsoft's Excel.

What made spreadsheets special, particularly for accountants and analysts, who, until then, had done everything on paper, was their ability to recalculate all values on a particular sheet after any individual cell was changed. Prior to the invention of spreadsheets making changes of this kind to forecast data could take hours with an eraser or correction fluid! The use of spreadsheets allowed for significant productivity gains. However, it also meant users became more ambitious, developing and using ever more complex spreadsheets to achieve their aims. This in turn led to the recognition of the problem of spreadsheet risk.

SPREADSHEET RISK

What then is spreadsheet risk? Put simply, this is the possibility that you are using the information in a spreadsheet to take economic decisions and the spreadsheet you are using contains errors *that you don't know about*. In extreme situations spreadsheet risk could (has) cost employees their jobs and their employers millions in losses.

The subject of spreadsheet risk has achieved some recognition in the academic world. I was first made aware of this many years ago when I was referred to a paper entitled 'What We Know About Spreadsheet Errors' published by Professor Raymond R. Panko at the University of Hawaii in 1998. This paper explained the problem of spreadsheet risk and pointed to a number of previous audits of spreadsheets in use in large businesses carried out by audit firms and others. At the time of writing this paper is still available on the Internet. These audits revealed that, without exception, in a given population of large spreadsheets in use there were a significant number of errors, with multiple errors often been present in individual spreadsheets.

Why is this error rate actually inevitable? There are a number of reasons. Firstly, unlike other commercial software, where inputs are controlled and validated by checksums and formatting limits, there are essentially *no controls* as to what a user can do in a spreadsheet. Any number (or label or formula) can be input to any cell at any time. For example the total at the bottom of a list of figures could be derived from anywhere else in the sheet. Even if the formula constituting a total is correctly coded to give the sum of the values above it may still not agree with the values displayed on the screen or printout (this being due to formatting issues which will be explained later).

Secondly, even though we have input the correct data we may make errors of logic in the structure of the model resulting in calculations that appear to result in valid output but in fact do not.

Thirdly, even if the information and logic in a spreadsheet is correct at one point in time, any cell can subsequently be overwritten. For example a cell may contain a formula, which, when the spreadsheet is presented to a user is overwritten by a value to illustrate some point. The rest of the sheet is still dynamic. However, the one cell overwritten is now fixed. Should the sheet be saved again this error becomes effectively permanent but is not visible when inspecting the output from the spreadsheet onscreen or in printed form.

Fourthly, there are risks associated with the misuse of a spreadsheet function called drag and drop. This enables the person constructing the sheet to quickly replicate whole groups of cells in adjacent parts of the spreadsheet. It is very easy to fail to drag the elements being written or overwritten to the precise location that was intended, so leaving parts of the sheet updated and others in their previous configuration.

Fifthly, we have known for many years prior to Professor Panko's paper about keying errors. Keying errors are the errors made by keyboard operators when inputting data. Numerous studies were made of this phenomenon in the 1980s and 1990s revealing that this is a persistent problem. It is not possible to input hundreds of keystrokes of data error free. If you are a regular user of computer keyboards you will be familiar with the number of corrections necessary as a document is typed due to errors when keying. When inputting numeric values this type of error is more difficult to detect, as it doesn't stand out as obviously wrong in the way a misspelled word does.

I hope by now you are sufficiently convinced by the above observations to accept that spreadsheet risk is a real problem. If you are not you should research the subject of spreadsheet risk further. There are many resources on the internet to enable you to do so until you are.

MANAGING SPREADSHEET RISK

So, spreadsheet risk exists. What can we do about it?

There are a number of risk management approaches we can adopt to try to reduce, and ideally eliminate, the risk of unknown errors in our spreadsheets.

Size and Complexity

Our cash flow model can be as simple or as complicated as circumstances and the resources available to build it and manage it warrant. However, remember KISS!

KISS stands for 'keep it simple, stupid!' It is a reminder that complexity *for the sake of it* is pointless. The optimum way to perform most tasks is usually the simplest.

There should always be an identifiable benefit when adding to the complexity in a model. If there is no benefit or payoff, don't bother. Transparency and clarity should always be more important than complexity. Increasing complexity and size in a model brings hidden dangers, which are explained in more detail later in this chapter.

Planning and Specification

As a tool for the analyst or accountant the spreadsheet programme is seductive. The ease with which we can start introducing information to a blank page simply by inserting a number of values and labels leads to a delusion. The delusion being that we can construct all spreadsheets simply by trial and error. This works fine for small spreadsheets where we can see and observe most of what's going on in a screen or so of information. However, as soon as our spreadsheet is a couple of hundred rows down the page and 10 worksheets deep we can no longer observe the cause and effect relationships as they occur when we change a cell. Very rapidly the whole spreadsheet can become unmanageable and at some point we may lose our way and be obliged to start again, because we have lost sight of how the spreadsheet works and broken the logic somewhere. Why does this outcome occur?

The logic of a typical spreadsheet model works as shown in Figure 19.1. We have some input data. We perform some calculations on the input data. This results in output data. When we develop a spreadsheet using trial and error we follow this route in developing our spreadsheet. If we make early design errors

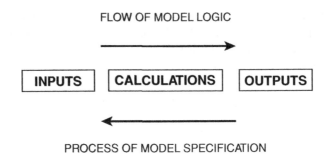

Figure 19.1   The information flow of a spreadsheet model

or compromises it may turn out to be difficult or impossible to get the output we need. What we should be doing is as follows:

1. Decide *exactly* what outputs we want.
2. Identify the inputs that are required and the calculations and logic required to achieve our output.
3. Code the model accordingly.

For anything but the smallest spreadsheet it is wise to adopt a more formal approach to the whole process of construction. The process I recommend contains the following steps:

A. Scope
B. Specify
C. Design
D. Build
E. Test
F. Document and Use

Scope
- Consider the objectives of the model. What is the model for? Who will use it? How will it be used? What is its estimated working life?
- Decide what needs to be in the model and what can be omitted.
- Consider the level of detail required in the input and logical assumptions. Understand in outline how all the logic in the model will work.
- Estimate the time and resources required to develop and test the model.
- Agree the above with all the main stakeholders.

A valuable step in these initial negotiations is to mock up the proposed output schedules in a spreadsheet to show stakeholders what the output will look like. This reduces the possibility of challenge later on in the construction process as to what was required. Put in the title, labels and some sample outputs formatted as you intend to present them and make sure this is what users are expecting. Get them to sign this off if necessary. Remember, users are usually only interested in the output and its information quality. The inputs and logic required to get to the output are typically the sole province of the person responsible for the development of the model.

Specify

Specify the structure and logic sufficiently to provide an unambiguous statement as to how the results or output will be generated. (If you don't know this before you commence coding the model you will not have the skills to make the model work without outside assistance or training.) Essentially, the developer should understand the inputs and calculations necessary to complete the whole model. There should be no surprises during the actual coding process, everything should have been researched and thought out at this stage.

If there are new or unusual features in the model that the developer is not familiar with it may be wise to try them out by constructing a pilot model. This is a prototype for the part of the model where there is any uncertainty about how the logic of the model will be constructed. It is a check that the functionality of the spreadsheet works as anticipated.

Design

Having completed all the intellectual preparation required, develop a plan of the actual layout and structure of the model.

Build

Only now should you load the spreadsheet programme and commence coding the model. There are a number of benefits in following this process. When you are coding you are only thinking about creating the layout structure and formulae required, there is no need to constantly consider the direction and overall logic because this has already been specified.

If the trial and error approach is adopted rather than the process recommended above the spreadsheet model development is actually starting at this point. The person coding is burdened with the need to develop the model logic on the fly as well as inputting the necessary labels, input fields and formulae. This tends to result in a model that is more complex than necessary and which takes longer to build because assumptions are made and functionality is created that is not needed later in the process to generate the required output.

Test

Once the model is complete it is important to test it by inputting simple data through the model. If it behaves as expected then follow this with extreme input value data to see whether the model is robust. Sometimes extreme, zero or negative values will break a model that works fine with typical or expected data values. If the logic and structure of the model is correct this should not be possible. Failure here implies formulae have been used that are incomplete or inappropriate for their purpose.

Another effective test is to have another person, take the model and review its function and try test data through it. New eyes may see flaws not evident to the original architect of the model.

Document and Use

Once the model is ready for use we should add narrative and guidance to the model.

This is usually achieved by adding a front sheet to the model containing a narrative of all the information required by the user to use the model.

The goal of the person preparing the model for use should be to make the model self-explanatory. There should be no need for any verbal guidance when a user is seeking to use the model; all the guidance required should be built into the model.

Timescales for Development

Here is a starting point for considering the time required for the various steps.

Scope	5%
Specify	25%
Design	10%
Build	25%
Test	25%
Document and use	10%

OWNERSHIP

Spreadsheets were originally designed as personal productivity tools. They were not designed for group working.

Those working with spreadsheet models tend to start with the assumption that when one person develops a model they understand how it works (because they built it). Even this may not be true unless the functionality of the spreadsheet has been documented at the time it was produced and is verifiable. If you spend a couple of weeks building a complex spreadsheet and then do not use it for some months, you will probably have forgotten some of how you made it work in the first place. This means that if you now make further changes to the model you may damage its functionality in ways you may not be aware of.

Where more than one person is involved in the construction of a spreadsheet model the risk of disaster is much higher.

If I build a complex spreadsheet model and then allow some other person to change its functionality without them showing me exactly what was done, then neither of us knows how the composite result works!

The safest approach to managing this problem is to have one person manage and maintain complex spreadsheet models. Others may propose changes and even suggest how they might be coded. However, only the model owner should actually make the changes. If this is not possible then the models under joint ownership must be properly documented and changes made in a controlled manner. The tools and approaches used by professional software programmers are relevant here – documenting, versioning and testing everything before releasing changes.

Even this approach is fraught with risk. At some point in the future the nominated person changes job, the business is then left with many complex spreadsheet models on which it depends for its operation with nobody employed who actually knows how they work.

If there is a need to develop and work as a group with spreadsheet type analysis, then there are other financial analysis software tools, that are not spreadsheets, available in the market that are designed for group use. Typically, the structure of these software tools is that the logic is designed by a group responsible for that task and then frozen. The users cannot change or interfere with the logic of the sheet because they do not have the necessary access. They can only input data and examine the resulting output.

CONCLUSIONS ABOUT SPREADSHEET RISK

The foregoing represents a summary of the major risk issues to consider before commencing a cash flow forecasting exercise using spreadsheet software. As further knowledge of spreadsheet forecasting is presented there will be many more methods, tips and tricks exposed to assist the spreadsheet model developer in avoiding spreadsheet risk.

It is impossible to be too structured or deliberate in the development of any complex spreadsheet model. The time spent in preparation is saved many times over in the debugging and completion phase.

GOOD SPREADSHEET TECHNIQUE

What follows is a primer of the most important risk issues to be aware of when developing spreadsheets or using spreadsheets developed by others.

There is a chicken and egg problem here in that I want readers who are less familiar with spreadsheets to understand the issues that result in the possibility of spreadsheet error; however, I am not seeking to teach readers how to code spreadsheets. There are many books written about the process of coding and using spreadsheets. The easiest way to become familiar with spreadsheet development is simply to start doing it. As with most software there is nothing to break if things go wrong. You can always delete and start again or go back a step (there is even a function that does this for you, called 'undo').

Whilst many of the actions required to make a spreadsheet are fairly intuitive, the way certain spreadsheet functionality operates is not intuitive and can result in unexpected difficulties.

Entering Data to Cells

Entering data to cells in a sheet is a potential minefield of errors and misunder-standing! It is essential to understand exactly what a spreadsheet actually does when handling cell data rather than making assumptions about what you guess might be happening.

Spreadsheets generally recognise four types of cell usage. A cell can contain a label, a number, which may be a date and/or time, or a formula.

Labels

Labels are generally text, so headings and other descriptive information are usually entered as labels. Text is defined as *any combination of numbers, spaces and nonnumeric characters.* So, 123abc is treated as text (because it contains non-numeric characters) as is 123 456 (because it contains a space).

There are situations in the real world where, as a spreadsheet user, you might deliberately want a spreadsheet to treat something it would recognise as a number by default as a text entry. Examples are inventory part numbers. If this is input as a number it will be checked for calculation every time the sheet recalculates so slowing the sheet down. If the number is input as text it no longer participates in the recalculation process (it is ignored). This also reduces the possibility of error (the number is actually a label so let's treat it as a label in the spreadsheet). So, if you want to force the spreadsheet to recognise a number as text (an inventory part number, for instance) you can force this by preceding the number with ' prior to entry. For example if I input '123456 to a cell it will treat the number as a text entry.

By default text is left justified, this means the text is displayed from the left hand side of the cell. You can change the alignment of the contents of a cell using the format cells command. However, I recommend that you do not do so until the very end of the worksheet development process (if at all). The fact that a left justified cell is a label by default is of considerable benefit when we are seeking to identify bugs and make our spreadsheet work. Change this at your peril!

The significance of items being treated as text is that all cells containing text are essentially ignored when the spreadsheet recalculates.

Numbers

The first thing to be aware of is that the basic input handling of numbers and dates in your version of the spreadsheet is typically defined when the operating system is installed, rather than in the spreadsheet programme itself. The defaults are found in the control panel or equivalent under the heading 'date, time, language and regional variations'. Thus, as is the convention in the UK, I am used to using the full stop symbol as my decimal separator, however, I have taught finance in other countries where the usual default decimal separator is a comma. This situation is also the case for the symbol used to separate the various elements of a date or time input such as /– and so on.

In Excel, for example, the only characters that can be used as numbers are 0 1 2 3 4 5 6 7 8 9 +–(), / $ % . E e. Generally, entering numbers is fairly intuitive. Any number without a preceding sign is assumed to be positive. Negative numbers can be entered with a preceding minus sign or by placing them in parentheses. Use of the dollar sign will change the cell format to a currency setting. Use of the % sign after the number when input will result in the value being identified and displayed as a percentage (21% also being decimal 0.21).

To avoid confusion regarding where the decimal should be I recommend that all values be input as decimal values. For example, a row may represent a percentage growth rate. I could enter the data in a cell as 25, meaning 25% and then construct formulae to apply this growth rate to sales values each period. If I subsequently change the formatting of the row to percentage the spreadsheet would display this as 2500%. It is better to input the growth rate as decimal, that is, 0.25 and construct formulas using this accordingly. Any change in formatting will still result in the value being recognised by the spreadsheet as 25%.

Dates and/or Time

Another surprise you may experience the first time a spreadsheet is used is the way it handles dates. If you commence entering a date in a cell using / or – as a separator the spreadsheet will recognise this as a date, format it and display it as a date. It stores it as a serial number commencing from 1 January 1900 if on a Windows machine and 2 January 1904 if on an Apple machine. A spreadsheet created in one machine environment is automatically converted to the second environment if opened there. For example inputting the date 01/01/2000 to a Windows machine results in the number 36526 being stored in the cell. This also happens if you input Jan–00. When I first came across this feature I was only seeking to display the date as a label and the way the spreadsheet kept changing my input was annoying. When trying to input dates as labels I learned to precede the input with 'to force the cell to text format.

The reason dates are converted to numbers is to facilitate their use in formulae; it is easier to do calculations involving them in this form.

By default, numbers are right justified in the cell, this means they appear to be adjacent to the right hand side of the cell. Once again it is a good idea not to change this default, so that the basic rule is labels are left justified and numbers (and dates and times) are right justified throughout the sheet.

Formulae

One of the most impressive things about spreadsheets is their power to effect complex arithmetic manipulations effortlessly. This is achieved by inputting formulae to the sheet. To signify that a cell is going to contain a formula any input is preceded by an equals sign =. I can input =2 + 3 –5 *10 to a cell, press enter and the spreadsheet will automatically solve the function and display the result (–45). Notice that the spreadsheet deals with the multiplication before the addition and subtraction, if you don't want this outcome use brackets to achieve the desired affect. This functionality, coupled with the use of cell references in formulae rather than numbers makes this feature incredibly powerful. So, if I input =A1 + A2 into cell A3 the spreadsheet will add the contents of cells A1 and A2 showing the result in cell A3.

There are over a hundred functions available that can be called as required by naming them in a formula. A function is a small pre-programmed formula that performs some arithmetic manipulation related to its name. They are listed in the Insert, Function menu item. If you intend to develop complex spreadsheets it is well worth expending the time required to get to know the functions that are relevant to your task and how they work. Each one is explained in the help menus. Do not assume you know how they work from their names; some of them are quite abstract in their actual operation.

One of the consequences of this architecture is that the formulae themselves are not normally visible in the sheet. The formula in a single cell can be observed by selecting the cell, the contents of the cell being displayed in the input line above the worksheet itself. All the formulas in a sheet can be displayed and/or printed by selecting the Tools, Options, View, Window options, Formulas tick box.

As with numbers, the default behaviour of the spreadsheet programme is that the output of formulae cells is right justified.

Data Entry Risks

By now it should be clear that a spreadsheet is more like a box of chocolates than a process. You pick what you like and use it as you wish. In developing spreadsheets the creators have striven to provide as much flexibility and functionality as they can with little regard to consistency. It is possible to create a list of numbers, format them as labels, right justify them and show a total at the bottom that appears to be the sum of the numbers but may not be, indeed it could be a label or a formula arising from anywhere else in the sheet or even another sheet. Changing any number in a column so created will not change the total when the spreadsheet recalculates. This could be right next to a column of numbers that are numbers and via a formula sum correctly to a total at the bottom. Changing any number in this second column resulting in the total being restated correctly.

Dates are evaluated and treated differently depending on the operating system environment in which the spreadsheet is opened.

In one sense spreadsheets could be viewed as a fraudsters paradise in that they can be made to look like anything you want. The fact that a spreadsheet appears to be laid out logically doesn't mean that it actually is! Remember that formulae are hidden in the normal view.

Before addressing how we might seek to minimise the possibility of spreadsheet error let us consider one other issue fundamental to our understanding of spreadsheet risk.

Formatting

Spreadsheet programmes allow you to change how the contents of a cell are displayed by *formatting* the cell. We have already come across a number of these possible formats in our earlier discussion of data entry. The default for numbers is a format called General, it allows display of up to 11 digits, it simply displays whatever you input unless it overflows the cell boundary in which case it truncates what is displayed and rounds up the last digit if above 0.5.

The maximum size a number can be in a cell is 15 digits, any additional digits arising being treated as zeros.

Selecting the Number format allows the user to decide how many digits are displayed in the cell after the decimal place. However, it does not suppress the remaining digits, they are still retained in the cell memory. This means you can input a series of decimal numbers, format them to whole numbers and then select a function to sum them. The total that arises will not agree with the numbers as displayed by the sheet because the hidden decimals that are not visible are added into the total.

This can be a problem when we use formulae to apply a percentage change value to a data number as is common in forecasting. This can easily generate trailing decimals which then mess up our totals as displayed. One way to deal with this is to suppress all trailing decimals when they arise in the model. There are a number of ways of doing this.

- Function INT – This rounds down the number input or generated by a formula to the nearest integer. You can nest INT in a formula so inputting to a cell =(INT(A1*0.15*100))/100 will generate a value of 15% of the number in cell A1 to 2 decimal places, the remainder always being rounded down. This is an elegant way of calculating VAT in a model without creating unwanted trailing decimals after the two decimal places required to display pence or cents.
- Function ROUND – This rounds a number to a specified number of digits. The format is =ROUND(number, num-digits). So ROUND(5.149, 1) will output 5.1. Unlike INT this function rounds 0.5 up and 0.49 down.
- Function ROUNDDOWN and ROUNDUP do what you would expect! =ROUNDDOWN(A1*0.15, 2) generates the same result as the INT function demonstrated earlier. There are other functions that perform similar manipulations such as FLOOR, CEILING, ODD and EVEN. When using such functions it is important to understand exactly how they work as this may not be as assumed, each function has a separate entry in the help menu explaining its functionality.

Another operation provided by the formatting menu is to change whether the contents of a cell are right or left justified or centred. As I have already stressed changing the defaults can result in cells appearing to be something they are not, so only do so if it improves the clarity or layout of a sheet. For example, I sometimes right justify date labels and currency symbols above columns so that they are directly above the values in the column itself.

CONCLUSIONS ABOUT SPREADSHEET RISK

The spreadsheet represents both heaven and hell. It can perform a mass of extremely complex calculations instantly and display the required output as numbers, in tables or as graphs. Recalculation after changing any input is normally trivial. Elegant, useful cash flow forecasting models can be constructed that add significantly to our understanding of the likely consequences of future events.

However, the lack of any controls on input and use means that the spreadsheet is vulnerable to malicious manipulation, error and mistake, the result being false or misleading outputs. The next chapter presents and discusses a number of ways to minimise this problem.

20

Good Practice Spreadsheet Development

DATA ENTRY, FORMATTING AND SPREADSHEET ERROR

Now that you are familiar with the innate vulnerabilities of spreadsheets and the ease and flexibility with which a spreadsheet can be made to appear exactly as the user wishes, we need to consider how to try to minimise the risk of spreadsheet error arising in our cash flow forecasts and models.

We will start by considering some general strategies to keep our spreadsheet efforts manageable and keep the risk of spreadsheet error to a minimum.

LAYOUT

There are certain conventions used when developing spreadsheets carried over from the original pen and paper world, which are good practice. This is to start with a logical and consistent layout, which is then used throughout a particular model even if it contains many different worksheets. (A worksheet is a single spreadsheet page, a complex spreadsheet model may consist of a number of linked worksheet pages in one or more files.)

Laying Out a Worksheet

Typically the first three or more lines of the sheet will contain headings about who, what and when. Who is it for, what is it, and when is the timescale or period covered? The financial headings will then usually run vertically down the sheet with time being dealt with horizontally across the sheet (Table 20.1).

When we commence laying out the data and formulae our goal is to make the layout clear, transparent and flowing. Ideally, the layout should always be self-explanatory; there should be no need to explain what is going on verbally to the user of a spreadsheet. This means the descriptions used on the labels on the left hand side should always be relevant and clear. Where a convention is adopted this should be explained in a front sheet attached to the model, together with any other important background information.

Table 20.1   Good practice layout illustration

Example Limited Cash flow forecast Year to 31st December 20XX	January $'000	February $'000	March $'000
CASH INFLOWS Deposits received from customers Receipts from trade debtors			
CASH OUFLOWS Payments in respect of trade creditors			

Here are some other guidelines.

There is Plenty of Room

A single worksheet is 65 536 rows vertically and 256 columns horizontally; there is plenty of room to do whatever is required. There is no need to economise on space, so, do not show constants as one number on the left, repeat them in each column in the assumptions area of the sheet. Break up the layout so the flow of logic and information through it remains absolutely clear. Don't use a complex formula in one row when the operation can be more clearly laid out in simpler steps over 10 rows. This practice aids in debugging the model as it makes it easier to see errors. Don't worry about what the output will look like for printing at this stage either. Creating a sheet to use for printing out can be done by linking all the cells in the calculation sheet to another sheet that is then separately prepared for printing by hiding unneeded rows and columns and creating additional subtotals or totals as required. This is discussed further later in the chapter.

Never Embed Data in Formulae

Even things like VAT rates can change. Show them at the top of the sheet in an area titled assumptions. Then refer to the cell reference when building the formula. Indeed things like the numbers of days in a month are better left in the assumptions section as well. Ideally formulae should contain only cell references and occasionally the odd mathematical constant (Table 20.2).

Keep Formulae Simple

Never do in one formula what you can do in three or four simpler formulae. When manipulating data it is better to display the steps being taken to arrive at the required output in a series of simple formulae so the intermediate results are

Table 20.2   Good practice assumptions layout illustration

Example Limited Cash flow forecast Year to 31st December 20XX	**January** **$'000**	**February** **$'000**	**March** **$'000**
ASSUMPTIONS			
Days in the month	31	28	31
Corporate tax rate	0.3	0.3	0.3
VAT rate	0.175	0.2	0.2

displayed in the sheet. This approach also facilitates the identification of errors and debugging. A good rule is if you need to get a calculator out to check a formula is working you are probably trying to do too much in one cell.

Keep Formulae Symmetrical, It Facilitates Error Recognition

Try to use the same formula for a particular operation right across the sheet. If data is brought forward the first column may be different to all the others, make a positive decision how to handle this, either have all of the first column different or use an IF function to allow the same formula in a row of cells to do two different things (the logic being if in column one do *this* otherwise do *this*).

Introduce Controls and Balancing Features Wherever Possible

Features such as making elements that have to balance with each other are a self-checking mechanism to expose errors. If the sheet doesn't balance, there is an error. This is one of the most elegant ways of achieving a more robust design, it also provides a way of justifying that the resulting output is valid to sceptical users.

Remember the cash flow template introduced in the first part of the book is a balancing template; this was a deliberate design decision on my part. If it is not in balance there is an error in its compilation or in the source data.

Calculation

By default whenever a number or formula cell is changed the whole spreadsheet is recalculated. This occurs when the revised entry is finalised by pressing the enter key or moving to another cell. Be aware this can be switched off in the Tools, Options, Calculation menu in which case recalculation only takes place when F9 is pressed.

This feature is included because it is possible to design sheets where the calculation process takes so much time that it is more convenient to input a number of changes before allowing recalculation to take place.

Don't Get Hung up about What It Will Look Like When Printing

Spreadsheet users often wish to achieve a layout that is convenient for printing. This is evident when the layout of a spreadsheet conveniently fits one or more pages of A4 paper.

In order to achieve this within a single spreadsheet, users may make design shortcuts such as concealing some of the spreadsheet logic within dense formulae to compress the number of cells required to get the required output. This is a mistake – the original spreadsheet used to develop the required output should be as large as is necessary without losing any transparency, clarity or flow.

It is easy to create a mirror of the original sheet by linking all the cells in the first sheet to a second worksheet. This is achieved by opening the second worksheet, inputting = and then pointing to the same cell in the original worksheet and pressing enter, (for example if you enter = in cell A1 of sheet 2 and then click on cell A1 of sheet 1 and press enter, cell A1 of sheet 2 will contain whatever is in cell A1 of sheet 1). The resulting formula is then dragged horizontally and vertically until it mirrors the original sheet.) The resulting mirror sheet changes whenever the original sheet is modified. Rows and columns can then be hidden or deleted and extra content introduced in the second spreadsheet to arrive at the layout required for printing.

Use a Filename Saving Hierarchy

If you continually save models in the same name as you incrementally improve them you are overwriting the previous version with your newer version each time. This means you lose the previous version. This is fine until you break your model with a formula or input that results in numerous errors throughout the model.

At this point you realise it would have been helpful to go back to a previous version of the model before you introduced the faulty logic that has caused the problem. So, rather than using the same name it is useful to have a system of filenames that means each save results in a new file. The simplest way of doing this is to call the files newmodel1.xls, newmodel2.xls, newmodel3.xls etc. Alternatively you can use date and time as part of the name. This sequence of files should be retained until you are sure the final model has adequate integrity and works the way you expect.

TYPES OF CASH FLOW SPREADSHEET MODELS

Businesses and others seek to forecast cash flows for a variety of different purposes. Here are four generic types of model:

- Forecast models to monitor and control monthly cash flows.
- Forecast models to decide whether to proceed with a capital project.
- Forecast models for strategy and planning purposes.
- Forecast models for cash flow valuation purposes.

Models for Cash Flow Monitoring and Management

These models typically consist of weekly, periodic or monthly forecasts of revenues and costs (essentially a forecast P&L account). The cash flow revenue part typically starts with one or more sales values and a lagging assumption to recognise the credit period granted to customers. It includes the VAT on sales as a separate item. The objective of the model being to capture as accurately as possible the expected cash inflow from revenues each period.

The cost part consists of a number of sections dealing with different kinds of cost. An elegant way to organise this section is to split costs into those that carry VAT and those that do not. This allows the model to identify the VAT inputs and outputs each month and predict the resulting payment that will be required each month or quarter.

These values are then used to derive a summary of the forecasted cash flows by applying a lagging assumption to the P&L data to reflect when cash is actually received or paid. Table 20.3 is an example of a small part of such a model.

Note that the second column describes what the assumptions represent. 'No' stands for number, so the days in a month are shown as a number. 'Dec' stands for decimal. In Chapter 19 I made it clear it is better to put all values into spreadsheets as decimals, it makes the formulae using them simpler. It also means that if the cells are reformatted to display the decimal as a percentage this works as expected (0.015 becoming 1.5%, if we had 1.5 in the cell this would become 150% on reformatting the cell).

As you can see in Table 20.3 we have identified the cash received each month from sales by using a proportional assumption. What proportion of sales is received as cash this month? What proportion of sales is received as cash next month? To make this work in the spreadsheet the rule is that the resulting proportions must add to one so that all the sales value is allocated to the cash flow forecast as time passes.

Table 20.3 shows all the cash collected over just three different months. However, this could easily be extended to cover as many months as is necessary. To keep the illustration of the logic clear I have left out the cash that would be received from sales in the previous year, which would of course be included in a real model.

Table 20.3 Sample of a cash flow forecasting model

Example Limited Cash flow forecast Year to 31st December 20XX		**Historic 20XX**	**Forecast Jan**	**Forecast Feb**	**Forecast Mar**
ASSUMPTIONS					
Days in the month	No		31	28	31
Inflation forecast	Dec		0.01	0.005	0.02
Real change in sales month	Dec		0.02	0.00	0.03
Sales paid for this month	Dec		0.1	0.15	0.2
Sales paid for next month	Dec		0.7	0.70	0.6
Sales paid for +2 months	Dec		0.2	0.25	0.2
CONTROL (must add to 1)	Dec		1	1	1
VAT RATE	Dec		0.175	0.20	0.20
PROFIT AND LOSS **ACCOUNT DATA**					
Sales		10 000	10 302	10 354	10 686
CASH FLOW DATA					
This month sales cash flow			1030	1553	2137
Last months sales cash flows				7200	7248
−2 months sales cash flow					2060
TOTAL CASH RECEIVED			1030	8753	11 445

Note: No = Number, Dec = Decimal.

The same strategy can be used to deal with the expenses of the business, forecast the monthly P&L cost and then lag it to show the normal payment behaviour of the business.

Those new to this should now be realising that the preparation of these models is not trivial, there will be many lines of assumptions and data to capture something that comes close to tracking the actual performance of a typical, well established business. Remember to add only as much complexity as you need and make the logic you have used as transparent as possible. Ideally someone else should be able to review the model and understand how it is constructed without any explanation from the creator.

The only items remaining required to make the cash flow forecasting part of the model complete are the capital (or balance sheet) inflows and outflows, these are normally sufficiently simple that they can be directly input to the model. The two main items are typically capital expenditure and debt repayment. Capital expenditure is typically an item that is scheduled many months before or otherwise known before being actually committed, so there is usually plenty of data available to provide values for the forecast. Likewise, scheduled debt repayment is usually known about many years in advance.

Finally we can add some logic, which identifies the monthly interest paid or received on the net cash/debt position each month. This typically looks something like Table 20.4.

Table 20.4 Sample of the interest treatment in a cash flow forecasting model

Example Limited Cash flow forecast Year to 31ˢᵗ December 20XX	**January $'000**	**February $'000**	**March $'000**
IN THE CASH INFLOWS PART			
Interest received on previous month closing balance		21	12
AT THE BOTTOM OF THE WORKSHEET			
Cash beginning of month	0	5000	3000
Movement in the month	5000	(2000)	6000
Cash end of month	5000	3000	9000

Forecast Models to Analyse Whether to Proceed with a Project

In the chapter introducing the subject of forecasting I suggested that the main pay-off from preparing forecasts was the facility to understand the cash flow consequences of changes to a project.

In deciding whether to proceed with a project we are, in addition, normally seeking to see if the project is actually viable. We want to know if the project will increase our wealth (cash).

We do this by forecasting all the cash outflows and inflows for the project and then discounting them to reflect the time cost of money. There are a series of steps to be followed, they are:

1. Identify the relevant project cash flows.
2. Summarise them to identify the periodic net cash flow relating to the project.
3. Discount the resulting values using an appropriate discount rate.
4. Sum the resulting values to identify the Net Present Value of the project.
5. Evaluate the result.

Identify the Relevant Poject Cash Flows

This is the most demanding part of the exercise; it might take weeks or months to gather all the necessary information for a large project. The remaining four steps can be completed in an afternoon.

Our objective is to identify and forecast all the cash inflows and outflows that the project will generate. If we are purchasing a machine to produce a product we are seeking to forecast the value of the output attributable to the work done by the machine. For example, if we purchase an injection moulding machine to produce say washing up bowls we would be interested in the value of a completed washing up bowl less the cost of the raw plastic that goes in it. This is the value generated by investing in the machine. So the cash inflow from the machine is likely to be the cash margin generated over the raw material cost times the number of bowls produced per measurement period (probably months for this example).

The relevant cash outflows would be the direct costs of operating the machine (electricity, gas, water etc.) and all other costs such as maintenance, servicing, premises, security and the cost of the tool to produce the washing up bowls. There would also be a labour cost in operating the machine.

So, even for this simple example, there are a lot of variables to consider. Just imagine what the forecast would look like for a toll bridge or power station with a timescale extending 25 to 40 years into the future.

Summarise Them to Identify the Periodic Net Cash Flow Relating to the Project

Having identified the relevant cash inflows and outflows we then need to summarise them into a spreadsheet. For a small project we might choose to do this by month or by quarter. For a large multi year project we might choose half years or full years.

Again, the issue here is, does the smaller measurement period add value to our analytical process? If it does not, do not do it. If quarters will give you what you need to know, do not produce a forecast in months.

Table 20.5 shows an example of the first year of the forecast for a simple project. Here we can see the capital cost of the machine and its installation costs, we are assuming it takes three months to install the machine. In the second quarter we see the value of the output of the machine, which then grows as sales increase over the next six months.

The duration of the forecast is important; it should reflect the life of the project. In our example this should probably be the predicted operating life of the machine as we are producing something that is unlikely to go out of fashion. This means we could be attempting to forecast 10 years or more into the future. This means our forecast is subject to more and more uncertainty as it goes forward. However, it is important to remember the points made in the introductory chapter on forecasting. We are not trying to predict the future. We are saying, if the future looks like this, what are the consequences for the cash inflows and cash outflows of the project?

If the product we are intending to produce on our machine is an item subject to fashion trends, then we may forecast the period we consider we will have demand

Table 20.5   Sample of the layout of a project evaluation model

Machine project Discounted cash flow forecast Year to 31st December 20XX		Forecast Jan–Mar	Forecast Apr–Jun	Forecast Jul–Sep	Forecast Oct–Dec
ASSUMPTIONS					
Days in the quarter	No		91	92	92
Inflation forecast	Dec		0.01	0.005	0.02
Cash inflows					
Cash margin from sales			10 000	15 000	20 000
Cash outflows					
Purchase of machine		100 000			
Installation cost		20 000			
Utility connection cost		6000			
Labour cost operation			2000	2100	2200
Utilities cost			2000	1800	2100
Maintenance cost			200	200	1000
Net Cash inflow/(outflow)		(126 000)	5800	10 900	14 700

for the product if we think demand for the product will cease before the life of the machine to produce it has expired. Remember to bring in the cash inflow from selling the machine (and the costs of decommissioning) at the end of the period if this is the scenario.

Discount the Resulting Values Using an Appropriate Discount Rate

Having identified the expected cash flows of the project we now need to discount them to reflect the time cost of money.

If interest rates are positive real, the value of a sum of money received some time in the future is lower than the value of the same sum of money received today.

If you are unfamiliar with the theory behind discounted cash flow and the time value of money I suggest you read an appropriate corporate finance textbook that explains this concept.

Generally we are seeking to apply to the project a discount rate that reflects the riskiness of the project. A good way of modelling this is to consider what it would cost to finance the project in equity and debt if it was taken to venture capitalists, business angels or banks for financing. In our example it might be possible to finance 80% of the purchase price of the machine by leasing it, the remainder being financed by equity. From this we can deduce a discount factor.

If the project is incremental to the activities of an existing business it may be reasonable to use the cost of capital of the existing business. This approach assumes the project is of similar risk to the level of business risk faced by that business.

If the forecast is quarterly we need to construct a quarterly discount factor to match the measurement period (Table 20.6).

Table 20.6 Sample illustrating the use of the discount factor in a project evaluation model

Machine project Discounted cash flow forecast Year to 31st December 20XX		Forecast Jan–Mar	Forecast Apr–Jun	Forecast Jul–Sep	Forecast Oct–Dec
ASSUMPTIONS					
Decimal year	No	0	0.25	0.5	0.75
Cash inflows					
Cash from sales			10 000	15 000	20 000
Cash Outflows					
Purchase of machine		100 000			
Installation cost		20 000			
Utility connection cost		6000			
Labour cost operation			2000	2100	2200
Utilities cost			2000	1800	2100
Maintenance cost			200	200	1000
Net Cash inflow/(outflow)		(126 000)	5800	10 900	14 700
Discount factor	0.1	1	0.976	0.953	0.931
Present value		(126 000)	5663	10 393	13 686

The easiest way to do this is to set up a formula that takes the annual discount factor from the position on the left, fix this location in the formula using the $ signs in front of the cell reference and take the power from the decimal period data assumption. You should end up with a formula that looks something like this. The ^ symbol means *to the power of* in Excel:

$$1/(1 + \text{Discount factor})^{\text{decimal period}}.$$

So for the April–June period the formula would be 1/(1 + 0.1) ^0.25 giving an answer of 0.976454.

Sum the Resulting Values to Identify the Net Present Value of the Project

Finally we sum the individual present values to end up with the Net Present Value of the project (Table 20.7).

Table 20.7 Sample of a part model illustrating the identification of the net present value of the project

Net Cash inflow/(outflow)		(126 000)	5800	10 900	14 700
Discount factor	0.1	1	0.976	0.953	0.931
Present value		(126 000)	5663	10 393	13 686
Project Net Present Value		154 963			

Bear in mind that the sample in Table 20.7 only displays the first four periods of the project, let us assume the full model forecasts out for 10 years. In our example we see a positive net present value for the project of 154 963. What does this actually signify?

Evaluate the Result

It means that if the project is executed and the cash flows arise as predicted the sponsor will be 154 963 better off than if they had not committed to the project. The interesting bit about discounting cash flows in this way is *when* you are better off. The answer is at the beginning of the project!

If you could borrow and lend at the same interest rate as the project, you could borrow 154 963 at the beginning of the project and spend it. Assuming the cash flows arise as predicted and interest rates are fixed the project would pay off the loan arising exactly. This is why the value is known as the Net Present Value of the project, it is the amount by which it increases your wealth now (at the beginning of the project).

So, in general, positive Net Present Values are good, they imply you will have more wealth by executing the project. Negative Net Present Values are bad; they imply you will lose wealth if you execute the project.

Conclusions about Discounting the Cash Flow of a Project

This technique is useful, but not because it predicts the future, (it does not). By completing a model of the cash inflows and cash outflows of a project it makes us consider the variability and risks associated with each individual cash flow and provides a model that can them be manipulated to look at the effects of delay, non-performance, cost inflation and other risks.

It also gives us some sense of the value to us of the project, for example a project may have a Net Present Value of £1000, but not be worth doing as it does not compensate us adequately for the other resources not necessarily captured in the cash flow forecast such as the management time required in order to complete the project.

Multi Year Models for Strategic Planning and Valuation

The final type of cash flow forecasting model we are going to consider are those used for strategic planning and valuation purposes. These typically consist of a multi year profit and loss account (P&L), a balance sheet and a summary cash flow.

Why is it typical to produce all three accounting statements?

Firstly, managers and entrepreneurs tend to think in terms of the profit and loss account (and balance sheet) rather than in terms of cash flow.

In running a manufacturing business, for example, managers typically target given levels of sales and costs, usually through some sort of budgeting process. They tend to think in terms of profit and loss account values. To a general manager, sales simply represent a given volume of output at a given price from the factory. For a production manager the challenge is to produce the volume required to satisfy the sales (within given cost constraints) within a set period.

If you ask a manger to predict the cash received in a period, he has no easy intuitive method of arriving at a value. However, if you ask a manager what the level of sales will be in a given month he is more likely to come up with a reasonable estimate based on his knowledge of the historic buying patterns and of the market served. This is partly because sales represents the actual physical goods delivered in a given period, and this is in some ways easier to visualise. If you also ask the manager what is the typical credit period taken by his customers he is likely to be able to give an answer very close to the likely future outcome most of the time.

From these two inputs the person developing the cash flow model can derive the forecast cash to be received each period.

So, the point is, when making multi year forecasts into the future, it does make sense to derive the future cash flows from a forecasted P&L and balance sheet, rather than in isolation. Managers will be better at arriving at useful forecast of the values required by starting with a P&L forecast, followed by the resulting balance sheet.

Secondly there is another benefit to producing a model that contains all three statements; the model can be constructed so that all three statements are linked through their actual real world relationships. In other words, if we produce a surplus in the profit and loss account this results in an increase in the assets or a decrease in the liabilities in the balance sheet and an equivalent change in the cash flows. The whole model can effectively be made so that all three statements are in balance at all times.

This can be very useful as it provides a reality check on the assumptions made about the future. For example, if a growth company forecasts aggressive levels of growth for the next five years it may discover it runs out of cash/debt facilities due to the increased investment required in fixed and working assets within 18 months. Likewise the growth scenario may reveal that fixed asset investment may need to double in order to keep capacity ahead of the required output. If the relationships between the statements are accurately modelled we can see the consequences in terms of assets and liabilities of changes to the forecasted P&L and observe the resulting cash flow behaviour.

The basic template to create this functionality is shown in Table 20.8. The steps required to complete the model are explained on each line.

This model illustrates the fundamental underlying logic required to create a three-statement model with each element balancing and linked to the other elements. It shown the minimum logic required to achieve this; there are essentially eleven inputs required.

Building these models is not trivial, it can take weeks to produce a model that is sufficiently tailored to a business to be realistic in the way it reflects changes in the assumptions into the statement values. This is the sort of model that requires the formal construction process I recommended in Chapter 19 on Spreadsheet Risk. The commentary that follows assumes the reader is an experienced user of spreadsheet software who already has some experience of attempting to create models of this type.

What follows is a guide to using this basic structure to create models of varying complexity. There a number of steps required to complete this model.

Enter EBITDA for the Year

Start by preparing a profit and loss account at the level of detail desired. Depending on your purpose this may be 10 to 20 lines or 100 to 200 lines. The first key value required for the three-statement logic is the value of EBITDA. The P&L can have as much sales, cost of sales and overhead detail as is required for purpose. Indeed, the modeller may choose to produce a model with sales and costs in a variety of separate worksheets, which summarise to the P&L worksheet as one or more totals.

Enter Depreciation

The assumptions required can be as simple as a percentage of sales assumption, or as complex as a full model to calculate depreciation by asset class for all existing and forecasted capital expenditure (a model like this is considerably more complicated to produce than the three statement model). The modeller can leave the decision as to how to drive this value until later in the process if preferred and

Table 20.8   Illustration of the logic required for a three statement model

Jury's master three statement model

Step	Spreadsheet operation	Profit & Loss Dr	Profit & Loss Cr	Cash Flow Dr	Cash Flow Cr	Balance Sheet Change Dr	Balance Sheet Change Cr
1	*Enter EBITDA for the year*		*50 000*	*50 000*	*0*		
2	*Enter depreciation*	*5000*				*0*	*5000*
3	*Enter interest*	*12 000*		*0*	*12 000*		
4	*Enter taxes*	*30 000*		*0*	*30 000*		
5	*Enter dividends*		*2000*	*0*	*2000*		
6	**Sum the two sides of the P&L & identify the profit and loss**	**49 000**	**50 000**				
7	**Profit or Loss for the period (transfer to the Balance Sheet)**	**1000**	**0**			**0**	**1000**
8	*Enter Capex for the year*				*20 000*	*20 000*	*0*
9	*Enter change in inventories*			*4000*		*0*	*4000*
10	*Enter change in debtors*				*1000*	*1000*	*0*
11	*Enter change in creditors*			*1500*		*0*	*1500*
12	*Enter new equity changes*			*2000*		*0*	*2000*
13	*Enter new debt changes*			*8000*		*0*	*8000*
14	**Sum the cash flows & balance the balance sheet**			**65 500**	**65 000**		
	Change in Debt/Cash for the period (transfer to the Balance Sheet)			**0**	**500**	**500**	**0**
15	**Sum the statements to ensure a balance**	**50 000**	**50 000**	**65 500**	**65 500**	**21 500**	**21 500**

simply enter a value in the spreadsheet for the moment if the first priority is to have a fully functioning three-statement model. I sometimes refer to these values as placeholders, they are there to allow the modeller to develop the rest of the model logic, and will be replaced with a more appropriate value (possibly derived from elsewhere) later in the process.

Enter Interest

Again the initial assumption driving this line is likely to be scheduled interest on any existing debt. Later on, after the model has been shown to work, we might create a deliberate circularity enabling us to calculate the interest received or paid on the net debt arising from the model each period. The modeller can leave the decision as to how to drive this value until later in the process if preferred and simply enter a value in the chosen location for the moment if the first priority is to have a fully functioning three-statement model.

Enter Taxes

A common way to drive this line in our model is to take a percentage of the profit before tax value as our expected taxation value, this percentage being known as the effective tax rate. Alternatively we can develop a full tax computation using appropriate values taken from other parts of the model such as Capex. The modeller can leave the decision as to how to drive this value until later in the process if preferred and simply enter a value in for the moment if the first priority is to have a fully functioning three-statement model.

Enter Dividends

If the business has traditionally paid a dividend we can initially put in a percentage payout assumption for the moment. As dividend payout policy is entirely under the control of management, the values (or percentages required) can simply be scheduled into the assumptions. The modeller can leave the decision as to how to drive this value until later in the process if preferred and simply put a value in for the moment if the first priority is to have a fully functioning three-statement model.

Complete the Profit and Loss Account Forecast

At this point the model should have a full profit and loss account. This can then be copied (dragged) to the right across the sheet to provide as many periods/years as is required for the purposes of the model. Strategy and planning models are typically 3–12 years into the future.

The issue of how long the forecast might be is dictated by things such as the product replacement cycle (this is 8–12 years for a business producing something like a motor car for example). This is another decision that is important, as we ideally want to capture cycle effects such as the effects of boom/recession and other sector cycle effects. The more uncertainty about the future the shorter the timescale of the planning model should be.

A valuation model should ideally have an explicit forecast period as long as possible as it reduces the significance of the terminal value in the whole process. I suggest 10 years as a good starting point.

Commence the Balance Sheet

We now start to build the logic for the balance sheet. Unless this is a new business project there will be an opening balance sheet in existence. The value each year in the forecast being built directly from this. What the assumptions in the three-statement model generate is balance sheet change values, these are then added or subtracted from the opening balance sheet values to get to the periodic forecast balance sheets.

Enter Capex for the Year

As Capex is generally planned well in advance, this should be straightforward. The main logic driving this is that there is sufficient capacity available from production to produce the forecasted sales; if we are forecasting significant sales growth it follows we expect higher Capex also. In most circumstances we can assume fixed asset disposal will be negligible in which case we can use the simpler logic of:

Opening fixed assets value $+$ Capex $-$ depreciation $=$ Closing fixed assets value

Alternatively we can model the whole of the fixed asset note and use the result to drive the forecast Capex and Fixed Asset values.

Enter Change in Inventories

The next task is to model the movements in the net working assets of the entity. The first item we deal with here is the change in inventory. If the business is mature with a stable product mix the assumption driving this value is unlikely to vary significantly year on year. The usual way of driving this value is by making an assumption about the number of days of sales the inventory represents (an inventory days assumption). We generate a value for the end of period inventory by taking a number of days of sales. So, if sales are increasing over time this implies inventory will increase in tandem. The change in inventory then comes into the cash flow statement as a working asset change item and into the current assets in the balance sheet.

Whilst one assumption will be sufficient in many cases, multiple assumptions can be used if there are different product lines with different inventory behaviours.

Enter Change in Debtors

Again, it is normal to deal with the change in debtors by expressing it as a number of days of sales, this means as sales levels change so does the amount invested in debtors. Depending on the need of the users it may be helpful to break this value up into trade debtors and other debtors or, indeed, further items; all of them can be driven in the same way unless there is better information elsewhere about the level of the value in the future in which case this can be used instead.

Enter Change in Creditors

The same logic applies to creditors, a number of days of sales assumption will usually work fine as it is a reasonable measure of volume change. Again it may help to split the item into trade creditors and other creditors. Further detail can be included if there is added value for users, the taxation and dividend creditor can be shown separately by incorporating the following logic into the sheet:

Opening taxation creditor + this year's tax − tax paid = Closing creditor

Opening dividend creditor
   + this year's dividend − dividend paid = Closing dividend creditor

Bear in mind we now need to drive the tax and dividend paid items in the cash flow with a unique assumption (probably last years P&L tax value). The dividend may be one dividend or an interim dividend in the current and a final dividend paid in the following period.

Enter Equity Changes

Here we can put in as an assumption showing the amount of equity increase or decrease we wish to have in the model. This allows us to introduce new capital should it be required in the forecast model as a scheduled fundraising. This may be necessary if the forecast shows the business is running out of funds due to the rate of growth.

Enter Debt Changes

The nature of debt is that the payments associated with it are normally known many years into the future. Thus it should be straightforward to identify these and incorporate them into the model. This should also be viable for variable rate debt as we will have a forecast variable interest rate (and margin) assumption for each separate element of debt in the model.

At this point we have all the information required to complete the balance sheet except the change in cash value, which will come from the completed cash flow statement.

So it is also time to complete the cash flow statement and link the resulting change in cash item to the balance sheet. If you have not made any errors of coding all three statement should now add up and balance as shown in the illustration of the three-statement model above.

Having made the model work, it can now be enhanced by improving the way individual assumptions are driven if this is needed. For example, we can improve the quality of the depreciation calculation, and taxation calculation to make them more realistic in the way they deal with changes in the other assumptions. Also the net debt can be summarised each period and the resulting cash debt balance used to identify the interest due on the period. The model can then be made circular by linking this to the interest value in the P&L. Alternatively, This can then be added manually if you do not like circularities in models.

It is also important to test the model with other data to make sure it does what is expected of it, try large, zero and negative values in the fields to ensure it operates as expected.

Conclusions about Strategic Planning and Valuation Forecasts

Building these multi year integrated models is both challenging and extremely satisfying. Whilst their construction is not trivial, if the guidelines regarding good modelling practice are adhered to there is no reason why an elegant model cannot be constructed over a couple of weeks.

The benefit of having such a model is that managers and others can examine the impact on an entity's future performance of changes in sales, margins, costs, working assets behaviour, interest rates, leverage and any other assumption in the model before taking any decision regarding the same.

One important issue is to think in scenarios rather than just changing one or more assumptions in isolation. For example, the onset of recession implies the following, a fall in sales and margins, an initial increase in inventory as sales slow, followed by a planned reduction in inventory, an increase in debtor days due to recession cash flow problems for customers, possible step change cost cutting and labour reduction if sales show a permanent fall to a lower value, a suspension of Capex and a rapid reduction in available debt capacity. So, in coming up with a scenario to examine the effects of recession all these assumptions should be manipulated in tandem to reflect the position.

The best way of using models like this is to come up with both positive and negative future scenarios that are related to possible future realities and examine the effect on the three statements of the changes made to the assumptions.

CONCLUSIONS ABOUT GOOD PRACTICE SPREADSHEET DEVELOPMENT

In this chapter I have tried to provide sufficient information about the four generic types of cash flow forecasting model for users new to the subject to develop the architecture of their own model built to satisfy their own particular needs.

It is difficult to standardise the cash flow forecast modelling process because every individual business is different. Issues such as precise nature of the business, size, sector and location all conspire to make our ideal model different to one that might be produced for a similar business elsewhere.

The best way of learning about the difficulties of spreadsheet modelling is simply to start doing it. As the process is normally non-destructive there is nothing to break!

21

The Use of Assumptions in Spreadsheet Models

INTRODUCTION

In the previous chapter, I illustrated the four generic types of model:

- Forecast models to monitor and control monthly cash flows.
- Forecast models to decide whether to proceed with a capital project.
- Forecast models for strategy and planning purposes.
- Forecast models for cash flow valuation purposes.

I hope by now it is clear that a model is only as good as the assumptions used to drive it. If these have been carefully researched so that their likely range and behaviour in different economic conditions are well understood, and they have been coded into the model with appropriate logic that behaves as desired, the model should be a useful tool to show us what future cash flow performance may look like given variations in the assumptions.

What follows is a more detailed discussion of some of the remaining issues involved in introducing assumptions to cash flow spreadsheet models.

HOW ASSUMPTIONS ARE USED IN A SPREADSHEET

The assumptions are there to allow us to create forecast values for the income, costs, balance sheet and hence cash flow. For example, the cash flow from sales is typically derived by adding a second assumption (debtor days) describing the time it takes customers to pay for the sales.

So, we might drive the sales line by showing an increase in sales of 5% for the first forecast period. The logic being the spreadsheet would then take the historic value and increase it by 5% to represent sales in the first forecast period.

In the second forecast period the forecasted percentage increase might by 10%. The logic being to take the first period forecast value and increase that by 10% to get the second forecast period value. This logic results in a daisy chain of formulae driving the sales line. This is the usual way of creating a multi period forecast (Table 21.1).

This is probably the simplest way of creating the forecast values required, the use of one simple assumption. In many situations this may be perfectly adequate.

Table 21.1 Illustration of the effect of a daisy chain assumption

Example Limited		Historic 20XX	Forecast 20X1	Forecast 20X2
Assumption				
Increase in sales year on year	%		5	10
Sales		10 000	10 500	11 550

If I change the percentage used as an assumption in the first forecast period it is important to remember that it will affect all the later periods (Table 21.2).

Table 21.2 Illustration of the effect of a change in a daisy chain assumption

Example Limited		Historic 20XX	Forecast 20X1	Forecast 20X2
Assumption				
Increase in sales year on year	%		10	10
Sales		10 000	11 000	12 100

If this is not considered desirable, the formulae can be constructed so the percentage change is always relative to the historic period sales (Table 21.3).

Table 21.3 Illustration of the effect of a non-daisy chain assumption

Example Limited		Historic 20XX	Forecast 20X1	Forecast 20X2
Assumption				
Increase in sales relative to 20XX	%		10	20
Sales		10 000	11 000	12 000

Notice how I have changed the description of the assumption to make this clear. The goal is always to construct and document the spreadsheet so that it is entirely self-explanatory. It is always important to ensure that the labels used for the assumptions are not misleading. If there is any doubt add a comment (Insert,Comment) to the cell explaining exactly what is going on.

THE SELECTION OF ASSUMPTIONS

In Chapter 18, I suggested the goal of a competent analyst was to produce forecast models that avoid unnecessary complexity and deal elegantly with the variables and assumptions used to drive the model.

One objective is to have the forecasted variables behave as we would expect given changes in the external and internal environment. This means we have to consider carefully what are the exact drivers of change. Some of these are internal (management actions) and some of these are external (the impact of an economic recession for example).

The next section deals with the introduction of macroeconomic assumptions to spreadsheets.

MACROECONOMIC ASSUMPTIONS

The main macroeconomic assumptions we will consider are:

- Inflation rates
- Interest rates
- Taxation rates
- Currency movements
- Commodity price changes

In preparing a model I may also add to this group of items any constants I may use in the sheet such as days in the month or decimal periods. I prefer to have all data shown as an assumption (even if it is considered a constant), rather than embedding data in formulae. It is better that all formulae simply consist of cell references (I make this a rule in spreadsheet preparation). The danger is that once data is in a formula and you wish to change it, it may be extremely time consuming to locate all instances of that same data in formulae throughout a number of large worksheets to correct the value, indeed failing to update the sheet properly may introduce spreadsheet error to the sheet. For example, if you embed the VAT rate in a formula, which is then subsequently changed (as has recently happened in the UK) you will then need to review all the formulae in the sheet that might contain the VAT rate for amendments to reflect the new VAT rate.

The Inflation Assumption

Inflation is a perennial feature of markets. It is best thought of as an exchange rate. It measures changes in the relationship between the value of money and the value of real assets.

Nominal Versus Real Forecasts

There are various schools of thought as to how best to deal with the effects of inflation in forecasting models.

One view is to ignore it, and forecast all values in terms of real (rather than nominal) money.

In order to use such a forecast to compare with actual performance, a user would have to either uplift the real forecast for the actual inflation experienced each period and then compare it with the actual performance values. Alternatively the user could rebase the current period actual values to the original forecast base date and compare the performance in real terms.

Creating a real forecast is reasonable where a project is essentially independent of local inflation effects. Examples are oil and gas projects where costs may be paid in a local currency but revenues are taken in US dollars when the oil or gas is sold into world markets, the construction of the original capital asset also being financed in US dollars.

The second view is to forecast the values in nominal terms and include in the model an inflation assumption. For example, the increase in sales each period would now have two components, the increase in sales due to inflation and the real increase achieved. This is illustrated in Table 21.4.

Table 21.4 Illustration of the effect of a percentage inflation assumption in a model

Example Limited		Historic 20XX	Forecast 20X1	Forecast 20X2
Assumption				
Inflation forecast	%		3	4
Real change in sales year on year	%		5	10
Sales		10 000	10 815	12 372

Looking at the above example it appears that inflation over the two year forecast is 7%. However, this is not the case as the values compound each period. The actual value is 7.12% (this being the sum of $(1.03 \times 1,04) -1$). This difference gets bigger if you compound more and more years.

One alternative to this layout is to use an inflation index (rather than an inflation rate) as an assumption. This is illustrated in Table 21.5. The index is easier to work with in formulae than a percentage periodic increase because the compounding is already built in. For example, to uplift the historic value by the inflation rate is simply:

Historic sales/historic index*forecast period index

10000/117.9*121.44

Table 21.5   Illustration of the use of an inflation index in a model

Example Limited		Historic 20XX	Forecast 20X1	Forecast 20X2
Assumption				
Inflation forecast	%		3	4
Inflation index		117.90	121.44	126.30
Real change in sales year on year	%		5	10
Sales		10 000	10 815	12 372

The same inflation value would be used to uplift costs each year and to identify the change in inventory, debtors and creditors due to inflation effects.

This approach is probably better for most projects where capital costs, borrowings, revenues and costs are all in the same local currency. Why is this?

The behaviour of consumers, markets and sectors changes as the level of inflation increases in a local currency. Variations in the periodic rate of inflation causes changes to consumer and business behaviour. When inflation is very low (say 2% or less) business and consumers tend to ignore it in most of their business dealings.

As inflation increases (which is normally accompanied by an increase in interest rates) the effect is to make the cost of providing credit to others more and more expensive. As a result trade credit starts to disappear and the cost of debt becomes prohibitive. Eventually a point is reached where no one wants to hold money when they get it because it is losing its value so quickly, so when they receive money they immediately buy real assets with it. A business may stop holding cash and instead buy more raw materials or commodities to shelter surpluses, as these will hold their value. The other option is to convert the money immediately into a harder currency if the business is located in a country where currency can be freely converted (some countries do not allow citizens to have bank accounts in foreign currencies).

So, the relationship between different assumptions in a forecasting model will change as economic circumstances change. By including inflation as an assumption, scenarios can be created that remain internally consistent as inflation increases.

Interest Rates

It is usual to have an interest rate assumption in forecasting models. This allows the model to calculate the cost of debt in the business and also to generate the value of interest receivable if the business has a cash surplus. Indeed if the business has a variety of different financing arrangements there may be many different rates of interest reflected as assumptions in the model.

Rather than assuming one rate for debt and another for cash surpluses it is more elegant to forecast the future base rate and show the margin paid over this for debt and the margin under this as a deposit rate. By designing the assumptions to work in this way it allows the model values to easily change as forecasted or actual base rates change (Table 21.6).

Table 21.6   Illustration of the use of interest rate assumptions in a model

Example Limited		Historic 20XX	Forecast 20X1	Forecast 20X2
Assumption				
Base rate (LIBOR)	%	4.5	5	6
Debt margin	%	2.5	2.5	2.0
Deposit margin		−1	−1	−1
Calculated variables				
Debt cost	%	7	7.5	8
Deposit interest rate	%	3.5	4	5

Taxation Rates

Most forecasting models will need a tax rate to drive the corporate tax due on profits value. One value is probably sufficient if the model if a multi year projection for strategy or valuation purposes.

If the forecast model is for monitoring and control purposes it may be necessary to include a VAT rate and possibly the average value of the deduction from wages and salaries in income taxes as a percentage. The level of detail required is largely driven by the variability of the values in the forecast. If the business being modelled is relatively stable there is less need for complexity in the model.

Currency Movements

If the business being modelled operates in a variety of currencies it is usual to view everything in terms of the reporting currency, this being the currency in which the annual report and accounts is prepared. Cash flows originating in other currencies need to be converted to the currency of the forecast. This requires us to have a view about future changes in exchange rates. Whatever assumptions are made need to be consistent with inflation expectations and the purchasing power parity model.

Commodity Price Changes

As well as the producers themselves, certain other kinds of business are very vulnerable to particular commodity costs. For example, a big cost for airlines is aviation fuel, which moves in price with the price of crude oil. Businesses who process plastics are in a similar position as most plastics are also derived from oil. Where a significant element of the cost of sales is represented by an input that is a commodity or is closely related to a commodity it may be more elegant to have the commodity price as an assumption and link the cost item to this.

THE APPROPRIATE AND INAPPROPRIATE USE OF ASSUMPTIONS

In the final part of this chapter we will discuss how to get the best out of our models when we use them. Remember that in Chapter 18, I introduced the idea that when we create these models to assist in management decision-making we are trying to develop *plausible future scenarios*.

Base Case

For example, if we are forecasting the future cash flows of a business for the next five years for strategic purposes we tend to start with what is referred to as the 'base case'.

This is the version of the model using the assumptions that management deems *most likely* to occur. The output is meant to give an impression of the likely future performance of the business given everything the managers know today (this of course excludes unknown or unexpected future events). By definition this is subjective (an opinion).

Even this may be contentious, owners and other capital providers may immediately express dissatisfaction with the expected outcome on the grounds that it is simply insufficient. They may seek more returns. The next set of scenarios we should consider are more positive scenarios.

Positive Scenarios

The next likely process is to develop some scenarios that produce higher returns in the future, usually by implementing more radical change in the business. Examples are:

- New product introduction
- Geographic expansion
- Capacity expansion
- Cost reduction and efficiency improvement
- Relocation
- Changes to the value chain (outsourcing, subcontracting etc.)
- Research and development
- Capital expenditure

The point being made here is that merely varying one or more assumptions to see the effect on profit may be a meaningless exercise. For example, we may note that increasing sales by an additional 5% over the entire forecast period results in an increase in 15% in profits.

However, we may have failed to add the additional incremental costs that might be required in extra salesman, advertising and promotion, travel costs and distribution to achieve this. In addition we may not have anticipated external effects such as competitor response that adversely impact the initiative.

So, varying a single assumption only has one useful benefit, it tells us by how much the situation improves (or deteriorates) assuming no other changes to the business. This is known as sensitivity analysis. It is useful to understand how much profit you lose each year if you allow gross margins to drop by 1% for example.

One exercise is to examine sensitivities using the base case model by varying each assumption by 1% or one unit. The outcome is usually interesting. Some assumptions have significant effects on returns and cash flow, other assumptions have very little effect. This is a useful exercise because it focuses attention on the assumptions to which the business is most sensitive.

Going back to the issue of positive scenarios, each scenario should ideally capture all the effects on the business of the possible initiative. So if we are examining geographic expansion we need to consider all the consequences of expanding our trading area, including cultural differences, language issues, distribution issues, taxes, competitor response, and so on. The scenario should be a complete entity in its own right.

Finally, we need to consider the degree of ambition inherent in a given scenario. As the upside plans become more ambitions they also become harder and harder to deliver in the real world. Running an existing business is relatively low risk because everything required is already happening. Launching new products, or developing or buying new businesses is far riskier, many of the risks being unknown – for example, new technology required, loss of key staff in a takeover, or competitor response to new product initiatives. So, while the very aggressive scenarios may look extremely financially attractive they may not be deliverable due to unexpected or unanticipated real world responses and difficulties.

Negative Scenarios

The same sorts of issue arise in examining negative or conservative scenarios. Once again, just to drop a single assumption by a few percent tells us little. Ideally we need to come up with a variety of plausible adverse scenarios and examine their effects on the business. A review of the history of the business can be helpful here. If the business is more than 10 years old it will have experienced recession in the past: what were the effects then and how did the business respond? Similarly other forms of disruption such as fires, strikes, disruption to the supply chain, and so on can be examined.

If direct competitors have experienced significant negative events financial analysis of the subsequent cost impact and other effects on their performance can be beneficial for creating more realistic scenarios.

We can usefully group negative scenarios as follows:

- Macro economic events, such as recession (economic cycles), interest rate increase, inflation increase, taxation increase, infrastructure problems.
- Sector level events such as raw material scarcity, labour scarcity, overcapacity (sector cycles), adverse competitive change, threat of substitutes, technological change.
- Legal and regulatory events such as adverse changes to laws and regulations increasing costs or reducing competitive advantages.
- Weather and peril related events such as earthquake, tsunami, hurricane, storms, other exceptional weather events, flood, fire, theft and others causing loss to the business directly or indirectly.

So, each of the above categories can be assessed for their possible impact on the business and, where possible, managers can effect risk management initiatives to try to eliminate or mitigate the effects of some of these risks. The point is to have a plan for these types of event, rather than to experience them as an act of god and react after the event. The objective of management should be to make the business as resilient as is cost effective to all known possible adverse events.

To make this clear I define a risk as anything that can disrupt the cash flows of the business. Managers should seek to have the business continue to operate successfully in virtually all conditions – indeed this can represent a competitive advantage, allowing the continuation of trade when other competitors are prevented from doing so by some adverse event.

Worst Case Scenarios

One of the problems with real life is that it is rarely predictable in the long run, if we are going to examine *worst case* scenarios the words should be taken seriously.

For example, in the world of credit everyone is aware of the impact of recessions. However, banks in general consistently fail to mitigate the consequences of recession in terms of bad debts and lost performance. One of the reasons for this is that the cause (or trigger) of each recession is different, so when things go wrong there is rarely one discrete cause, rather there are a number of apparently disconnected events occurring simultaneously that cause the recession and hence losses, the causes only being identified with hindsight. For this reason prudent lenders will, before lending, consider the effects on their proposed loan servicing and repayment of:

- Economic cycles (recession)
- Sector overcapacity

- Adverse legal or regulatory change
- Loss of key management/employees

However, examining the worst case means considering the effects of *all these adverse events occurring at the same time*.

So in coming up with a worst case scenarios we should be looking at not one but a number of adverse events impacting the entity being examined, at the same time.

CONCLUSIONS ABOUT FORECASTING CASE FLOWS

The forecasting of cash flows is a powerful tool for the analyst, investor, lender, entrepreneur, or manager to have at their disposal.

A well developed forecast, that successfully mimics the actual behaviour of a business as variables change, is a valuable tool because it is proactive (it looks forward into the future) rather than reactive (telling us about the past).

Used intelligently it enables the user to examine the effects of adverse events on the business before they occur so giving management the opportunity to mitigate risks as far as is possible. Examining the positive scenarios allows managers to assess the most cost effective ways of improving performance.

CONCLUSIONS ABOUT CASH FLOW ANALYSIS

This is the end of the book, if you have got this far you should now know significantly more about cash flow analysis.

Business is about cash flow. Without it a business dies. Lenders and investors are rewarded with cash returns. It follows that a cash flow centric approach to managing, lending and investing is not only sensible but also absolutely essential!

I have written this book to help people manage and lend and invest smarter. I hope it adds value to your endeavours in the future.

Index

Printed and bound by CPI Group (UK) Ltd, Croydon, CR0 4YY

16/04/2025

14658500-0004